THE POETRY OF TENNYSON

THE
POETRY OF TENNYSON

BY
HENRY VAN DYKE

University Press of the Pacific
Honolulu, Hawaii

The Poetry of Tennyson

by
Henry van Dyke

ISBN: 1-4102-1189-4

Reprinted from the 1915 edition

University Press of the Pacific
Honolulu, Hawaii
http://www.universitypressofthepacific.com

TO

A YOUNG WOMAN

OF AN OLD FASHION

WHO LOVES ART

NOT FOR ITS OWN SAKE

BUT BECAUSE IT ENNOBLES LIFE

WHO READS POETRY

NOT TO KILL TIME

BUT TO FILL IT WITH BEAUTIFUL THOUGHTS

AND WHO STILL BELIEVES

IN GOD AND DUTY AND IMMORTAL LOVE

I DEDICATE

THIS BOOK

PREFACE

TO THE TENTH EDITION.

THIS book is a study of the growth of a
poet's mind and of the perfecting of his art.
Such a subject cannot be treated without
reference to personality and environment.
The man, if he be true, stands revealed in
his work; and the work, if it be vital, re-
flects the age in which it is produced, and
the literature of other lands and times to
which it is related.

These pages, therefore, if they are to have
any value, must contain something about
Tennyson's life and character; something
about the intellectual and spiritual tenden-
cies of the Victorian Age; and something
about poetry in its broader aspects as the
inspirer and consoler of humanity in all
ages. But I have tried not to follow these
lines so far afield as to lose sight of my

definite purpose, which was to give as clear and fair a view as possible of the poetry of Tennyson in its real significance, its distinctive quality, and its permanent worth.

It must be confessed, however, that nothing so large as this was contemplated or proposed when the book was begun. In fact, it was not planned at all, nor built after a regular design. It grew out of a personal experience. And perhaps this may be as good a time and place as any, now that the tenth edition is going to the press, to tell how the book came to be written, and thus to explain its form and its limitations.

It began with a birthday gift of a dollar which a little boy received on his fourteenth birthday, from a very pleasant old lady. His fortune led him into a bookstore to spend this money, which burned in his pocket; and his guardian angel, I must suppose, directed his unconscious choice to a book called *Enoch Arden*. It was a pirated edition, and therefore cheap, for this happened in the days when the American publishers still practised literary brigandage, and the American people were still willing to be.

lieve that it was more desirable to get
books at a low price than to get them in
a fair way. But the boy was not far enough
out of the age of barbarism to feel any
moral scruple on a point like this, and the
guardian angel said nothing about it,—
probably intending to overrule the evil for
good. So the book was bought, and it be-
came the key which let that happy boy into
the garden and palace of poetry, there to
find a new beauty in the world, a new
meaning in life, and a new joy in living.

Not that this was his first book of poems.
He had lived in a library, and was already
the proprietor of a small bookcase of his
own. But hitherto poetry had seemed to
him like something foreign and remote,
much less interesting than fiction, and even
than some kinds of history. He had read
plenty of poems, of course, and had tried
his hand at making verses. But the formal
and artificial side of poetry was still the
most prominent to his mind. It was some-
thing to be translated and scanned and
parsed. It belonged to the tedious, profit-
able world of education and examination.

But *Enoch Arden* evidently belonged to
life. It was a story about real people. And
then, it was so beautifully told. There was
such a glow in it, such splendid colour, such
a swing and sweep of musical words, such a
fine picture of a brave man, and at the end
such a sad touch to bring the tears into your
eyes, — all by yourself, you understand,
when no one could see you and laugh at
you. Why, this was as good as any novel,
— yes, somehow it was better, for there
was a charm in the very movement of the
verse, the rise and fall, the ebb and flow,
the stately, measured cadence, that seemed
to stir the feelings and make them deeper
and fuller.

So the boy became a lover of poetry,
perceiving that it was a living thing ; and
he began to look around him for other
poems which should give him the same
kind of pleasure through the quickening of
his feelings, and the brightening of his
thoughts, and the interpreting of life and
nature in music. Of course, he found many
of them, ancient and modern. His capacity
of enjoyment increased, as his taste broad-

ened. He passed along the lines of new
sympathies from one poet to another, dis-
covered the touch of life in books which he
had thought were dry and dead, and learned
to appreciate beauties of which he had not
suspected the existence. Even the poets of
Greece and Rome began to say something
to his heart which it was neither necessary
nor possible to translate. They were no
longer shadows of mighty names, but real
makers of real things in the enduring world
of poesy.

The boy came to understand, as he grew
into man's estate, that there were other,
and a few yet loftier, masters in the realm
of song; but Tennyson still held the first
place in his affections. There was a singular
charm in the manner and accent of this
poet, so melodious, so fluent, so clear, and
yet so noble and powerful. Tennyson
seemed to be the one, among all the Eng-
lish poets, who was in closest sympathy
with the sentiments, the aspirations, the
conflicts, and the hopes of the modern
world. He not only led the boy for the first
time into the regions of poetry; he also

kept company, through all the experiences,
of life, with the young man.

When love began to speak in his heart,
it found an echo in *Maud*, and *Locksley
Hall*, and *The Princess*. When doubt be-
gan to trouble his mind, he turned to *Two
Voices* and *In Memoriam*, to learn that it
was no new thing for faith to have to fight
for her life. When the larger problems of
human duty and destiny began to press
upon him, he saw them nobly pictured in
the *Idylls of the King* and *The Palace of
Art ;* and he read a splendid answer to them
in such poems as *Will*, and *Wages*, and the
Ode on the Death of the Duke of Wellington.
When he began to take that deeper, broader
interest in human character which only
comes with maturity, he found in *Ulysses*
and *Lucretius* and *St. Simeon Stylites* and
The Northern Farmer and *Rizpah*, convinc-
ing portraits of living souls. And when at
last, after many happy years, sorrow entered
his house and filled his heart, he turned
again to *In Memoriam*, and it brought him
more comfort than any book in the world
save One.

It was not unnatural, then, that this man should be a Tennysonian, not as a matter of theory, but as an affair of experience. And the time came when he felt the wish to make some acknowledgment of the debt which he owed to this poet, to set in order some more careful estimate of the influences which have flowed from his poetry into the life of the present age, and to give some reasons for thinking that Tennyson stands among the great poets, if not on a level with the greatest.

So an essay was written comparing and contrasting *Tennyson and Milton*, and entering, for the first time, a claim for Tennyson as third in rank among the English poets. This essay was printed in 1883. It was followed by another which contained a critical study of the successive changes in *The Palace of Art*, as indicating the growth of Tennyson's genius and the spirit of his poetry. Then, after intervals of a year or two, essays on *The Idylls of the King*, *The Bible in Tennyson*, and *Locksley Hall Sixty Years After*, were written. At last it seemed as if a book could be made out of these chapters, with the addition of others, to complete the outline, which might give some pleasure to a few readers among the lovers of Tennyson, and perhaps make a few converts among those who had not yet appreciated the significance of his poetry. A chronology of the poet's life and a bibliography of the Tennyson literature were prepared, imperfectly enough, to be sure, but yet with far more fulness and accuracy than had hitherto been attempted; and with these additions the volume was printed and published in 1889.

This was the way in which I came to be the author of this book; and the story may serve at once to make its spirit and purpose clear to the reader, and to explain, if not to excuse, the imperfections and defects of its method.

The call for successive editions was equally surprising and agreeable. It afforded the opportunity of correcting some errors, revising some hasty judgments, and incorporating some new material. It also offered the temptation, too strong to be resisted, to add several prefaces and notes which did not enhance the typographical beauty of the volume. In 1897 these incumbrances were removed and the book was brought out in a smaller form, in the Cameo Series, without the chronology, the bibliography, or the list of Biblical references, but with a new chapter on *In Memoriam.*

But there is still a demand for the book in its original form by those who wish to have the fuller materials for study. I have therefore made this final revision and enlargement.

The various prefaces to the former editions give place to this preface. The chapter on *In Memoriam* from the Cameo edition is inserted, and some of the other chapters are slightly altered. The chronological and bibliographical appendix is fully revised and completed, so that it may serve as a guide to those who wish to study the life and works and critical estimates of Tennyson, more in detail. The list of Biblical references is re-arranged and much enlarged.

With these changes I close my work upon the book, and send it out for the last time to take its chances in the world. If it shall still find readers who like it, or dislike it, enough to turn from its pages to the poems of Tennyson, it will do well.   For I am quite sure, however poorly I may have succeeded in proving it, that poetry is the noblest form of literature and a vital element in human existence.   The critic who leads or drives men to read a great poet has served his purpose in the order of the universe.

HENRY VAN DYKE.

NEW YORK,
October 1st, 1898.

CONTENTS.

THE FIRST FLIGHT

THE POETRY OF TENNYSON.

THE FIRST FLIGHT.

THE first appearance of a true poet usually bears at least one mark of celestial origin — he "cometh not with observation." A small volume is printed on some obscure press. The friends to whom it is sent, "with the compliments of the author," return thanks for it in words which compromise truth with affection. The local newspaper applauds it in a perfunctory way; some ogre of a critic, whose appetite for young poets is insatiable, may happen to make a hasty and savage meal of it; or some kindly reviewer, who is always looking on the hopeful side of literature, may discover in it the buds of promise. But this is mainly a matter of chance; the certainty is that there will be few to buy the book with hard cash, and fewer still to read it, except from curiosity or friendship, and that the great world will roll on its way as serenely as if nothing of consequence had occurred.

Somewhat after this fashion most of the leading English poets have arrived. There was no great stir made by the publication of *Descriptive Sketches*, or *Hours of Idleness*. The announcement of *Original Poems by Victor and Cazire* did not produce any excitement. Even *Venus and Adonis* failed to inform the public that the creator of *Hamlet* and *Othello* had appeared. The recognition of genius in a first flight rarely takes place at the proper time ; it is reserved for those prophets who make their predictions after the event.

But surely there never was a poet of rank who slipped into print more quietly than the junior author of *Poems by Two Brothers*. The book was published in 1827 for J. & J. Jackson, of Louth, and W. Simpkin & B. Marshall, of London. The title-page bore a modest motto from Martial : " *Hæc nos novimus esse nihil.*" The preface repeated the same sentiment in more diffuse language.

" The following Poems were written from the ages of fifteen to eighteen, not conjointly, but individually, which may ac-

count for their differences of style and
matter. To light upon any novel combi-
nation of images, or to open any vein of
sparkling thought, untouched before, were
no easy task; indeed, the remark itself is
as old as the truth is clear; and no doubt,
if submitted to the microscopic eye of
periodical criticism, a long list of inaccu-
racies and imitations would result from
the investigation. But so it is; we have
passed the Rubicon, and we leave the
rest to fate, though its edict may create a
fruitless regret that we ever emerged from
' the shade' and courted notoriety."

That was surely a most gentle way of
passing the Rubicon. The only suggestion
of a flourish of trumpets was the capital
P in " Poems." Fate, who sat smiling on
the bank, must have been propitiated by a
bow so modest and so awkward. Not even
the names of the young aspirants for pub-
lic favor were given, and only the friends
of the family could have known that the
two brothers who thus stepped out, hand
in hand, from " the shade " were Charles
and Alfred Tennyson.

It is difficult to conjecture — unless, in-
deed, we are prepared to adopt some wild

theory of the disinterested benevolence of
publishers — what induced the Jacksons to
pay twenty pounds for the privilege of
printing this book. But if they were alive
to-day, and had kept a sufficient number
of the first edition on their shelves, their
virtue would have its reward ; for I must
confess to having paid half as much for a
single copy as they gave for the copyright,
and, as prices go, it was an excellent
bargain.

Here it is — a rather stout little volume
of two hundred and twenty-eight pages,
paper not of the finest, print not without
errors.   It contains one hundred and two
pieces of verse, in all kinds of metres, and
imitated after an amazing variety of models.
There is nothing very bad and nothing
very inspiring. *The Literary Chronicle
and Weekly Review* came as near to the
truth as one can expect of a newspaper
when it said: "This volume exhibits a
pleasing union of kindred tastes, and con-
tains several little pieces of considerable
merit." That is the only contemporary
criticism which has been exhumed. And
it would be absurd, at this late day, to
urn the "microscopic eye," of which the

brothers were so needlessly afraid, upon
their immature production.

And yet, to one who can find a pleasure
in tracing the river to its narrow source
among the hills, this book is precious
and well worth reading. For somewhere
between these covers, hardly to be distin-
guished from the spring of that twin
rivulet of verse which ran so brief a course
in the *Sonnets* and *Small Tableaux* of
Charles Tennyson, lies the fountain-head
of that deeper, clearer stream which has
flowed forth into *In Memoriam* and the
Idylls of the King, and refreshed the Eng-
lish-speaking world for more than sixty
years with the poetry of Alfred Tennyson.
Here, then, we may pause for a moment
and glance at some of the impulses which
led him to commence poet, and the influ-
ences which directed his earliest efforts.

It seems to me that the most interesting
and significant thing about this little book
is the fact that the two brothers appear in
it together; for this tells us a great deal
in regard to the atmosphere of the home
in which Tennyson's boyhood was passed.
The seven sons and four daughters of the
rector of Somersby were not ordinary chil-

dren; nor was their education conducted
in that dull, commonplace, Gradgrind spirit
which so often crushes all originality out
of a child. The doors of the ideal world
were opened to them very early; they
were encouraged to imagine as well as to
think; they peopled their playgrounds with
lofty visions of kings and knights, and
fought out the world-old battles of right
and wrong in their childish games, and
wove their thoughts of virtue and courage
and truth into long romances with which
they entertained each other in turn at the
dinner-table. The air of the house was
full of poetry. Charles, the second son,
was probably the leader in this life of
fancy. It was he, at all events, who first
directed his brother Alfred, his junior by
a year, into the poetic path. One Sunday
morning, when Alfred was to be left at
home alone, Charles gave him a slate and
bade him write some verses about the
flowers in the garden. The task was
eagerly accepted, and when the family had
returned from church, the little boy came
with his slate all written over with lines of
blank verse, to ask for his brother's ap-
proval. Charles read them over gravely

and carefully, with the earnestness of a
childish critic. Then he gave the slate
back again, saying, " Yes, you can write."
It was a very kindly welcome to the world
of poetry, and I doubt whether Alfred Ten-
nyson ever heard a word of praise that
filled him with more true delight than
this fraternal recognition.

Having found each other as kindred
spirits, the two boys held closely together.
They were intimate friends. They helped
and cheered and criticised each other in
their common studies and writings. It is
a good omen for genius when it is capable
of fraternity. It is the best possible safe-
guard against eccentricity and morbidness
and solitary pride. Charles Lamb was
right when he wrote to Coleridge: " O my
friend, cultivate the filial feelings ! and let
no man think himself released from the
kind charities of relationship." Tennyson's
best work has never lost the insight of
the heart. And if there were no other
reason for valuing these *Poems by Two
Brothers*, we should still prize them as the
monument of a brotherly love to which the
poet has paid this exquisite tribute in *In
Memoriam :*

> But thou and I are one in kind,
>   As moulded like in Nature's mint;
>   And hill and wood and field did print
> The same sweet forms on either mind.
>
> For us the same cold streamlet curl'd
>   Thro' all his eddying coves; the same
>   All winds that roam the twilight came
> In whispers of the beauteous world.
>
> At one dear knee we proffer'd vows;
>   One lesson from one book we learn'd,
>   Ere childhood's flaxen ringlet turn'd
> To black and brown on kindred brows.

Another noticeable feature in this book is the great number of quotations from modern and classical authors. Almost all of the poems have mottoes. I glance over them at random, and find scraps from Virgil, Addison, Gray, Clare, Cicero, Horace, Moore, Byron, Milton, Racine, Claudian, Rousseau, Scott, Hume, Ossian, Lucretius, Sallust, and *The Mysteries of Udolpho.* These school-boys must have loved their books well, if not wisely.

Moreover, there are foot-notes in which they tell us that " PIGHT is a word used by Spenser and Shakespeare," and that "none but the priests could interpret the Egyptian hieroglyphics," and that " Ponce de Leon discovered Florida when he was in

search of the fabled fountain of youth,"
and that "Apollonius Rhodius was not
born at Alexandria, but at Naucratis."
The display of learning is so immense that
it becomes amusing. But it is not without
significance, for it distinctly marks Tenny-
son as one of those who, like Milton, were
students before they were poets, and whose
genius did not develop in solitude, but in

> Converse with all forms
> Of the many-sided mind.

The volume abounds, as I have already
said, in imitations ; indeed, there is hardly
a piece in it which does not sound like an
echo of some other poet. The influence
which is most clearly marked is that of
Byron. He is quoted six times. There is
a strong flavour of his dramatic melancholy
in such lines as,

> I wander in darkness and sorrow,
> Unfriended and cold and alone;

or,

> I stand like some lone tower
>   Of former days remaining,
> Within whose place of power
>   The midnight owl is plaining.

It is evident that this grief could not
have been very real to a school-boy be-

tween fifteen and eighteen. It was like
the gloom of Shakespeare's young gentle-
man of France who was " sad as night only
for wantonness." And the fashion of the
sadness was learned from the author of
Childe Harold. His metrical manner also
is copied with undisguised enthusiasm. The
lad who wrote,

Thou shalt come like a storm when the moonlight is dim,
And the lake's gloomy bosom is full to the brim;
Thou shalt come like the flash in the darkness of night,
When the wolves of the forest shall howl with affright,

had certainly been captured by the As-
syrian who came down like the wolf on the
fold.

After reading all this it is interesting
to hear Tennyson tell in his own words,
spoken many years afterward, how the
news of Byron's death had affected him:
" Byron was dead. I thought the whole
world was at an end. I thought every-
thing was over and finished for every one
— that nothing else mattered. I remem-
ber, I walked out alone and carved ' Byron
is dead ' into the sandstone."

The spell of this passionate devotion
soon passed away, but perhaps we can see
some lingering trace of its effects in poems

as late as *Locksley Hall* and *Maud.* Indeed,
I think the influence of Byron upon Tenny-
son has been generally underrated, if not
completely ignored.

There are a few other points of interest
in this little volume. For instance, the
variety of metrical forms indicates an un-
usual freedom and catholicity of taste. The
result of such a miscellaneous admiration
of all styles, from the finish of Horace to
the formlessness of Ossian, might possibly
be nothing better than a facility in general
imitation, the fluency of a successful paro-
dist. But if a boy had real genius it would
lead him on to try experiments in many
metres until he mastered those which were
best fitted to express his thoughts, and
gave new life to obsolete forms of verse,
and finally, perhaps, created some original
form. And this, in fact, is what Alfred
Tennyson has done. He has attempted
almost every kind of measure. And though
his early efforts were so irregular that
Coleridge remarked that " Tennyson had
begun to write poetry without knowing
what metre was," yet in the end he made
himself one of the most musical of English
singers.

In 1893, sixty-seven years after the orig-
inal publication, a new edition of *Poems
by Two Brothers* was brought out, with a
preface by Hallam, Lord Tennyson, the
poet's son.   In this edition the poems were
attributed, as far as possible, to their re-
spective authors, on the evidence of the
differences in the handwriting of the
manuscript and the recollections of Mr.
Frederick Tennyson, who, it now appears,
contributed four or five poems to his
brothers' volume.

It is interesting to note that the pieces
which show the greatest freedom and ra-
pidity, and also, it must be admitted, the
greatest irregularity of metrical movement,
are those which bear the initials A. T.
The rule which is so painfully familiar
to those who are learning to skate seems
to hold good for those who are learning to
write verse.   Success is impossible without
a good many tumbles.

Scattered through these early verses we
find a number of thoughts and phrases
which Tennyson used again in his more
mature poems.   I will give a few illustra-
tions of these parallel passages.

In *Remorse* we find the lines :

> To life, whose every hour to me
> Hath been increase of misery.

The Two Voices gives us the same thought:

> Thou art so full of misery,
> Were it not better not to be ?

In *Midnight* there is a reference to

> the glutting wave
> That saps eternally the cold gray steep;

which reminds us of

> Break, break, break,
> On thy cold gray stones, O Sea!

In *Switzerland* the poet cries :

> O ! when shall Time
> Avenge the crime ?

and in *The Vision of Sin* he says again :

> It was a crime
> Of sense, avenged by sense that wore with time.

In the poem on *Sublimity* we find the phrase " holds communion with the dead," which occurs again in one of the most beautiful passages of *In Memoriam.*

In *Egypt* we find :

> The first glitter of his rising beams
> Falls on the broad-bas'd pyramids sublime.

The epithet recurs in *A Fragment*, printed in an annual in 1830 :

> The great pyramids,
> Broad-bas'd amid the fleeting sands.

Other passages might be quoted to show
the connection between Tennyson's earlier
and later work. It is one of his charac-
teristics that he uses the same image more
than once, and that the repetition is almost
always an improvement. But it will be
more profitable to close this brief intro-
ductory essay with a few lines which are
worthy to be remembered for their own
merits, and which belong to the first genu-
ine poetry of Alfred Tennyson.   True and
broad descriptive power is shown in such
lines as these:

> Like some far fire at night
> *Along the dun deep streaming.*

> *A wan, dull, lengthen'd sheet of swimming light*
> Lies the broad lake —

> *The thunder of the brazen prows*
> *O'er Actium's ocean rung.*

But the passage which exhibits the most
sustained vigour of expression is found in
the poem entitled *Persia*.   It is a descrip-
tion of the great king contemplating the
ruin of his empire.   He spreads the dust
upon his laurelled head, as he is forced

> To view the setting of that star
> Which beam'd so gorgeously and far
> O'er Anatolia, and the fane
> Of Belus, and Caïster's plain,

> And Sardis, and the glittering sands
>   Of bright Pactolus, and the lands
> Where Crœsus held his rich domain;
> And further east, where broadly roll'd
> Old Indus pours his streams of gold;
> And southward to Cilicia's shore,
> Where Cydnus meets the billows' roar;
> And northward far to Trebizonde,
>   Renown'd for kings of chivalry,
> Where Ilyssus rolling from the strand
>   Disgorges in the Euxine Sea —
> The Euxine, falsely named, which whelms
> The mariner in the heaving tide —
> To high Sinope's distant realms,
> Where cynics rail'd at human pride.

This is not perfect poetry, but it is certainly strong verse. It is glorified nomenclature. Milton himself need not have blushed to acknowledge it. The boy who could write like this before he was eighteen years old knew something, at least, of the music and magic of names. If we may read our history, like our Hebrew, backward, we can detect the promise of a great poet in the swing and sweep of these lines, and recognize the wing-trial of genius in Tennyson's first flight.

THE PALACE OF ART

THE PALACE OF ART.

THE year of our Lord eighteen hundred and thirty-three was a period of waiting and uncertainty in English literature. Twelve years had passed since the brief. bright light of Keats went out at Rome; eleven years, since the waters of Spezzia's treacherous bay closed over the head of Shelley; nine years, since the wild flame of Byron's heart burned away at Missolonghi; a few months, since the weary hand of Scott had at last let fall the wizard's wand. The new leaders were dead; the old leaders were silent. Wordsworth was reclining on the dry laurels of his *Ecclesiastical Sonnets* at Rydal Mount; Coleridge was pacing up and down the garden-path at Highgate talking transcendental metaphysics; Southey had ceased writing what he called poetry; Thomas Moore was warbling his old songs to an audience which had almost begun to weary of them. The coming man had not yet arrived. Dickens was a short-hand reporter in the House of Commons; Thackeray was running through his property in the ruinous dissipation of newspaper-publishing; Carlyle was wrestling with poverty and the devil at Craigenputtock; Robert Browning, a youth of twenty, was travelling in Italy; Matthew Arnold and Arthur Clough were boys at Rugby; William Morris and Algernon Charles Swinburne were yet unborn. In this somewhat barren and unpromising interval, the poetical reputation of Mr. Alfred Tennyson, late of the University of Cambridge, was trembling in the balance of Criticism.

Criticism with a large C, you will please to observe; for the reign of their mighty Highnesses, the Reviewers, was still unshaken. Seated upon their lofty thrones in London and Edinburgh, they weighed the pretensions of all new-comers into their realms with severity if not with impartiality, and meted out praise and blame with a royal hand. In those rude days there was no trifling with a book in little "notices" of mild censure or tepid approbation, — small touches which, if unfavourable, hardly hurt more than pin-pricks, and if favourable, hardly help more than gentle pats upon

the head. That is the suave, homœopathic
method of modern times : but then — in
the days of Herod the king — it was either
the accolade or decapitation. Many an in-
nocent had the dreadful Gifford slaughtered,
and though he had done his last book, there
were other men, like Wilson and Croker
and Lockhart, who still understood and
practiced the art of speedy dispatch. *Black-
wood* and *The Quarterly* still clothed them-
selves with Olympian thunder,

" And that two-handed engine at their door,
   Stood ready to smite once and smite no more."

It was before this stern tribunal that
young Tennyson had made his appearance
in 1830 with a slim volume of *Poems,
Chiefly Lyrical.* They were fifty-three in
number, and covered only one hundred and
fifty-four pages ; yet within that narrow
compass at least a score of different metres
were attempted with amazing skill, and the
range of subjects extended from *The Mer-
man* to *Supposed Confessions of a Second-
rate Sensitive Mind not in Unity with It-
self.* One can easily imagine the confusion
and scorn which the latter title must have
excited in the first-rate unsensitive mind of
an orthodox Edinburgh Reviewer. Nor were

the general style and quality of the poems calculated to mollify these feelings. Dainty in finish, pre-raphaelite in their minute painting of mosses and flowers and in their super-subtle shading of emotions, musical yet irregular, modern in sentiment, yet tinged with some archaic mannerisms, the poems taken altogether concealed the real strength of some of them (such as *Mariana*, *The Poet*, *Ode to Memory*, and *The Deserted House*,) under an appearance of delicacy and superficiality. Arthur Henry Hallam praised them, but that counted for nothing, because he was Tennyson's friend. *The Westminster Review* praised them, but that counted for little, because it belonged to the party of literary revolt. Leigh Hunt praised them, but that counted for worse than nothing, because he was the arch-heretic of poetry, the leader of the so-called " Cockney school." The authoritative voice of Criticism was not heard until " Christopher North " took up the new poet in *Blackwood*, and administered the castigation which he thought most necessary and salutary. Mingling a little condescending encouragement with his condemnation, and holding out the hope that if " Alfred " would only

reform his style and get rid of his cockney
admirers he might some day write something
worth reading, the stern magister set to work
in the meantime to demolish the dainty lyrics.
Drivel, and more dismal drivel, and even
more dismal drivel was what he called them;
and in winding up his remarks upon the
song entitled *The Owl*, he said: "Alfred
himself is the greatest owl; all he wants is
to be shot, stuffed, and stuck in a glass case,
to be made immortal in a museum."

Truly this was Criticism of the athletic
order; and the humour of it lies in the
unconscious absence of wit. Six months
after this article was printed, in Decem-
ber, 1832, Mr. Tennyson put out his sec-
ond volume. Its title-page ran as follows:
Poems by Alfred Tennyson. London:
Edward Moxon, 64, New Bond Street.
MDCCCXXXIII. It is, therefore, prop-
erly speaking, the edition of 1833.

It lies on my desk now, a slender vol-
ume of one hundred and sixty-three pages,
with Barry Cornwall's autograph on the fly-
leaf, and his pencil-marks running all along
the margins. It contains only thirty poems,
but among them are *The Lady of Shalott*,
The Miller's Daughter, *Œnone*, *The Palace*

of Art, *The Lotos-Eaters*, and *A Dream of Fair Women.*

It was evident at once that the young poet had not changed his style, though he had enriched it. Fuller and stronger were his notes, more manly and of a wider range; but his singing was still marked by the same lyrical freedom, the same delicacy of imagination, the same exquisite and unconventional choice of words, the same peculiar blending of the classic with the romantic spirit, — qualities which to us have become so familiar that we can hardly realize how fresh and strange they must have seemed to the readers of half a century ago. It was clear enough that this new writer was no mere disciple of Leigh Hunt, or neophyte of the Cockney school, to be frightened back into the paths of propriety by brutal thunders. He might be moving on the same lines which Keats had begun to follow, but he was going beyond his leader; he was introducing a new spirit and method into English verse; he bid fair to become the master of a new school of poetry. In the opinion of the reviewers he needed to be dealt with mildly, but firmly. And this time it was not "crusty Christopher," but a more dangerous critic who undertook the task. The review of Tennyson's poems which appeared in the *Quarterly* for July, 1833, is one of the cleverest and bitterest things ever written, and though unacknowledged, it has always been attributed to the editor, James Gibson Lockhart, sometimes called "the scorpion," because of a certain peculiarity in the latter end of his articles.

He begins in a tone of ironical compliment, apologizing for never having seen Mr. Tennyson's first volume, and proposing to repair his unintentional neglect by now introducing to the admiration of sequestered readers "a new prodigy of genius, another and a brighter star of that galaxy or *milky way* of poetry of which the lamented Keats was the harbinger." He proceeds to offer what he calls "a tribute of unmingled approbation," and selecting a few specimens of Mr. Tennyson's singular genius, "to point out now and then the peculiar brilliancy of some of the gems that irradiate his poetical crown." This means, in plain words, to hold up the whole performance to ridicule by commending its weakest points in extravagant mock-laudation, and passing over its best points in silence. A method

more unfair and exasperating can hardly be
imagined. It is like applauding a musician
for every false note. Lockhart's "unmin-
gled approbation" was a thousand times
more severe than old Christopher's blunt
and often clumsy abuse. It was as if one
had praised Pope for his amiable temper, or
Wordsworth for his keen sense of humour.

And yet, — after all, — in spite of the
malicious spirit and the unjust method of
the article, — we may as well be honest and
confess that on many points Lockhart was
right. His hard, formal, opinionated, Cale-
donian mind could not possibly appreciate
the merits of Tennyson, but it could and it
did detect the blemishes of his earlier work.
In almost every case the shaft of the re-
viewer's irony found the joint in the poet's
armour and touched some vulnerable spot.

The proof of this is furnished by Tenny-
son himself. For ten years he preserved an
almost unbroken silence. When at length
he published his *Poems, in Two Volumes*,
in 1842, he was recognized immediately as
the poet, not of a coterie, but of England.
The majestic blank-verse of *Morte d'Arthur*,
the passionate force of *Locksley Hall*, the
sweet English beauty of *Dora, The Garden-*

er's Daughter, and *The Talking Oak*, the
metaphysical depth and human intensity of
The Two Voices and *The Vision of Sin*, —
and perhaps more than all the simple, magi-
cal pathos of that undying song,

> Break, break, break
> On thy cold gray stones, O Sea!

won the admiration of readers of every
class, and Tennyson was acknowledged, in
the language of Wordsworth, as decidedly
the first of our living poets. But no less
significant than these new poems, in the his-
tory of his genius, was the form in which
his earlier poems were reprinted. The edi-
tion of 1842 contained a selection from the
edition of 1833; and it is most remarkable
that all of the weaker pieces which Lockhart
had criticised most severely were omitted,
while those which were retained had been
so carefully pruned and corrected as to seem
almost rewritten. There is an immense im-
portance, for example, in such a slight
change as the omission of the accent from
words like *charmèd* and *apparellèd*. It in-
dicates a desire to avoid even the appear-
ance of affectation. Or take this passage
from *The Miller's Daughter* in its first
form : —

Remember you that pleasant day
  When after roving in the woods,
('Twas April then), I came and lay
  Beneath the gummy chestnut-buds
That glistened in the April blue.
  Upon the slope so smooth and cool
I lay and never thought of *you*
  But angled in the deep mill-pool.

A water-rat from off the bank
  Plunged in the stream.   With idle care
Downlooking through the sedges rank
  I saw your troubled image there.
Upon the dark and dimpled beck
  It wandered like a floating light,
A full fair form, a warm white neck
  And two white arms — how rosy white !

These are very pretty lines, and doubtless
quite true to nature, for the buds of the
chestnut are very sticky in April, and the
water-rat has a habit of diving suddenly into
the water.   But as Mr. Lockhart politely
observed, the accumulation of such tender
images as the gummy buds and the plun-
ging rat was somewhat unusual and disturb-
ing.   Tennyson saw the justice of the crit-
icism.   He recognized that the canon of
truth to nature must be supplemented by the
canon of symmetry in art, and that facts
which are incongruous and out of harmony
must not be recorded.   The water-rat was

not profoundly suggestive of love at first
sight. Moreover, one who was looking up
at the chestnut-buds would not have noticed
their stickiness, but only their shining as
they were moved by the wind. Here, then,
is the new version of the passage, quite as
true but far more poetical, and made sim-
pler by a more careful art : —

> But, Alice, what an hour was that,
>   When after roving in the woods
> ('Twas April then), I came and sat
>   Below the chestnuts, when their buds
> Were glistening to the breezy blue;
>   And on the slope, an absent fool
> I cast me down, nor thought of you,
>   But angled in the higher pool.
>
> Then leapt a trout. In lazy mood
>   I watch'd the little circles die;
> They past into the level flood,
>   And there a vision caught my eye;
> The reflex of a beauteous form,
>   A glowing arm, a gleaming neck,
> As when a sunbeam wavers warm
>   Within the dark and dimpled beck.

Now a poet who could take criticism in
this fashion and use it to such good purpose,
was certainly neither weak nor wayward.
Weighed in the balance, he was not found
wanting but steadily growing. He would
not abandon his art at the voice of censure,

but correct and perfect it, until it stood com-
plete and sound beyond the reach of censure.
The method and the result of this process of
self-criticism — which Tennyson has prac-
ticed more patiently and successfully than
any other poet — may be traced most clearly
in the history of *The Palace of Art*, the long-
est and most important of the 1833 poems.
Nor can I think of any better way to study
the unfolding of his genius and the develop-
ment of his style, than to observe carefully
the number and nature and purpose of the
changes which he has made in this poem.

The poem is an allegory. Its meaning
is clearly defined in the dedication to an
unnamed friend. Its object is to exhibit a
gifted but selfish soul, in its endeavours to
live alone in its own enchanted world of re-
fined and consummate pleasures, without car-
ing for the interests or the sufferings of the
great world of mankind. The lesson which
the poet desires to teach is that such a life
must be a failure and carry its punishment
within itself. It is an æsthetic protest
against æstheticism. But it is worthy of
notice that, while the dedication in the first
edition was addressed to a member of the
æsthetic class. —

You are an artist, and will understand
Its many lesser meanings, —

in the second edition these lines have disap-
peared. It is as if the poet desired to give
a wider range to his lesson; as if he would
say, "You are a man, and no matter what
your occupation may be, you will feel the
truth of this allegory."

This first alteration is characteristic. It
shows us the transformation of Tennyson's
feelings and purposes during those eventful
ten years of silence. He had grown broader
and deeper. He was no longer content to
write for a small and select circle of readers.
His sympathies were larger and more hu-
mane. He began to feel that he had a coun-
try, and patriotism inspired him to write for
England. He began to feel that the lives
of common men and women were full of ma-
terials for poetry, and philanthropy inspired
him to speak as a man to his fellow-men.
This change was prophesied in the first
conception of *The Palace of Art,* but when
the fulfilment came, it was so thorough that
it had power to remould the form of the
prophecy itself.

The Palace which the poet built for his
soul is described as standing on a lofty table-

land, secure and inaccessible, for his first
object was to dwell apart from the world.
Then follows, in the original edition, a de-
scription of its long-sounding corridors,

> Roofed with thick plates of green and orange glass,
> Ending in stately rooms.

In the second edition the architect's good
taste has discarded this conservatory effect
and these curiously assorted colors. He
describes instead the surroundings of the
Palace, with its four great courts and its
foaming fountains, its smooth lawns and
branching cloisters. He draws a gilded par-
apet around the roof, and shows the distant
landscape. In following this order he has
given reality and dignity to his structure, so
that it seems less like a picture-gallery and
more like a royal mansion.

Then he leads the soul through the differ-
ent rooms, and describes the tapestries on
the walls. As the poem stood at first these
included the Madonna, Venus Anadyomene,
St. Cecily, Arthur in the valley of Avilion,
Kriemhilt pouring the Nibelungen gold into
the Rhine, Europa, with her hand grasping
the golden horn of the bull, and Ganymede
borne upward by the eagle, together with
landscapes of forest and pasture, sea-coast,

mountain-glen, and woodland, interspersed
with gardens and vineyards. When the
Palace was changed, Venus and Kriemhilt
disappeared, and Europa occupied a smaller
place. Pictures of Numa and his wise
wood-nymphs, Indian Cama seated on his
summer throne, and the porch of Moham-
med's Paradise thronged with houris, were
added. And among the landscapes there
were two new scenes, one of cattle feeding
by a river, and another of reapers at their
sultry toil.

The soul pauses here, in the first edition,
and indulges in a little rhapsody on the evo-
lution of the intellect. This disappears in
the second edition, and we pass directly from
the chambers hung with arras into the great
hall, the central apartment of the Palace.
Here the architect had gathered, at first, a
collection of portraits of great men which
was so catholic in its taste as to be almost
motley. Lockhart laughed derisively when
he saw the group. "Milton, Shakespeare,
Dante, Homer, Michael Angelo, Martin Lu-
ther, Francis Bacon, Cervantes, Calderon,
King David, the Halicarnassean (*quære*,
which of them?), Alfred himself (presum-
ably not the poet),

> Isaiah with fierce Ezekiel,
>   Swarth Moses by the Coptic sea,
> Plato, Petrarca, Livy, Raphaël,
>   And eastern Confutzee."

This reminds the critic of a verse in that
Hibernian poem, *The Groves of Blarney*,
and he wonders whether Mr. Tennyson was
not thinking of the Blarney collection —

> " Statues growing that noble place in
>   Of heathen goddesses most rare ;
> Homer, Plutarch, and Nebuchadnezzar,
>   All standing naked in the open air."

But in the revised Palace all these have been
left out, except the first four, and the archi-
tect has added a great

>   mosaic choicely plann'd
>   With cycles of the human tale
> Of this wide world, the times of every land
>   So wrought, they will not fail.
>
> The people here, a beast of burden slow,
>   Toil'd onward, prick'd with goads and stings ;
> Here play'd a tiger, rolling to and fro
>   The heads and crowns of kings ;
>
> Here rose an athlete, strong to break or bind
>   All force in bonds that might endure,
> And here once more like some sick man declin'd
>   And trusted any cure.

This mosaic covered the floor, and over these
symbols of struggling humanity the vainglo-
rious soul trod proudly as she went up to

take her throne between the shining win-
dows on which the faces of Plato and Veru-
lam were blazoned. In the first edition
there was a gorgeous description of the ban-
quet with which she regaled herself; piles
of flavorous fruits, musk - scented blooms,
ambrosial pulps and juices, graceful chalices
of curious wine, and a service of costly jars
and bossed salvers. Thus she feasted in
solitary state, and

> ere young night divine
> Crowned dying day with stars,
>
> Making sweet close of his delicious toils,
>   She lit white streams of dazzling gas,
> And soft and fragrant flames of precious oils
>   In moons of purple glass.

This was written when the use of gas for
illuminating purposes was new, and not con-
sidered unromantic. When the Palace was
remodelled the gas was turned off, and the
supper was omitted. The soul was lifted
above mere sensual pleasures, and sat listen-
ing to her own song and rejoicing in her
royal seclusion.

There are a great many minor alterations
scattered through the poem, which I have
not time to notice. Some of them are mere
changes of spelling, like Avilion, which be-

comes Avalon; and Cecily, which is changed
to Cicely in 1842, and back again to Cecily
in later editions; and sweet Europa's man-
tle, which at first " blew unclasped," and
then lost its motion and got a touch of colour,
becoming "blue, unclasped," and finally re-
turned to its original form. (Some one has
said that a painter would not have been
forced to choose between colour and motion,
for he could have made the mantle at once
blue and blowing.) Corrections and re-cor-
rections such as these show how carefully
Mr. Tennyson seeks the perfection of lan-
guage.

But the most interesting change yet to be
noted is directly due to Lockhart's sharp
criticism; at least, it was he who first pointed
out the propriety of it, in his usual sarcastic
way. " In this poem," said he, "we first
observed a stroke of art which we think very
ingenious. No one who has ever written
verses but must have felt the pain of eras-
ing some happy line, some striking phrase,
which, however excellent in itself, did not
exactly suit the place for which it was des-
tined. How curiously does an author mould
and remould the plastic verse in order to fit
in the favorite thought; and when he finds

that he cannot introduce it, as Corporal
Trim says, *any how*, with what reluctance
does he at last reject the intractable, but
still cherished, offspring of his brain. Mr.
Tennyson manages this delicate matter in a
new and better way. He says, with great
candour and simplicity, ' If this poem were
not already too long *I should have added the
following stanzas*,' and then *he adds them ;*
or, ' I intended to have added something on
statuary, but I found it very difficult; but
I have finished the statues of Elijah and
Olynpias ; judge whether I have succeeded ;'
and then *we have those two statues.* This
is certainly the most ingenious device that
has ever come under our observation for
reconciling the rigour of criticism with the
indulgence of parental partiality."

The passages to which Mr. Lockhart al-
ludes in this delicious paragraph are the
notes appended to pages 73 and 83 of the
original edition. The former of these con-
tains four stanzas on sculptures ; the latter
gives a description of one of the favourite
occupations of the self-indulgent soul, which
is too fine to be left unquoted. Above the
Palace a massive tower was built :

Hither, when all the deep unsounded skies
  Were shuddering with silent stars, she clomb,
And, as with optic glasses, her keen eyes
  Pierced thro' the mystic dome,

Regions of lucid matter taking forms,
  Brushes of fire, hazy gleams,
Clusters and beds of worlds, and bee-like swarms
  Of suns, and starry streams.

She saw the snowy poles of moonless Mars,
  That marvellous round of milky light
Below Orion, and those double stars
  Whereof the one more bright

Is circled by the other.

But, however admirable these lines may seem, and however much we may regret their loss, there can be no doubt that the manner of their introduction was incongruous and absurd. It was like saying, "This Palace is not to have a hall of statues, but I will simply put on a small wing as a sample of what is not to be done. And there is no room for an observatory, but I will construct one in order that you may see what it would have been like." The poet himself seems to have recognized that the device was too "ingenious" to be dignified; and in 1842 he restored the symmetry of the Palace by omitting the annex-buildings entirely.

And now let us sum up the changes which have been made in the Palace since it was first constructed. For this purpose it will be better to take Macmillan's edition of 1884 (which probably represents the final text) and lay it beside the edition of 1833.

In 1833 the poem, including the notes, contained eighty-three stanzas; in 1884 it has only seventy-five. Of the original num ber thirty-one have been entirely omitted — in other words, more than a third of the structure has been pulled down; and, in place of these, twenty-two new stanzas have been added, making a change of fifty-three stanzas. The fifty-two that remain have almost all been retouched and altered, so that very few stand to-day in the same shape which they had at the beginning. I suppose there is no other poem in the language, not even among the writings of Tennyson, which has been worked over so carefully as this.

But what is the significance of all this toilsome correction and remodelling? How does the study of it help us to a better comprehension of the poet? I think it shows us, first of all, the difference between the intellectual temper of Tennyson and that of a man who is possessed by his theories, instead

of possessing them, and whom they carry
away into eccentricity. Suppose, for exam-
ple, that such an article as Lockhart's had
been written about Wordsworth's early
work, what would he have done? Or rather,
for the case is not adscititious but actual,
what did he do when the Philistines fell
upon him? He replied to the attacks upon
Goody Blake by publishing *Peter Bell;*
he insisted upon using the language of
common life even when he had nothing to
say; he justified his poem upon an idiot
and his pony, by producing a much longer
one upon a pedlar and his ass. But with
Tennyson the effect of criticism was differ-
ent. He had the saving sense of humour,
and could see the point of a clever jest even
when it was directed against himself. He
was willing to learn even from an enemy,
and he counted no pains too great to take if
only he could succeed in cleansing his work
from blemishes and freeing it from "the de-
fects of its virtues." The result of this,
merely from a technical point of view, is
seen in the *Palace of Art.* It has gained
in rebuilding. The omission of unnecessary
decoration is a good rule for the architect.
And though we lose many rich and polished

details, beautiful as the capitals of Corin-
thian pillars, their absence leaves the Palace
standing more clear and noble before the
inward eye.

But when we look at the alterations from
a higher point, when we consider their ef-
fect upon the meaning of the poem, we see
how immense has been the gain. The new
lines and stanzas are framed, almost with-
out exception, with a wondrous skill to in-
tensify the allegory. Touch after touch
brings out the picture of the self-centred
soul : the indifference that hardens into
cruel contempt, the pride that verges on in-
sanity, the insatiate lust of pleasure that de-
vours all the world can give and then turns
to feed upon itself, the empty darkness of
the life without love. It seems as if the poet
had felt more deeply, as he grew older, the
need of making this picture clear and strong.
Take for instance these two stanzas which he
has added to the poem, describing the exul-
tation of the soul in her exclusive joy : —

> O God-like isolation which art mine,
>   I can but count thee perfect gain,
> What time I watch the darkening droves of swine
>   That range on yonder plain.

In filthy sloughs they roll a prurient skin,
  They graze and wallow, breed and sleep;
And oft some brainless devil enters in,
  And drives them to the deep.

These lines are essential to the understand-
ing of the poem. They touch the very core
of the sin which defiled the Palace and de-
stroyed the soul's happiness. It was not
merely that she loved beauty and music and
fragrance; but that in her love for these
she lost her moral sense, denied her human
duties, and scorned, instead of pitying and
helping, her brother-men who lived on the
plain below. This is the sin of selfish pride,
the sin which drives out the Christ because
He eats with publicans and sinners, the un-
pardonable sin which makes its own hell.
And it is just this sin, the poet declares, that
transforms the Palace of Art into a prison
of despair.

Is not this a lesson of which the age has
need? The chosen few are saying to their
disciples that the world is a failure, humanity
a mass of wretchedness, religion an outworn
dream, — the only refuge for the elect of
wealth and culture is in art. Retreat into
your gardens of pleasure. Let the plague
take the city. Delight your eyes with all

things fair and sweet. So shall it be well
with you and your soul shall dwell at ease
while the swine perish. It is the new gospel
of pessimism which despairs of the common
people because it despises them, — nay, the
old gospel of pessimism which seeks to se-
crete a selfish happiness in " the worst of
all possible worlds." Nebuchadnezzar tried
it in Babylon; Hadrian tried it in Rome;
Solomon tried it in Jerusalem; and from all
its palaces comes the same voice: *vanitas
vanitatum et omnia vanitas.*

It is not until the soul has learned a better
wisdom, learned that the human race is one,
and that none can really rise by treading on
his brother-men, learned that true art is not
the slave of luxury but the servant of hu-
manity, learned that happiness is born, not
of the lust to possess and enjoy, but of the
desire to give and to bless, — then, and
not until then, when she brings others with
her, can the soul find true rest in her Palace.

Tennyson has learned, as well as taught,
this consecration of art. He has always
been an artist, but not for art's sake; a
lover of beauty, but also a lover of humanity;
a singer whose music has brightened and
blessed thousands of homes wherever the

English tongue is spoken, and led the feet
of young men and maidens, by some Or-
phean enchantment, into royal mansions and
gardens, full of all things pure and lovely
and of good report.

MILTON AND TENNYSON

A COMPARISON AND A CONTRAST.

MILTON AND TENNYSON.

COMPARISON has long been recognized as one of the fruitful methods of criticism. But in using this method one needs to remember that it is the least obvious comparison which is often the truest and the most suggestive. The relationship of poets does not lie upon the surface; they receive their spiritual inheritance from beyond the lines of direct descent. Thus a poet may be most closely connected with one whose name we never join with his, and we may find his deepest resemblance to a man not only of another age, but of another school.

Tennyson has been compared most frequently with Keats; sometimes, but falsely, with Shelley; and sometimes, more wisely, with Wordsworth. Our accomplished American critic, Mr. Edmund Clarence Stedman, who touches nothing that he does not adorn, has a chapter in his *Victorian Poets* on Tennyson and Theocritus. But the best comparison, — one which runs far below the out-

ward appearance into the profound affini-
ties of genius — yet remains to be carefully
traced. Among all poets, — certainly among
all English poets, — it seems to me that
Tennyson's next of kin is Milton.

By this I do not mean to say that they
are equally great or exactly alike. For so
far as perfect likeness is concerned, there is
no such thing among the sons of men.
Every just comparison involves a contrast.
And when we speak of greatness, Milton's
place as the second poet of England is not
now to be called in question by any rival
claim. Yet even here, when we ask who is
to take the third place, I think there is no
one who has such a large and substantial
title as the author of In Memoriam and
The Idylls of the King. The conjunction
of the names of Milton and Tennyson will
be no unfamiliar event for the future ; and
for the present there is no better way of
studying these two great poets than to lay
their works side by side, and trace their
lives through the hidden parallel of a kin-
dred destiny.

I.

There are two direct references to Milton
in the works of Tennyson ; and these we

must examine first of all, in order that we
may understand the attitude of his mind to-
wards the elder master. The first is in *The
Palace of Art.* The royal daïs on which
the soul set up her intellectual throne is
described as having above it four portraits of
wise men.

> There deephaired Milton like an angel tall
>   Stood limnèd, Shakespeare bland and mild,
> Grim Dante pressed his lips, and from the wall
>   The bald blind Homer smiled.

Thus ran the verse in the 1833 edition;
and it tells us the rank which Tennyson, in
his twenty-fourth year, assigned to Milton.
But there is hardly an instance in which the
fineness of Tennyson's self - correction is
more happily illustrated than in the change
which he has made in this passage. In the
later editions it reads as follows : —

> For there was Milton like a seraph strong,
>   Beside him, Shakespeare bland and mild;
> And there the world-worn Dante grasped his song
>   And somewhat grimly smiled.
>
> And there the Ionian father of the rest;
>   A million wrinkles carved his skin;
> A hundred winters snowed upon his breast,
>   From cheek and throat and chin.

Let those who think that poetic expression

is a matter of chance ponder upon this pas-
sage. Every alteration is an improvement;
and most of all the change in the first line.
For now the poet has formed a true picture of
Milton's genius, and shows a profound com-
prehension of its essential quality. Its sign
is strength, but strength seraphic; not the
rude, volcanic force of the Titan, but a power
serene, harmonious, beautiful; a power of
sustained flight, of far-reaching vision, of
lofty eloquence, such as belongs to the sera-
phim alone. Mark you, the word is not
" angel," for the angels are lower beings, fol-
lowers in the heavenly host, some weak, and
some fallen; nor is the word " cherub," for
the cherubim, in the ancient Hebrew doc-
trine, are silent and mysterious creatures, not
shaped like men, voiceless and inapproach-
able; but the word is "seraph," for the ser-
aphim hover on mighty wings about the
throne of God, chanting His praise one to
another, and bearing His messages from
heaven to earth. This, then, is the figure
which Tennyson chooses, with the precision
of a great poet, to summon the spirit of Mil-
ton before us, — *a seraph strong*. That one
phrase is worth more than all of Dr. John-
son's ponderous criticisms.

The second reference is found among the *Experiments in Quantity* which were printed in the *Cornhill Magazine* in 1863. We have here the expression of Tennyson's mature opinion, carefully considered, and uttered with the strength of a generous and clear conviction; an utterance well worth weighing, not only for the perfection of its form, but also for the richness of its contents and the revelation which it makes of the poet's own nature. Hear with what power and stateliness the tone-picture begins, rising at once to the height of the noble theme ; —

> O, mighty-mouth'd inventor of harmonies,
> O, skill'd to sing of Time or Eternity,
>   God-gifted organ-voice of England,
>   Milton, a name to resound for ages ;
> Whose Titan angels, Gabriel, Abdiel,
> Starr'd from Jehovah's gorgeous armouries,
>   Tower, as the deep-domed empyrean
>   Rings to the roar of an angel onset, —
> Me rather all that bowery loneliness
> The brooks of Eden mazily murmuring
>   And bloom profuse and cedar arches
>   Charm, as a wanderer out in ocean,
> Where some refulgent sunset of India
> Streams o'er a rich ambrosial ocean isle,
>   And crimson-hued the stately palm-woods
>   Whisper in odorous heights of even.

Thus the brief ode finds its perfect close,

the rich, full tones dying away in the pro-
longed period, as the strains of some large
music are lost in the hush of twilight.   But
one other hand could have swept these grand
chords and evoked these tones of majestic
sweetness, — the hand of Milton himself.

It was De Quincey, that most nearly in-
spired, but most nearly insane, of critics, who
first spoke of the Miltonic movement as
having the qualities of an organ voluntary.
But the comparison which with him was little
more than a fortunate and striking simile is
transformed by the poet into a perfect
metaphor.

The great organ, pouring forth its melo-
dious thunders, becomes a living thing,
divinely dowered and filled with music, —
an instrument no longer, but a *voice*, majes-
tic, potent, thrilling the heart, — the voice of
England pealing in the ears of all the world
and all time.   Swept on the flood of those
great harmonies, the mighty hosts of angels
clash together in heaven-shaking conflict.
But it is the same full tide of music which
flows down in sweetest, lingering cadence
to wander through the cool groves and fra-
grant valleys of Paradise.   Here the younger
poet will more gladly dwell, finding a deeper

delight in these solemn and tranquil melodies
than in the roar and clang of battles, even
though angelic.

Is it not true? True, not only that the
organ voice has the twofold gift of beauty
and grandeur; true, not only that Tenny-
son has more sympathy with the loveliness
of Eden than with the mingled splendours
and horrors of the celestial battlefields; but
true, also, that there is a more potent and
lasting charm in Milton's description of the
beautiful than in his description of the sub-
lime. I do not think that *L'Allegro, Il
Penseroso*, and *Comus* have any lower place
in the world, or any less enduring life, than
Paradise Lost. And even in that great
epic there are no passages more worthy to be
remembered, more fruitful of pure feelings
and lofty thoughts, than those like the Hymn
of Adam, or the description of the first even-
ing in Eden, which show us the fairness and
delightfulness of God's world. We have
forgotten this; we have thought so much of
Milton's strength and sublimity that we
have ceased to recognize what is also true,
that he, of all English poets, is by nature
the supreme lover of beauty.

II.

This, then, is the first point of vital sympathy between Tennyson and Milton : their common love of the beautiful, not only in nature, but also in art. And this we see most clearly in the youth and in the youthful writings of the two poets.

There is a close resemblance in their early life. Both were born and reared in homes of modest comfort and refined leisure, under the blended influences of culture and religion. Milton's father was a scrivener ; deprived of his heritage because he obeyed his conscience to become a Protestant, but amassing a competence by his professional labor, he ordered his house well, softening and beautifying the solemnity of Puritan ways with the pursuit of music and literature. Tennyson was born in a country rectory, one of those fair homes of peace and settled order which are the pride and strength of England, — homes where " plain living and high thinking " produce the noblest types of manhood. His father also, like Milton's, was a musician, and surrounded his seven sons with influences which gave them poetic tastes and impulses. It is

strange to see how large a part music has
played in the development of these two
poets. Milton, even in his poverty, would
have an organ in his house to solace his dark
hours. Tennyson, it is said, often called one
of his sisters to play to him while he com-
posed ; and in his dedication of the *Songs
of the Wrens* to Sir Ivor Guest, he speaks
of himself as " wedded to music."

It is of course no more than a coincidence
that both of the young poets should have
been students in the University of Cam-
bridge. But there is something deeper in
the similarity of their college lives and stud-
ies. A certain loftiness of spirit, an habitual
abstraction of thought, separated them from
the mass of their fellow-students. They were
absorbed in communion with the great minds
of Greece and Rome. They drank deep at
the springs of ancient poesy. Not alone the
form, but the spirit, of the classics became
familiar to them. They were enamoured of
the beauty of the old-world legends, the
bright mythologies of Hellas, and Latium's
wondrous histories of gods and men. For
neither of them was this love of the ancient
poets a transient delight, a passing mood.
It took strong hold upon them ; it became

a moulding power in their life and work.
We can trace it in all their writings. Allu-
sions, themes, illustrations, similes, forms
of verse, echoes of thought, conscious or
unconscious imitations, — a thousand tokens
remind us that we are still beneath the in-
fluence of the old masters of a vanished
world, —

  "The dead, but sceptered sovereigns, who still rule
  Our spirits from their urns."

And here, again, we see a deep bond of
sympathy between Tennyson and Milton:
they are certainly the most learned, the most
classical, of England's poets.

Following their lives beyond the univer-
sity, we find that both of them came out into
a period of study, of seclusion, of leisure, of
poetical productiveness. Milton retired to
his father's house at Horton, in Bucking-
hamshire, where he lived for five years.
Tennyson's home at Somersby, in Lincoln-
shire, was broken up by his father's death in
1831 ; and after that, as Carlyle wrote to
Emerson, " he preferred clubbing with his
Mother and some Sisters, to live unpro-
moted and write Poems ; . . now here, now
there ; the family always within reach of
London, never in it ; he himself making rare

and brief visits, lodging in some old com-
rade's rooms." The position and circum-
stances of the two young poets were wonder-
fully alike. Both were withdrawn from the
whirl and conflict of active life into a world
of lovely forms, sweet sounds, and enchant-
ing dreams; both fed their minds with the
beauty of nature and of ancient story,
charmed by the music of divine philosophy,
and by songs of birds filling the sweet Eng-
lish air at dawn or twilight; both loved to
roam at will over hill and dale and by the
wandering streams; to watch the bee, with
honeyed thigh, singing from flower to flower,
and catch the scent of violets hidden in the
green; to hear the sound of far-off bells
swinging over the wide-watered shore, and
listen to the sighing of the wind among the
trees, or the murmur of the waves on the
river-bank; to pore and dream through long
night-watches over the legends of the past,
until the cold winds woke the gray-eyed
morn, and the lark's song startled the dull
night from her watch-tower in the skies.
They dwelt as idlers in the land, but it was
a glorious and fruitful idleness, for they
were reaping

> The harvest of a quiet eye
> That broods and sleeps on his own heart

How few and brief, and yet how wonder-
ful, how precious, are the results of these
peaceful years. *L'Allegro*, *Il Penseroso*,
Arcades, *Comus*, *Lycidas ; Isabel*, *Recol-
lections of the Arabian Nights*, *Ode to
Memory*, *The Dying Swan*, *The Palace of
Art*, *A Dream of Fair Women*, *Mariana*,
The Lady of Shalott, *The Lotos-Eaters*,
Œnone, — these are poems to be remem-
bered, read, and re-read with ever fresh de-
light, the most perfect things of their kind
in all literature. Grander poems, more pas-
sionate, more powerful, are many ; but there
are none in which the pure love of beauty,
Greek in its healthy symmetry, Christian in
its reverent earnestness, has produced work
so complete and exquisite as the early poems
of Milton and Tennyson.

Their best qualities are the same. I am
more impressed with this the more I read
them. They are marked by the same exact
observation of Nature, the same sensitive
perception of her most speaking aspects, the
same charm of simple and musical descrip-
tion. Read the *Ode to Memory*, — for in-
stance, the description of the poet's home : —

> Come from the woods that belt the gray hillside,
> The seven elms, the poplars four
> That stand beside my father's door;

And chiefly from the brook that loves
To purl o'er matted cress and ribbed sand
Or dimple in the dark of rushy coves,
Drawing into his narrow earthen urn,
    In every elbow and turn,
The filtered tribute of the rough woodland.
    O! hither lead my feet!
Pour round my ears the livelong bleat
Of the thick-fleeced sheep from wattled folds
    Upon the ridged wolds,
When the first matin-song hath waken'd loud,
Over the dark dewy earth forlorn,
What time the amber morn
Forth gushes from beneath a low-hung cloud.

Compare with this some lines from *L'Alle-gro* : —

To hear the lark begin his flight,
And singing startle the dull night
From his watch-tower in the skies,
Till the dappled dawn doth rise!
   .   .   .   .   .   .
Some time walking, not unseen,
By hedge-row elms, on hillocks green,
Right against the eastern gate
Where the great sun begins his state,
Rob'd in flames and amber light,
The clouds in thousand liveries dight;
While the ploughman, near at hand,
Whistles o'er the furrow'd land,
And the milkmaid singeth blithe,
And the mower whets his scythe,
And every shepherd tells his tale
Under the hawthorn in the dale.
Straight mine eye hath caught new pleasures
While the landscape round it measures;

> Russet lawns and fallows gray,
> Where the nibbling flocks do stray;
> Mountains on whose barren breast
> The labouring clouds do often rest;
> Meadows trim with daisies pied,
> Shallow brooks and rivers wide.

Here are the same breadth of vision, delicacy of touch, atmospheric effect; the same sensitiveness to the simplest variations of light and sound; the same power to shed over the quiet scenery of the English country the light of an ideal beauty. It is an art far beyond that of the landscape painter, and all the more perfect because so well concealed.

Another example will show us the similarity of the two poets in their more purely imaginative work, the description of that which they have seen only with the dreaming eyes of fancy. Take the closing song, or epilogue of the Attendant Spirit, in *Comus* : —

> To the ocean now I fly
> And those happy climes that lie
> Up in the broad fields of the sky.
> There I suck the liquid air,
> All amidst the gardens fair
> Of Hesperus, and his daughters three,
> That sing about the golden tree :
> Along the crisped shades and bowers
> Revels the spruce and jocund Spring;

The graces and the rosy-bosomed Hours
Thither all their bounties bring;
There eternal summer dwells,
And west-winds, with musky wing,
About the cedarn alleys fling
Nard and cassia's balmy smells.
Iris there with humid bow
Waters the odourous banks, that blow
Flowers of more mingled hue
Than her purfled scarf can shew,
And drenches with Elysian dew
Beds of hyacinths and roses.

Compare this with Tennyson's *Recollections of the Arabian Nights :*—

Thence thro' the garden I was drawn—
A realm of pleasance, many a mound,
And many a shadow-chequer'd lawn
Full of the city's stilly sound,
And deep myrrh-thickets blowing round
The stately cedar, tamarisks,
Thick rosaries of scented thorn,
Tall orient shrubs, and obelisks
    Graven with emblems of the time,
    In honour of the golden prime
        Of good Haroun Alraschid.

With dazed vision unawares
From the long alley's latticed shade
Emerged, I came upon the great
Pavilion of the Caliphat.
Right to the carven cedarn doors
Flung inward over spangled floors,
Broad-based flights of marble stairs
Ran up with golden balustrade,

After the fashion of the time,
And humour of the golden prime
Of good Haroun Alraschid.

Here is more than a mere resemblance of
words and themes, more than an admiring
imitation or echoing of phrases; it is an
identity of taste, spirit, temperament. But
the resemblance of forms is also here. We
can trace it even in such a minor trait as the
skilful construction and use of double-words.
This has often been noticed as a distinguish-
ing feature of Tennyson's poetry. But Mil-
ton uses them almost as freely and quite
as magically. In *Comus*, which has a few
more than a thousand lines, there are fifty-
four double-epithets; in *L'Allegro* there are
sixteen to a hundred and fifty lines; in *Il
Penseroso* there are eleven to one hundred
and seventy lines. Tennyson's *Ode to Mem-
ory*, with a hundred and twenty lines, has
fifteen double-words; *Mariana*, with eighty
lines, has nine; the *Lotos-Eaters*, with two
hundred lines, has thirty-two. And if I
should choose at random fifty such words
from the early poems, I do not think that
any one, not knowing them by heart, could
tell at first glance which were Milton's and
which Tennyson's. Let us try the experi-
ment with the following list: —

Low-thoughted, empty-vaulted, rosy-white, rosy-bo-
somed, violet-embroidered, dew-impearled, over-exquisite,
long-levelled, mild-eyed, white-handed, white-breasted,
pure-eyed, sin-worn, self-consumed, self-profit, close-
curtained, low-browed, ivy-crowned, gray-eyed, far-
beaming, pale - eyed, down - steering, flower - inwoven,
dewy-dark, moon-loved, smooth-swarded, quick-falling,
slow-dropping, coral-paven, lily-cradled, amber-dropping,
thrice-great, dewy-feathered, purple-spiked, foam-foun-
tains, sand-built, night-steeds, full-flowing, sable-stoled,
sun-steeped, star-led, pilot-stars, full-juiced, dew-fed,
brazen-headed, wisdom-bred, star-strown, low-embowed,
iron-worded, globe-filled.

It will puzzle the reader to distinguish
with any degree of certainty the authorship
of these words. And this seems the more
remarkable when we remember that there
are two centuries of linguistic development
and changing fashions of poetic speech be-
tween *Comus* and *Œnone*.

Not less remarkable is the identity of
spirit in Tennyson and Milton in their deli-
cate yet wholesome sympathy with Nature,
their perception of the relation of her moods
and aspects to the human heart. This, in
fact, is the keynote of *L'Allegro* and *Il
Penseroso*. The same world, seen under
different lights and filled with different
sounds, responds as deeply to the joyous, as
to the melancholy, spirit. There is a pro-

found meaning, a potent influence, in the
outward shows of sky and earth. While
the Lady of Shalott dwells in her pure se-
clusion, the sun shines, the lily blossoms on
the river's breast, and the blue sky is un-
clouded ; but when she passes the fatal line,
and the curse has fallen on her, then

> In the stormy eastwind straining,
> The pale yellow woods are waning,
> The broad stream in his banks complaining,
> Heavily the low sky raining,
>   Over tower'd Camelot.

Thus, also, when the guilty pair in Eden
had transgressed that sole command on which
their happiness depended, —

> Sky lowered, and muttering thunder, some sad drops
> Wept at completing of the mortal sin.

Mr. Ruskin says that this is " the pathetic
fallacy ; " for, as a matter of fact, the clouds
do not weep, nor do the rivers complain,
and he maintains that to speak of them as
if they did these things is to speak with a
certain degree of falsehood which is un-
worthy of the highest kind of art. But Mr.
Ruskin may say what he pleases about Mil-
ton and Tennyson without much likelihood
of persuading any sane person that their
poetry is not profoundly true to Nature, —

and most true precisely in its recognition of
her power to echo and reflect the feelings of
man. All her realities are but seemings ;
and she does seem to weep with them that
weep, and to rejoice with them that do re-
joice. Nothing can be more real than that.
The chemistry of the sun is no more true
than its message of joy ; the specific gravity
of the rain is of no greater consequence than
its message of sadness. And for the poet
the first necessity is that he should be able
to feel and interpret the sentiment of nat-
ural objects. The art of landscape-poetry,
I take it, consists in this : the choice and
description of such actual images of external
nature as are capable of being grouped and
coloured by a dominant idea or feeling. Of
this art the most perfect masters are Tenny-
son and Milton. And here I have reversed
the order of the names, because I reckon
that on this point Tennyson stands first.
Take, for example, the little poem on *Mari-
ana*, — that wonderful variation on the
theme of loneliness suggested by a single
line in *Measure for Measure.* Here the
thought is the weariness of waiting for one
who does not come. The garden has grown
black with moss, the nails in the wall are

rusted, the thatch is full of weeds on the forsaken house; the moat is crusted over with creeping marsh - plants, the solitary poplar on the fen trembles eternally in the wind ; slowly pass the night-hours, marked by the distant sounds of crowing cocks and lowing oxen ; slower still the hours of day, while the fly buzzes on the window-pane, the mouse shrieks in the wainscot, the sparrow chirps on the roof ; everything in the picture belongs to a life sunken in monotony, lost in monotony, forgotten as a dead man out of mind.   Even the light that falls into the moated grange is full of dust.

> But most she loathed the hour
>   When the thick-moted sunbeam lay
>   Athwart the chambers, and the day
> Downsloped, was westering in his bower.
>   *Then*, said she, " I am very dreary,
>   He will not come," she said ;
>   She wept, " I am aweary, aweary,
>   Oh God, that I were dead."

Now all this is perfect painting of the things in nature which respond exactly to the sense of depression and solitude and intolerable, prolonged neglect, in a human soul. For an illustration of the opposite feeling turn to the description of the May morning in *The Gardener's Daughter*. The

passage is too long to quote here; but it is
beyond doubt one of the most rich and joy-
ous pictures in English verse. The world
seems to be overflowing with blossom and
song as the youth draws near to the maiden.
It is love set to landscape. And yet there
is not a single false touch; all is true and
clear and precise, down to the lark's song
which grows more rapid as he sinks to-
wards his nest, and the passing cloud whose
moisture draws out the sweet smell of the
flowers.

Another trait common to the earlier
poems of Milton and Tennyson is their
purity of tone. They are sensuous, — indeed
Milton declared that all good poetry must
be sensuous, — but never for a moment, in a
single line, are they sensual.

Look at the Lady in *Comus.* She is the
sweet embodiment of Milton's youthful ideal
of virtue, clothed with the fairness of open-
ing womanhood, armed with the sun-clad
power of chastity. Darkness and danger
cannot

> Stir the constant mood of her calm thoughts.

Evil things have no power upon her, but
shrink abashed from her presence.

> So dear to heaven is saintly chastity
> That when a soul is found sincerely so,
> A thousand liveried angels lackey her,
> Driving far off each thing of sin and guilt;
> And in clear dream and solemn vision,
> Tell her of things that no gross ear can hear,
> Till oft converse with heavenly habitants
> Begin to cast a beam on th' outward shape,
> The unpolluted temple of the mind,
> And turns it by degrees to the soul's essence,
> Till all be made immortal.

And now, beside this loveliest Lady, bring
Isabel, with those

> Eyes not down-dropt nor over-bright, but fed
> With the clear-pointed flame of chastity,
> Clear, without heat, undying, tended by
> Pure vestal thoughts in the translucent fane
> Of her still spirit.

Bring also her who, for her people's good,
passed naked on her palfrey through the
city streets, — Godiva, who

> Rode forth, clothed on with chastity;
> The deep air listen'd round her as she rode,
> And all the low wind hardly breathed for fear.

These are sisters, perfect in purity as in
beauty, and worthy to be enshrined forever
in the love of youth. They are ideals which
draw the heart, not downward, but upward
by the power of " *das ewig Weibliche.*"

There are many other points of resem-
blance between the early poems of Milton

and Tennyson on which it would be pleasant
to dwell. Echoes of thought like that son-
net, beginning

> Check every outflash, every ruder sally
> Of thought and speech : speak low, and give up wholly
> Thy spirit to mild-minded melancholy, —

which seems almost as if it might have been
written by Il Penseroso. Coincidences of
taste and reading such as the fondness for
the poet to whom Milton alludes as

> Him that left half told
> The story of Cambuscan bold,
> Of Camball and of Algarsife
> And who had Canace to wife, —

and whom Tennyson calls

> Dan Chaucer, the first warbler, whose sweet breath
> Preluded those melodious bursts that fill
> The spacious times of great Elizabeth
> With sounds that echo still.

Likenesses of manner such as the imitation
of the smooth elegiac poets in *Lycidas* and
Œnone. But a critic who wishes his con-
clusions to be accepted cheerfully and with
a sense of gratitude must leave his readers
to supply some illustrations for themselves.
And this I will be prudent enough to do ;
expressing only the opinion that those who
study the subject carefully will find that
there is no closer parallel in literature than

that between the early poems of Milton and
Tennyson.

III.

There are two causes which have power
to change the natural or premeditated course
of a man's life, — the shock of a great out-
ward catastrophe, and the shock of a pro-
found inward grief. When the former
comes, it shatters all his cherished plans,
renders the execution of his favorite pro-
jects impossible, directs the current of his
energy into new channels, plunges him
into conflict with circumstances, turns his
strength against corporeal foes, and produces
a change of manner, speech, life, which is
at once evident and tangible. With the
latter, it is different. The inward shock
brings with it no alteration of the visible
environment, leaves the man where he stood
before, to the outward eye unchanged, free
to tread the same paths and pursue the same
designs; and yet, in truth, not free; most
deeply, though most subtly, changed; for
the soul, shaken from her serene repose, and
losing the self-confidence of youth, either
rises into a higher life or sinks into a
lower; meeting the tremendous questions
which haunt the shade of a supreme

personal bereavement, she finds an answer
either in the eternal Yes or in the eternal
No; and though form and accent and mode
of speech remain the same, the thoughts and
intents of the heart are altered forever.

To Milton came the outward conflict; to
Tennyson, the inward grief. And as we
follow them beyond the charmed circle of
their early years, we must trace the parallel
between them, if indeed we can find it at
all, far below the surface; although even
yet we shall see some external resemblances
amid many and strong contrasts.

Milton's catastrophe was the civil war,
sweeping over England like a flood. But
the fate which involved him in it was none
other than his own conscience. This it was
that drew him, by compulsion more strong
than sweet, from the florid literary hospital-
ity of Italian mutual laudation societies into
the vortex of tumultuous London, made him
" lay aside his singing robes " for the heavy
armour of the controversialist, and leave his
" calm and pleasant solitariness, fed with
cheerful and confident thoughts, to embark
on a troubled sea of noises and harsh dis-
putes." His conscience, I say, not his
tastes : all these led him the other way.

But an irresistible sense of duty caught him, and dragged him, as it were, by the neck to the verge of the precipice, and flung him down into the thick of the hottest conflict that England has ever seen.

Once there, he does not retreat. He quits himself like a man. He is not a Puritan. He loves many things that the mad Puritans hate, — art, music, fine literature, nature, beauty. But one thing he loves more than all, — liberty ! For that he will fight, — fight on the Puritan side, fight against anybody, desperately, pertinaciously, with grand unconsciousness of possible defeat. He catches the lust of combat, and "drinks delight of battle with his peers." The serene poet is transformed into a thundering pamphleteer. He launches deadly bolts against tyranny in Church, in State, in society. He strikes at the corrupt clergy, at the false, cruel king, at the self-seeking bigots disguised as friends of freedom. He is absorbed in strife. Verse is forgotten. But one brief strain of true poetry bursts from him at the touch of personal grief. The rest is all buried, choked down, concealed. The full stream of his energy, unstinted, undivided, flows into the struggle

for freedom and truth; and even when the
war is ended, the good cause betrayed by
secret enemies and foolish friends, the free-
dom of England sold back into the hands
of the treacherous Stuarts, Milton fights on,
like some guerilla captain in a far mountain
region, who has not heard, or will not be-
lieve, the news of surrender.

The blow which fell on Tennyson was
secret. The death of Arthur Henry Hal-
lam, in 1833, caused no great convulsion in
English politics, brought no visible disaster
to church or state, sent only the lightest
and most transient ripple of sorrow across
the surface of society; but to the heart of
one man it was the shock of an inward
earthquake, upheaving the foundations of
life and making the very arch of heaven
tremble. Bound to Hallam by one of those
rare friendships passing the love of women,
Tennyson felt his loss in the inmost fibres
of his being. The world was changed, dark-
ened, filled with secret conflicts. The im-
portunate questions of human life and des-
tiny thronged upon his soul. The ideal
peace, the sweet, art-satisfied seclusion, the
dreams of undisturbed repose, became im-
possible for him. He must fight, not for a

party cause, but for spiritual freedom and immortal hopes, not against incorporate and embattled enemies, but against unseen foes, — thrones, principalities, and powers of darkness.

I think we have some record of this strife in poems like *Two Voices*, and *The Vision of Sin*. The themes here treated are the deepest and most awful that can engage the mind. The worth of life, the significance of suffering, the reality of virtue, the existence of truth, the origin and end of evil, human responsibility, Divine goodness, mysteries of the now and the hereafter, — these are the problems with which the poet is forced to deal, and he dares to deal with them face to face. I will not say that he finds, as yet, the true solution ; there is a more profound and successful treatment of the same problems to follow in *In Memoriam*. But I think that, so far as they go, these poems are right and true; and in them, enlightened by grief, strengthened by inward combat, the poet has struck a loftier note than can be heard in the beautiful poems of his youth.

For this, mark you, is clear. The poet has now become a man. The discipline of sorrow has availed. Life is real and earnest

to him. He grapples with the everlasting
facts of humanity. Men and women are
closer to him. He can write poems like
Dora, *Ulysses*, *St. Simeon Stylites*, as won-
derful for their difference in tone and sub-
ject as for their common virility and abso-
lute truth to nature. He has learned to feel
a warm sympathy with

> Men, my brothers, men, the workers:

to care for all that touches their welfare; to
rejoice in the triumphs of true liberty; to
thunder in scorn and wrath against the social
tyrannies that crush the souls of men, and

> The social lies that warp us from the living truth.

It is true that there is no actual and visi-
ble conflict, no civil war raging to engulf
him. He is not called upon to choose be-
tween his love of poetry and his love of
country, nor to lay aside his singing-robes
even for a time. It is his fortune, or mis-
fortune, to have fallen upon an age of peace
and prosperity and settled government. But
in that great unseen warfare which is ever
waging between truth and error, right and
wrong, freedom and oppression, light and
darkness, he bears his part and bears it well,
by writing such poems as *Locksley Hall*,

Sea Dreams, *Enoch Arden*, *Aylmer's Field;* and these entitle him to high rank as a poet of humanity.

Are they then so far apart, Milton and Tennyson, the Latin Secretary of Cromwell and the Poet Laureate of Queen Victoria, — are they so far apart in the spiritual activity of their lives as their circumstances seem to place them ? Are they as unlike in the fact, as they are in the form, of their utterance on the great practical questions of life? I think not. Even here, where the lines of their work seem to diverge most widely, we may trace some deep resemblances, under apparent differences.

It is a noteworthy fact that a most important place in the thought and writing of both these men has been occupied by the subject of marriage. How many of Tennyson's poems are devoted to this theme! *The Miller's Daughter*, *The Lord of Burleigh*, *Lady Clare*, *Edwin Morris*, *The Brook*, *The Gardener's Daughter*, *Love and Duty*, *Locksley Hall*, *The Princess*, *Maud*, *Enoch Arden*, *Aylmer's Field*, *The Golden Supper*, *The Window*, *The First Quarrel*, *The Wreck*, *The Flight*, and *The Idylls of the King*, all have the thought of union between

man and woman, and the questions which
arise in connection with it, at their root.

In *The Coming of Arthur*, Tennyson
makes his chosen hero rest all his power
upon a happy and true marriage: —

> What happiness to reign a lonely king
> Vext with waste dreams ? For saving I be join'd
> To her that is the fairest under heaven,
> I seem as nothing in the mighty world,
> And cannot will my will nor work my work
> Wholly, nor make myself in mine own realm
> Victor and lord. But were I join'd with her,
> Then might we live together as one life,
> And reigning with one will in everything,
> Have power on this dark land to l¹ghten it,
> And power on this dead world to make it live.

Compare with this Adam's complaint in
Paradise : —

> In solitude
> What happiness ? Who can enjoy alone ?
> Or all enjoying what contentment find ?

his demand for a companion equal with him-
self, " fit to participate all rational delight ; "
and his description of his first sight of Eve :

> She disappeared and left me dark. I wak'd
> To find her, or forever to deplore
> Her loss, and other pleasures all abjure.

Mark the fact that those four tremendous
pamphlets on Divorce with which Milton

horrified his enemies and shocked his friends,
have underlying all their errors and extrava-
gances the great doctrine that a genuine
marriage must be a true companionship and
union of souls — a doctrine equally opposed
to the licentious, and to the conventional,
view of wedlock. This is precisely Tenny-
son's position. His bitterest invectives are
hurled against marriages of convenience and
avarice. He praises " that true marriage,
that healthful and holy family life, which
has its roots in mutual affection, in mutual
fitness, and which is guarded by a constancy
as strong as heaven's blue arch and yet as
spontaneous as the heart-beats of a happy
child." But in praising this, Tennyson
speaks of what he has possessed and known :
Milton could have spoken only of what he
had desired and missed. A world-wide dif-
ference, more than enough to account for
anything of incompleteness or harshness in
Milton's views of women.

What gross injustice the world has done
him on this point ! Married at an age when
a man who has preserved the lofty ideals and
personal purity of youth is peculiarly liable
to deception, to a woman far below him in
character and intellect, a pretty fool utterly

unfitted to take a sincere and earnest view
of life or to sympathize with him in his
studies; deserted by her a few weeks after
the wedding-day; met by stubborn refusal
and unjust reproaches in every attempt to
reclaim and reconcile her; accused by her
family of disloyalty in politics, and treated
as if he were unworthy of honourable consid-
eration; what wonder that his heart experi-
enced a great revulsion, that he began to
doubt the reality of such womanhood as he
had described and immortalized in *Comus*,
that he sought relief in elaborating a doc-
trine of divorce which should free him from
the unworthy and irksome tie of a marriage
which was in truth but an empty mockery?
That divorce doctrine which he propounded
in the heat of personal indignation, dis-
guised even from himself beneath a mask of
professedly calm philosophy, was surely false,
and we cannot but condemn it. But can we
condemn his actual conduct, so nobly incon-
sistent with his own theory? Can we con-
demn the man, as we see him forgiving and
welcoming his treacherous wife driven by
stress of poverty and danger to return to the
home which she had frivolously forsaken;
welcoming also, and to the best of his ability

sheltering, her whole family of Philistines, who were glad enough, for all their pride, to find a refuge from the perils of civil war in the house of the despised schoolmaster and Commonwealth-man; bearing patiently, for his wife's sake, with their weary presence and shallow talk in his straitened dwelling-place until the death of the father-in-law, whose sense of honour was never strong enough to make him pay one penny of his daughter's promised marriage-portion, — can we condemn Milton as we see him acting thus? And as we see him, after a few months of happy union with a second wife, again left a widower with three daughters, two of whom, at least, never learned to love him; blind, poor, almost friendless; disliked and robbed by his undutiful children, who did not scruple to cheat him in the market-ings, sell his books to the rag-pickers, and tell the servants that the best news they could hear would be the news of their father's death; forced at length in very instinct of self-protection to take as his third wife a plain, honest woman who would be faithful and kind in her care of him and his house; can we wonder if, after this experience of life, he thought somewhat doubtfully of women?

But of woman, woman as God made her
and meant her to be, woman as she is in the
true purity and unspoiled beauty of her na-
ture, he never thought otherwise than nobly
and reverently. Read his sonnet to his sec-
ond wife, in whom for one fleeting year his
heart tasted the best of earthly joys, the joy
of a perfect companionship, but who was lost
to him in the birth of her first child : —

Methought I saw my late espoused saint
  Brought to me like Alcestis from the grave,
  Whom Jove's great son to her glad husband gave,
Rescued from death by force though pale and faint.
Mine, as whom washed from spot of child-bed taint
  Purification in the old Law did save,
  And such as yet once more I trust to have
Full sight of her in Heaven, without restraint,
Came vested all in white, pure as her mind;
  Her face was veiled, yet to my fancied sight
Love, sweetness, goodness in her person shined
  So clear as in no face with more delight.
But O, as to embrace me she inclined,
  I waked, she fled, and day brought back my night.

Surely there is no more beautiful and heart-
felt praise of perfect womanhood in all liter-
ature than this; and Tennyson has never
written with more unfeigned worship of
wedded love.

It is true, indeed, that Milton declares that
woman is inferior to man " in the mind and

inward faculties," but he follows this decla-
ration with the most exquisite description
of her peculiar excellences :

> When I approach
> Her loveliness, so absolute she seems
> And in herself complete, so well to know
> Her own, that what she wills to do or say
> Seems wisest, virtuousest, discreetest, best :
> Authority and reason on her wait
> As one intended first, not after made
> Occasionally ; and to consummate all,
> Greatness of mind and nobleness their seat
> Build in her loveliest, and create an awe
> About her as a guard angelic placed.

It is true that he teaches, in accordance
with the explicit doctrine of the Bible, that
it is the wife's duty to obey her husband, to
lean upon, and follow, his larger strength
when it is exercised in wisdom. But he
never places the woman below the man,
always at his side ; the divinely - dowered
consort and counterpart, not the same, but
equal, supplying his deficiencies and solac-
ing his defects,

> His likeness, his fit help, his other self,

with whom he may enjoy

> Union of mind or in us both one soul.

And love like this

> Leads up to heaven ; is both the way and guide.

Compare these teachings with those of
Tennyson in *The Princess*, where under a
veil of irony, jest mixed with earnest, he
shows the pernicious folly of the modern
attempt to change woman into a man in
petticoats, exhibits the female lecturer and
the sweet girl graduates in their most de-
lightfully absurd aspect, overthrows the vis-
ionary towers of the Female College with a
baby's touch, and closes the most good-hu-
moured of satires with a picture of the true
relationship of man and woman, so beautiful
and so wise that neither poetry nor philoso-
phy can add a word to it.

> For woman is not undevelopt man,
> But diverse : could we make her as the man,
> Sweet Love were slain ; his dearest bond is this,
> Not like to like, but like in difference.
> Yet in the long years liker must they grow ;
> The man be more of woman, she of man ;
> He gain in sweetness and in moral height,
> Nor lose the wrestling thews that throw the world ;
> She mental breadth, nor fail in childward care,
> Nor lose the childlike in the larger mind ;
> Till at the last she set herself to man
> Like perfect music unto noble words.
>
> . . . .
>
> Then comes the statelier Eden back to men :
> Then reign the world's great bridals, chaste and calm
> Then springs the crowning race of humankind.
> May these things be !

A second point in which we may trace a deep resemblance between Milton and Tennyson is their intense love of country. This is not always a prominent characteristic of great poets. Indeed, we may question whether there is not usually something in the poetic temperament which unfits a man for actual patriotism, makes him an inhabitant of an ideal realm rather than a citizen of a particular country; inclines him to be governed by disgusts more than he is inspired by enthusiasms, and to withdraw himself from a practical interest in the national welfare into the vague dreams of Utopian perfection. In Goethe we see the cold indifference of the self-centred artistic mind, careless of his country's degradation and enslavement, provided only the all-conquering Napoleon will leave him his poetic leisure and freedom. In Byron we see the wild rebelliousness of the poet of passion, deserting, disowning, and reviling his native land in the sullen fury of personal anger. But Milton and Tennyson are true patriots — Englishmen to the heart's core. They do not say, " My country, right or wrong ! " They protest in noble scorn against all kinds of tyrannies and hypocrisies. They

are not bound in conscienceless servility
to any mere political party. They are
the partisans of England, and England to
them means freedom, justice, righteous-
ness, Christianity. Milton sees her " rous-
ing herself like a strong man after sleep,
and shaking her invincible locks ; " or " as
an eagle, mewing her mighty youth, and
kindling her undazzled eyes at the full mid-
day beam ; purging and scaling her long-
abused sight at the fountain itself of heav-
enly radiance ; while the whole noise of
timorous and flocking birds, with those also
that love the twilight, flutter about amazed
at what she means, and in their envious
gabble would prognosticate a year of sects
and schisms." Tennyson sings her praise as

> the land that freemen till,
> That sober-suited Freedom chose,
> The land where, girt with friends or foes,
> A man may speak the thing he will.

He honours and reveres the Queen, but it
is because her power is the foundation and
defense of liberty; because of her it may
be said that

> Statesmen at her council met
> Who knew the season when to take
> Occasion by the hand, and make
> The bounds of freedom wider yet,

By shaping some august decree,
  Which kept her throne unshaken still,
  Broad-bas'd upon the people's will,
And compass'd by the inviolate sea.

Think you he would have written thus if
Charles Stuart, bribe-taker, extortioner,
tyrant, dignified and weak betrayer of his
best friends, had been his sovereign? His
own words tell us on which side he would
have stood in that great revolt. In the
verses written on *The Third of February*,
1852, he reproaches the Parliament for their
seeming purpose to truckle to Napoleon,
after the *coup d'état*, and cries :

Shall we fear *him*? Our own we never feared.
  From our first Charles by force we wrung our claims.
Pricked by the Papal spur, we reared,
  We flung the burthen of the second James.

And again, in the poem entitled *England
and America in 1782*, he justifies the Amer-
ican Revolution as a lesson taught by Eng-
land herself, and summons his country to
exult in the freedom of her children.

But thou, rejoice with liberal joy !
  Lift up thy rocky face,
And shatter, when the storms are black,
In many a streaming torrent back,
  The seas that shock thy base.

Whatever harmonies of law
  The growing world assume,

The work is thine, — the single note
From the deep chord that Hampden smote
  Will vibrate to the doom.

Here is the grand Miltonic ring, not now
disturbed and roughened by the harshness
of opposition, the bitterness of disappoint-
ment, the sadness of despair, but rounded
in the calm fulness of triumph. "The
whirligig of Time brings in his revenges."
The bars of oppression are powerless to stay
the tide of progress.

The old order changeth, giving place to new,
And God fulfils Himself in many ways.

If Milton were alive to-day he would find
his ideals largely realized ; freedom of wor-
ship, freedom of the press, freedom of edu-
cation, no longer things to be fought for, but
things to be enjoyed ; the principle of pop-
ular representation firmly ingrained in the
constitution of the British monarchy (which
Tennyson calls " a crowned Republic "), and
the spirit of " the good old cause," the peo-
ple's cause which seemed lost when the sec-
ond Charles came back, now victorious and
peacefully guiding the destinies of the na-
tion into a yet wider and more glorious
liberty.

But what would be the effect of such an

environment upon such a character as his?
What would Milton have been in this nine-
teenth century? If we can trust the prophe-
cies of his early years; if we can regard the
hints of his own preferences and plans, from
whose fruition a stern sense of duty, like a
fiery-sworded angel, barred him out, we must
imagine the course of his life, the develop-
ment of his genius, as something very differ-
ent from what they actually were.   An age
of peace and prosperity, the comfort and
quietude of a well-ordered home, freedom to
pursue his studious researches and cultivate
his artistic tastes to the full, an atmos-
phere of liberal approbation and encourage-
ment, — circumstances such as these would
have guided his life and work into a much
closer parallel with Tennyson, and yet they
never could have made him other than him-
self.   For his was a seraphic spirit, strong,
indomitable, unalterable; and even the most
subtile influence of surroundings could never
have destroyed or changed him fundamen-
tally.   So it was true, as Macaulay has said,
that "from the Parliament and from the
court, from the conventicle and from the
Gothic cloister, from the gloomy and sepul-
chral rites of the Roundheads, and from

the Christmas revel of the hospitable cava-
lier, his nature selected and drew to itself
whatever was great and good, while it re-
jected all the base and pernicious ingre-
dients by which these finer elements were
defiled." And yet the very process of re-
jection had its effect upon him. The fierce
conflicts of theology and politics in which
for twenty years he was absorbed left their
marks upon him for good and for evil. They
tried him as by fire. They brought out all
his strength of action and endurance. They
made his will like steel. They gave him
the God-like power of one who has suffered
to the uttermost. But they also disturbed,
at least for a time, the serenity of his men-
tal processes. They made the flow of his
thought turbulent and uneven. They nar-
rowed, at the same time that they intensi-
fied, his emotions. They made him an in-
veterate controversialist, whose God must
argue and whose angels were debaters.
They crushed his humour and his tender-
ness. Himself, however, the living poet, the
supreme imagination, the seraphic utterance,
they did not crush, but rather strengthened.
And so it came to pass that in him we have
the miracle of literature, — the lost river of

poetry springing suddenly, as at Divine com-
mand, from the bosom of the rock, no trick-
ling and diminished rill, but a sweeping
flood, laden with richest argosies of thought.

IV.

How to speak of *Paradise Lost* I know
not. To call it a master-work is superfluous.
To say that it stands absolutely alone and
supreme is both true and false. Parts of it
are like other poems, and yet there is no
poem in the world like it. The theme is
old; had been treated by the author of
Genesis in brief, by Du Bartas and other
rhymers at length. The manner is old, in-
herited from Virgil and Dante. And yet,
beyond all question, *Paradise Lost* is one
of the most unique, individual, unmistaka-
ble poems in the world's literature. Imita-
tions of it have been attempted by Mont-
gomery, Pollok, Bickersteth, and other pious
versifiers, but they are no more like the
original than St. Peter's in Montreal is like
St. Peter's in Rome, or than the pile of
coarse - grained limestone on New York's
Fifth Avenue is like the Cathedral of
Milan, with its

Chanting quires,
The giant windows' blazoned fires,
The height, the space, the gloom, the glory,
A mount of marble, a hundred spires!

Imitation may be the sincerest flattery, but imitation never produces the deepest resemblance. The man who imitates is concerned with that which is outward, but kinship of spirit is inward. He who is next of kin to a master-mind will himself be too great for the work of a copyist; he will be influenced, if at all, unconsciously; and though the intellectual relationship may be expressed also in some external traits of speech and manner, the true likeness will be in the temper of the soul and the sameness of the moral purpose. Such likeness, I think, we can discern between *Paradise Lost* and Tennyson's greatest works, *The Idylls of the King* and *In Memoriam.*

I shall speak first and more briefly of the Idylls, because I intend to make them the subject of another study from a different point of view. At present we have to consider only their relations to the work of Milton. And in this connection we ought not to forget that he was the first to call attention to the legend of King Arthur as a

fit subject for a great poem. Having made
up his mind to write a national epic which
should do for England that which Tasso and
Ariosto had done for Italy, " that which the
greatest and choicest wits of Athens and
Rome, and those Hebrews of old did for
their country," Milton tells us that he enter-
tained for a long time a design to

> Revoke into song the kings of our island,
> Arthur yet from his underground hiding stirring to war-
>   fare,
> Or to tell of those that sat round him as Knights of his
>   Table ;
> Great-souled heroes unmatched, and (O might the spirit
>   but aid me),
> Shiver the Saxon phalanxes under the shock of the Bri-
>   tons.

The design was abandoned : but it was a
fortunate fate that brought it at last into the
hands of the one man, since Milton died,
who was able to carry it to completion.

Compare the verse of the *Idylls* with that
of *Paradise Lost.*

Both Milton and Tennyson have been led
by their study of the classic poets to under-
stand that rhyme is the least important ele-
ment of good poetry ; the best music is made
by the concord rather than by the unison
of sounds, and the coincidence of final con-

sonants is but a slight matter compared with
the cadence of syllables and the accented
harmony of long vowels. Indeed it may be
questioned whether the inevitable recurrence
of the echo of rhyme does not disturb and
break the music more than it enhances it.
Certainly Milton thought so, and he frank-
ly took great credit to himself for setting
the example, "the first in English, of an-
cient liberty recovered to heroic poems from
the troublesome and modern bondage of
riming."

There were many to follow him in this
path, but for the most part with ignominious
and lamentable failure. They fell into the
mistake of thinking that because unrhymed
verse was more free it was less difficult, and,
making their liberty a cloak of poetic li-
cense, they poured forth floods of accurately
measured prose under the delusion that they
were writing blank-verse. The fact is that
this is the one form of verse which requires
the most delicate ear and the most patient
labour. In Cowper, Coleridge, Southey,
Wordsworth, Browning, these preconditions
are wanting. And with the possible excep-
tion of Matthew Arnold's *Sohrab and Rus-
tum*, the first English blank-verse worthy

to compare with that of *Paradise Lost* is
found in Tennyson's *Idylls of the King.*

There is a shade of contrast in the move-
ment of the two poems. Each has its own
distinctive quality. In Milton we observe
a more stately and majestic march, more of
rhythm: in Tennyson a sweeter and more
perfect tone, more of melody. These quali-
ties correspond, in verse, to form and colour
in painting. We might say that Milton is
the greater draughtsman, as Michael An-
gelo; Tennyson the better colourist, as Ra-
phael. But the difference between the two
painters is always greater than that between
the two poets. For the methods by which
they produce their effects are substantially
the same; and their results differ chiefly as
the work of a strong, but sometimes heavy,
hand differs from that of a hand less power-
ful, but better disciplined.

De Quincey has said, somewhere or other,
that finding fault with Milton's versification
is a dangerous pastime. The lines which you
select for criticism have a way of justifying
themselves at your expense. That which
you have condemned as a palpable blunder,
an unpardonable discord, is manifested in
the mouth of a better reader as majestically

right and harmonious. And so, when you attempt to take liberties with any passage of his, you are apt to feel as when coming upon what appears to be a dead lion in a forest. You have an uncomfortable suspicion that he may not be dead, but only sleeping; or perhaps not even sleeping, but only shamming. Many an unwary critic has been thus unpleasantly surprised. Notably Drs. Johnson and Bentley, and in a small way Walter Savage Landor, roaring over Milton's mistakes, have proved themselves distinctly asinine.

But for all that, there are mistakes in *Paradise Lost.* I say it with due fear, and not without a feeling of gratitude that the purpose of this essay does not require me to specify them. But a sense of literary candour forces me to confess the opinion that the great epic contains passages in which the heaviness of the thought has infected the verse, passages which can be read only with tiresome effort, lines in which the organ-player's foot seems to have slipped upon the pedals and made a ponderous discord. This cannot be said of the Idylls. Their music is not broken or jangled. It may never rise to the loftiest heights, but it

never falls to the lowest depths. Tennyson
has written nothing so strong as the flight
of Satan through Chaos, nothing so sublime
as the invocation to Light, nothing so rich
as the first description of Eden; but taking
the blank-verse of the Idylls through and
through, as a work of art, it is more finished,
more expressive, more perfectly musical than
that of *Paradise Lost.*

The true relationship of these poems lies,
as I have said, beneath the surface. It con-
sists in their ideal unity of theme and
lesson. For what is it in fact with which
Milton and Tennyson concern themselves?
Not the mere story of Adam and Eve's
transgression; not the legendary wars of
Arthur and his knights; but the everlasting
conflict of the human soul with the adver-
sary, the struggle against sin, the power of
the slightest taint of evil to infect, pollute,
destroy all that is fairest and best. Both poets
tell the story of a paradise lost, and lost
through sin; first, the happy garden designed
by God to be the home of stainless inno-
cence and bliss, whose gates are closed for-
ever against the guilty race; and then, the
glorious realm of peace and love and law
which the strong and noble king would

make and defend amid the world's warfares,
but which is secretly corrupted, undermined,
destroyed at ast in blackening gloom.

To Arthur, as to Adam, destruction comes
through that which seems, and indeed is,
the loveliest and the dearest. The beauteous
mother of mankind, fairer than all her daugh-
ters since, drawn by her own highest desire of
knowledge into disobedience, yields the first
entrance to the fatal sin; and Guinevere,
the imperial-moulded queen, led by degrees
from a true friendship into a false love for
Lancelot, infects the court and the whole
realm with death. Vain are all safeguards
and defenses; vain all high resolves and
noble purposes; vain the instructions of
the archangel charging the possessors of
Eden to

> Be strong, live happy, and love! but first of all
> Him whom to love is to obey!

vain the strait vows and solemn oaths by
which the founder of the Table bound his
knights

> To reverence the King as if he were
> Their conscience, and their conscience as their King,
> To break the heathen and uphold the Christ.

All in vain! for sin comes creeping in; and
sin, the slightest, the most seeming-venial,

the most beautiful, is the seed of shame and
death. This is the profound truth to which
the *Idylls of the King* and *Paradise Lost*
alike bear witness. And to teach this, to
teach it in forms of highest art which should
live forever in the imagination of the race,
was the moral purpose of Milton and Ten-
nyson.

But there is another aspect of this theme,
which is hardly touched in the *Idylls*. Sin
has a relation to God as well as to man,
since it exists in His universe. Is it stronger
than the Almighty? Is His will wrath? Is
His purpose destruction? Is darkness the
goal of all things, and is there no other sig-
nificance in death; no deliverance from its
gloomy power? In *Paradise Lost*, Milton
has dealt with this problem also. Side by
side with the record " of man's first disobe-
dience " he has constructed the great argu-
ment whereby he would

> Assert eternal Providence
> And justify the ways of God to men.

The poem has, therefore, parallel with its
human side, a divine side, for which we shall
look in vain among the *Idylls of the King*.
Tennyson has approached this problem from
another standpoint in a different manner.

And if we wish to know his solution of it, his answer to the mystery of death, we must look for it in *In Memoriam.*

This poem is an elegy for Arthur Hallam, finished throughout its seven hundred and twenty-four stanzas with all that delicate care which the elegiac form requires, and permeated with the tone of personal grief, not passionate, but profound and pure. But it is such an elegy as the world has never seen before, and never will see again. It is the work of years, elaborated with such skill and adorned with such richness of poetic imagery as other men have thought too great to bestow upon an epic. It is the most exquisite structure ever reared above a human grave, more wondrous and more immortal than that world-famous tomb which widowed Artemisia built for the Carian Mausolus. But it is also something far grander and better. Beyond the narrow range of personal loss and loneliness, it sweeps into the presence of the eternal realities, faces the great questions of our mysterious existence, and reaches out to lay hold of that hope which is unseen but abiding, whereby alone we are saved. Its motto might well be given in the words of St. Paul: *For our light*

*affliction which is but for a moment worketh
for us a far more exceeding and eternal
weight of glory; while we look not at the
things which are seen, but at the things
which are not seen; for the things which
are seen are temporal, but the things which
are not seen are eternal.*

At first sight it may seem almost absurd
to compare the elegy with the epic, and im-
possible to discover any resemblance between
those long-rolling, thunderous periods of
blank-verse and these short swallow-flights
of song which " dip their wings in tears and
skim away." The comparison of *In Memo-
riam* with *Lycidas* would certainly appear
more easy and obvious; so obvious, indeed,
that it has been made a thousand times, and
is fluently repeated by every critic who has
had occasion to speak of English elegies.
But this is just one of those cases in which
an external similarity conceals a fundamental
unlikeness. For, in the first place, Edward
King, to whose memory *Lycidas* was dedi-
cated, was far from being an intimate friend
of Milton, and his lament has no touch of
the deep heart-sorrow which throbs in *In
Memoriam*. And, in the second place, *Ly-
cidas* is in no sense a metaphysical poem,

does not descend into the depths or attempt to answer the vexed questions. But *In Memoriam* is, in its very essence, profoundly and thoroughly metaphysical; and this brings it at once into close relation with *Paradise Lost*. They are the two most famous poems — with the exception of Dante's *Divine Comedy* — which deal directly with the mysteries of faith and reason, the doctrine of God and immortality.

There is a point, however, in which we must acknowledge an essential and absolute difference between the great epic and the great elegy, something deeper and more vital than any contrast of form and metre. *Paradise Lost* is a theological poem, *In Memoriam* is a religious poem. The distinction is narrow, but deep. For religion differs from theology as life differs from biology. Milton approaches the problem from the side of reason, resting, it is true, upon a supernatural revelation, but careful to reduce all its contents to a logical form, demanding a clearly-formulated and closely-linked explanation of all things, and seeking to establish his system of truth upon the basis of sound argument. His method is distinctly rational; Tennyson's is emotional. He has no linked

chain of deductive reasoning ; no sharp-cut
definition of objective truths. His faith is
subjective, intuitive. Where proof fails him,
he will still believe. When the processes
of reason are shaken, disturbed, frustrated ;
when absolute demonstration appears im-
possible, and doubt claims a gloomy empire
in the mind, then the deathless fire that God
has kindled in the breast burns toward that
heaven which is its source and home, and the
swift answer of immortal love leaps out to
solve the mystery of the grave. Thus Ten-
nyson *feels* after God, and leads us by the
paths of faith and emotion to the same goal
which Milton reaches by the road of reason
and logic.

Each of these methods is characteristic
not only of the poet who uses it, but also of
the age in which it is employed. *Paradise
Lost* does not echo more distinctly the age
of the Westminster divines than *In Memo-
riam* represents the age of Maurice and
Kingsley and Robertson. It is a mistake to
think that the tendency of our day is toward
rationalism. That was the drift of Milton's
time. Our modern movement is toward
emotionalism, a religion of feeling, a sub-
jective system in which the sentiments and

affections shall be acknowledged as lawful
tests of truth. This movement has undoubt-
edly an element of danger in it, as well as
an element of promise. It may be carried to
a false extreme. But this much is clear, —
it has been the strongest inspiration of the
men of our own time who have fought most
bravely against atheism and the cold nega-
tions of scientific despair. And the music
of it is voiced forever in *In Memoriam*. It
is the heart now, not the colder reason, which
rises to

> Assert eternal Providence
> And justify the ways of God to men.

But the answer is none other than that
which was given by the blind poet. The
larger meanings of *In Memoriam* and *Par-
adise Lost* — whatever we may say of their
lesser meanings — find their harmony in
the same

> Strong Son of God.

Is Tennyson a Pantheist because he speaks
of

> One God, one law, one element,
> And one far-off divine event
> To which the whole creation moves?

Then so is Milton a Pantheist when he
makes the Son say to the Father, —

> Thou shalt be all in all, and I in thee
> Forever, and in me all whom thou lovest.

Is Tennyson an Agnostic because he speaks of the "truths that never can be proved," and finds a final answer to the mysteries of life only in a hope which is hidden "behind the veil"? Then so is Milton an Agnostic, because he declares

> Heaven is for thee too high
> To know what passes there. Be lowly wise;
> Think only what concerns thee and thy being.
> Solicit not thy thoughts with matters hid;
> Leave them to God above.

Is Tennyson a Universalist because he says,

> Oh, yet we trust that somehow good
>   Will be the final goal of ill
>   To pangs of nature, sins of will,
> Defects of doubt, and taints of blood?

Then so is Milton a Universalist when he exclaims, —

> O, goodness infinite, goodness immense,
> That all this good of evil shall produce,
> And evil turn to good!

The faith of the two poets is one; the great lesson of *In Memoriam* and *Paradise Lost* is the same. The hope of the universe is in the Son of God, whom Milton and Tennyson both call "Immortal Love." To Him through mists and shadows we must look up,

> Gladly behold, though but his utmost skirts
> Of glory, and far-off his steps adore.

Thus our cry out of the darkness shall be answered. Knowledge shall grow from more to more.

> Light after light well-used we shall attain,
> And to the end persisting safe arrive.

But this can come only through self-surrender and obedience, only through the consecration of the free-will to God who gave it; and the highest prayer of the light-seeking, upward-striving human soul is this: —

> O, living will that shalt endure,
>   When all that seems shall suffer shock,
>   Rise in the spiritual Rock,
> Flow through our deeds and make them pure,
>
> That we may lift from out the dust
>   A voice as unto him that hears,
>   A cry above the conquered years,
> To one that with us works and trust,
>
> With faith that comes of self-control,
>   The truths that never can be proved
>   Until we close with all we love,
> And all we flow from, soul in soul.

THE PRINCESS AND MAUD

THE PRINCESS AND MAUD.

It was somewhere in the forties of this
century that Edgar Allan Poe put forth a
new doctrine of poetry, which, if I remem-
ber rightly, ran somewhat on this wise:
'The greatest poems must be short. For
the poetic inspiration is of the nature of a
flash of lightning and endures only for a
moment. But what a man writes between
the flashes is worth comparatively little.
All long poems are therefore, of necessity,
poor in proportion to their length, — or at
best they are but a mass of pudding in which
the luscious plums of poetry are embedded
and partially concealed.'

This ingenious theory (which has a slight
air of special pleading) has never been gen-
erally accepted. Indeed, at the very time
when Mr. Poe was propounding it, and using
the early poems of Tennyson as an illus-
tration, the world at large was taking for
granted the truth of the opposite theory, and
demanding that the newly discovered poet

should prove his claim to greatness by writing something long. "We want to see," said one of the best of the critics in 1842, "a poem of power and *sustained energy.* Mr. Tennyson already enjoys a high position; let him aim at one still higher; why not the highest?"

I believe that it was, at least partly, in answer to demands of this kind that *The Princess* appeared in 1847. Mr. Poe might have claimed it as an illustration of his theory. For it certainly adds more to the bulk of Tennyson's poems than it contributes to the lasting fame of his poetry. Its length is greater than its merit. There are parts of it in which the style falls below the level of poetry of the first rank; and these are the very parts where the verse is most diffuse and the story moves most slowly through thickets of overgrown description. The "flash of lightning theory" of poetic inspiration, although it is very far from being true and complete as a whole, appears to fit this poem with peculiar nicety; for the finest things in it are quite distinct, and so much better than the rest that they stand out as if illumined with sudden light.

I know that there are some ardent admirers of Tennyson who will dispute this opinion. They will point out the admirable moral lesson of *The Princess*, which is evident, and dwell upon its great influence in advancing the higher education of women, which is indisputable. They will insist upon its manifest superiority to other contemporary novels in verse, like *Lucile* or *The Angel in the House*. Let us grant all this. Still it does not touch the point of the criticism. For it is Tennyson himself who gives the standard of comparison. If Giulio Romano had painted the *Madonna di Foligno*, we might call it a great success — for him. But beside *La` Sistina*, or even beside the little *Madonna del Granduca*, it suffers. *Enoch Arden, Dora, Aylmer's Field, Locksley Hall*, are all shorter than *The Princess*, but they are better. Their inspiration is more sustained. The style fits the substance more perfectly. The poetic life in them is stronger and more enduring. One might say of them that they have more soul and less body. In brief, what I mean to say is this: *The Princess* is one of the minor poems of a major poet.

But there is poetry enough in it to make

the reputation of a man of ordinary genius.
And what I want to do in this little essay is
to value this element of genuine poetry at
its true worth, and to distinguish it, if I
can, from the lower elements which seem to
me to mar the beauty and weaken the force
of the poem.

The Princess has for its theme the eman-
cipation of woman, — a great question, cer-
tainly, but also a vexed question, and one
which is better adapted to prose than to
poetry, at least in the present stage of its
discussion. It has so many sides, and such
humorous aspects, and such tedious compli-
cations in this Nineteenth Century, that it is
difficult to lift it up into the realm of the
ideal; and yet I suppose the man does not
live, certainly the poet can hardly be found,
who would venture to treat it altogether as
a subject for realistic comedy. That would
be a dangerous, perhaps a fatal experiment.
Tennyson appears to have felt this difficulty.
He calls his story of the Princess Ida, who
set out to be the deliverer of her sex by
founding a Woman's University, and ended
by marrying the Prince who came to woo
her in female disguise, "a Medley." He
represents the imaginary poet, who appears

in the Prologue, and who undertakes to
dress up the story in verse for the ladies
and gentlemen to whom it was told at a pic-
nic, as being in a strait betwixt two parties
in the audience: one party demanding a bur-
lesque; the other party wishing for some-
thing "true-heroic." And so he says, —

> I moved as in a strange diagonal,
> And maybe neither pleased myself nor them.

This diagonal movement may have been
necessary; but it is unquestionably a little
confusing. One hardly knows how to take
the poet. At one moment he is very much in
earnest; the next moment he seems to be
making fun of the woman's college. The
style is like a breeze which blows northwest
by southeast; it may be a very lively breeze,
and full of sweet odours from every quarter;
but the trouble is that we cannot tell which
way to trim our sails to catch the force of
it, and so our craft goes jibing to and fro,
without making progress in any direction.

I think we feel this uncertainty most of all
in the characters of the Princess and the
Prince, — and I name the Princess first be-
cause she is evidently the hero of the poem.
Sometimes she appears very admirable and
lovable, in a stately kind of beauty; but

again she seems like a woman from whom a
man with ordinary prudence and a proper
regard for his own sense of humour would
promptly and carefully flee away, appreciat-
ing the truth of the description which her
father, King Gama, gives of her, —

> Awful odes she wrote,
> Too awful sure for what they treated of,
> But all she says and does is awful.

There is a touch of her own style, it seems
to me, here and there in the poem. The
epithets are somewhat too numerous and too
stately. The art is decidedly arabesque;
there is a surplus of ornament; and here,
more than anywhere else, one finds it difficult
to defend Tennyson from the charge of over-
elaboration. For example, he says of the
eight " daughters of the plough," who worked
at the woman's college, that

> Each was like a Druid rock;
> Or like a spire of land that stands apart
> Cleft from the main, and wail'd about with mews.

The image is grand, — just a little too
grand for a group of female servants, sum-
moned to eject the three masculine intruders
from the university.

The Princess was the first of Tennyson's
poems to become widely known in America,
and it is a curious fact that the most favour-

able, as well as the most extensive, criticisms of it have come from this side of the Atlantic. First, there was Professor James Hadley's thoughtful review in 1849; then Mr. Edmund Clarence Stedman's eloquent paragraphs in " Victorian Poets;" then Mr. S. E. Dawson's admirable monograph published in Montreal; and finally Mr. William J. Rolfe's scholarly " variorum " edition of *The Princess*, with notes. Mr. Dawson's excellent little book was the occasion of drawing from Tennyson a letter, which seems to me one of the most valuable, as it is certainly one of the longest, pieces of prose that he has ever given to the public. It describes his manner of observing nature and his practice of making a rough mental note in four or five words, like an artist's sketch, of whatever strikes him as picturesque, that is to say, fit to go into a picture. *The Princess* is full of the results of this kind of work, scattered here and there like flowers in a tangle of meadow-grass. For example, take these two descriptions of dawn: —

> Notice of a change in the dark world
> Was lispt about the acacias, and a bird
> That early woke to feed her little ones
> Sent from her dewy breast a cry for light. —

Morn in the white wake of the morning star
Came furrowing all the orient into gold.—

These are as different in feeling as possible,
yet each is true, and each is fitted to the
place in which it stands; for the one de-
scribes the beginning of a day among the
splendours of the royal college before it was
broken up; the other describes the twilight
of the morning in which the Princess began
to yield her heart to the tender touch of love.
Or take again these two pictures of storm:—

And standing like a stately pine
Set in a cataract on an island-crag,
When storm is on the heights, and right and left
Suck'd from the dark heart of the long hills roll
The torrents, dash'd to the vale.—

As one that climbs a peak to gaze
O'er land and main, and sees a great black cloud
Drag inward from the deeps, a wall of night,
Blot out the slope of sea from verge to shore,
And suck the blinding splendour from the sand,
And quenching lake by lake and tarn by tarn,
Expunge the world.—

Tennyson says that the latter of these pas-
sages is a recollection of a coming tempest
watched from the summit of Snowdon.
Work like this, so clear, so powerful, so
exact, would go far to redeem any poem,
however tedious.

But better still is the love-scene in the
last canto, where the poet drops the tantal-
izing vein of mock-heroics, and tells us his
real thought of woman's place and work in
the world, in words which are as wise as
they are beautiful. I have quoted them in
another place and may not repeat them here.
But there is one passage which I cannot
forbear to give, because it seems to describe
something of Tennyson's own life.

> Alone, from earlier than I know,
> Immersed in rich foreshadowings of the world,
> I loved the woman: he that doth not, lives
> A drowning life, besotted in sweet self,
> Or pines in sad experience worse than death,
> Or keeps his wing'd affections clipt with crime:
> Yet was there one thro' whom I loved her, one
> Not learned, save in gracious household ways,
> Not perfect, nay, but full of tender wants,
> No angel, but a dearer being, all dipt
> In angel instincts, breathing Paradise,
> Interpreter between the gods and men,
> Who look'd all native to her place, and yet
> On tiptoe seemed to touch upon a sphere
> Too gross to tread, and all male minds perforce
> Sway'd to her from their orbits as they moved,
> And girded her with music. Happy he
> With such a mother! faith in womankind
> Beats with his blood, and trust in all things high
> Comes easy to him, and tho' he trip and fall
> He shall not blind his soul with clay.

This is worthy to be put beside Words-
worth's —

"A creature not too bright or good
For human nature's daily food."

But the very best things in the poem are,
"Tears, idle tears," the "small, sweet Idyl,"
and the songs which divide the cantos. Ten-
nyson tells us in a letter that these songs
were not an after-thought; that he had de-
signed them from the first, but doubted
whether they were necessary, and did not
overcome his laziness to insert them until the
third edition in 1850. It may be that he
came as near as this to leaving out the jew-
els which are to the poem what the stained-
glass windows are to the confused vastness
of York Minster, — the light and glory of
the structure. It would have been a fatal
loss. For he has never done anything more
pure and perfect than these songs, clear and
simple and musical as the chime of silver
bells, deep in their power of suggestion as
music itself. Not a word in them can be
omitted or altered, neither can they be trans-
lated. The words *are* the songs. "Sweet
and low," "Ask me no more," and "Blow,
bugle, blow" will be remembered and sung,
as long as English hearts move to the sweet
melody of love and utter its secret meanings
in the English tongue.

I have put *Maud* and *The Princess* to-
gether, because it seems to me that they have
some things in common. They are both
intensely modern; both deal with the pas-
sion of romantic love; in both, the story
is an important element of interest. But
these points of resemblance only serve to
bring out more clearly the points of contrast.
The one is epic; the other is dramatic. The
one is complicated; the other is simple. The
style of the one is narrative, diffuse, deco-
rated; the style of the other is personal, di-
rect, condensed. In the one you see rather
vague characters, whose development de-
pends largely upon the unfolding of the plot;
in the other you see the unfolding of the plot
controlled by the development of a single,
strongly-marked character. In fact, Tenny-
son himself has given us the only true start-
ing-point for the criticism of each of these
poems in a single word, by calling the *Prin-
cess* "a Medley," and *Maud* "a Mono-
drama."

I will confess frankly, although frank con-
fession is not precisely fashionable among
critics, that for a long time I misunderstood
Maud and underrated it. This came from
looking at it from the wrong point of view.

I was enlightened by hearing the poet read it aloud.

Tennyson's reading was extraordinary. His voice was deep, strong, masculine, limited in its range, with a tendency to monotone, broadening and prolonging the vowels and rolling the *r*'s; it was not flexible, nor melodious in the common sense of the word, but it was musical in a higher sense, as the voice of the sea is musical. When he read he forgot all the formal rules of elocution, raised his voice a little higher than his usual tone in speaking, and poured out the poem in a sustained rhythmic chant. He was carried away and lost in it. In the passionate passages his voice rose and swelled like the sound of the wind in the pine-trees; in the lines which express grief and loneliness it broke and fell like the throbbing and murmuring of the waves on the beach. I felt the profound human sympathy of the man, the largeness and force of his nature. I understood the secret of the perfection of his lyrical poems. Each one of them had been composed to a distinct music of its own. He had heard it in his mind before he had put it into words. I saw also why his character-pieces were so strong. He had been absorbed in each one of them. The living personality had been real to him, and he had entered into its life.

All this came home to me as I sat in the evening twilight in the study at Aldworth, and listened to the poet, with his massive head outlined against the pale glow of the candles, his dark, dreamy eyes fixed closely upon the book, lifted now and then to mark the emphasis of a word or the close of a forceful line, and his old voice ringing with all the passion of youth, as he chanted the varying cantos of the lyrical drama of *Maud.* I understood why he loved it, and what it meant. I felt that, although it may not be ranked with his greatest works, like *In Memoriam* and the *Idylls of the King*, it is certainly one of his most original poems.

You must remember always, in reading it, what it is meant to be — a lyrical drama. It shows the unfolding of a lonely, morbid soul, touched with inherited madness, under the influence of a pure and passionate love. Each lyric is meant to express a new moment in this process. The things which seem like faults belong not so much to the poem as to the character of the hero.

He is wrong, of course, in much that he
says. If he had been always wise and just
he would not have been himself. He be-
gins with a false comparison — " blood-red
heath."   There is no such thing in nature;
but he sees the heather tinged like blood
because his mind has been disordered and
his sight discoloured by the tragedy of his
youth. He is wrong in thinking that war
will transform the cheating tradesman into
a great-souled hero, or that it will sweep
away the dishonesties and lessen the miser-
ies of humanity. The history of the Crimea
proves his error. But this very delusion is
natural to him : it is in keeping with his
morbid, melancholy, impulsive character to
seek a cure for the evils of peace in the
horrors of war.

He is wild and excessive, of course, in
his railings and complainings. He takes
offense at fancied slights, reviles those
whom he dislikes, magnifies trifles, is sub-
ject to hallucinations, hears his name
called in the corners of his lonely house,
fancies that all the world is against him.
He is not always noble even in the expres-
sion of his love at first. He sometimes
strikes a false note and strains the tone of

passion until it is almost hysterical. There is at least one passage in which he sings absurdly of trifles, and becomes, as he himself feared that he would, "fantastically merry." But all this is just what such a man would do in such a case. The psychological study is perfect, from the first outburst of moody rage in the opening canto, through the unconscious struggle against love and the exuberant joy which follows its entrance into his heart and the blank despair which settles upon him when it is lost, down to the wonderful picture of real madness with which the second part closes. It is as true as truth itself. But what is there in the story to make it worth the telling? What elements of beauty has the poet conferred upon it? What has he given to this strange and wayward hero to redeem him? Three gifts.

First, he has the gift of exquisite, delicate, sensitive perception. He sees and hears the wonderful, beautiful things which only the poet can see and hear. He knows that the underside of the English daisy is pink, and when Maud passes homeward through the fields he can trace her path by the upturned flowers, —

> For her feet have touch'd the meadows
> And left the daisies rosy.

He sees how the tops of the trees on a windy morning are first bowed by the wind and then tossed from side to side, —

> Caught and cuff'd by the gale.

He has noted the colour of the red buds on the lime-tree in the spring, and how the green leaves burst through them, —

> A million emeralds break from the ruby-budded lime.

He has heard the " broad-flung shipwrecking roar of the tide " and the sharp " scream " of the pebbles on the beach dragged down by the receding wave. He has listened to the birds that seem to be calling, " Maud, Maud, Maud, Maud," — and he knows perfectly well that they are not nightingales, but rooks, flying to their nests in the tall trees around the Hall. The poem is rich in observations of nature.

The second gift which is bestowed upon the hero of *Maud* is the power of song. And in bestowing this the poet has proved the fineness and subtlety of his knowledge. For it is precisely this gift of song which sometimes descends upon a wayward, unsound life,—as it did upon Shelley's,—and draws from it tones of ravishing sweetness; not harmonies, for harmony belongs to the broader, saner mind, but melodies, which catch the heart and linger in the memory forever. Strains of this music come to us from *Maud:* the song of triumphant love,—

> I have led her home, my love, my only friend.
> There is none like her, none,—

the nocturne that rises like the breath of passion from among the flowers,—

> Come into the garden, Maud,—

and the lament,—

> O that 't were possible.

These lyrics are magical, unforgetable; they give an immortal beauty to the poem.

The third gift, and the greatest, which belongs to the hero of *Maud,* is the capacity for intense, absorbing, ennobling love. It is this that makes Maud love him, and saves him from himself, and brings him out at last from the wreck of his life, a man who has awaked to the nobler mind and knows—

> It is better to fight for the good than rail at the ill.

How clearly this awakening is traced through the poem! His love is tinged with selfishness at first. He thinks of the smile of Maud as the charm which is to make the world sweet to him; he says:

> Then let come what come may
> To a life that has been so sad,
> I shall have had my day.

But unconsciously it purifies itself. He looks up at the stars and says: —

> But now shine on, and what care I,
> Who in this stormy gulf have found a pearl
> The countercharm of space and hollow sky,
> And do accept my madness, and would die
> To save from some slight shame one simple girl.

And at last, when his own fault has destroyed his happiness and divided him from her forever, his love does not perish, but triumphs over the selfishness of grief.

> Comfort her, comfort her, all things good,
> While I am over the sea!
> Let me and my passionate love go by,
> But speak to her all things holy and high,
> Whatever happen to me!
> Me and my harmful love go by;
> But come to her waking, find her asleep,
> Powers of the height, Powers of the deep,
> And comfort her tho' I die.

This is the meaning of *Maud.* Love is the power that redeems from self.

IN MEMORIAM

IN MEMORIAM.

MANY beautiful poems, and some so noble that they are forever illustrious, have blossomed in the valley of the shadow of death. But among them all none is more rich in significance, more perfect in beauty of form and spirit, or more luminous with the triumph of light and love over darkness and mortality, than *In Memoriam*, the greatest of English elegies.

How splendid is the poetic company in which it stands! Milton's stately and solemn lament for *Lycidas*; Gray's pure and faultless *Elegy in a Country Churchyard*; Shelley's musical and mournful *Adonaïs*; Matthew Arnold's pensive *Thyrsis*, and his deeper *Lines at Sunset in Rugby Chapel*; Emerson's profound, passionate, lovely *Threnody* on the death of his little son, — these all belong to the high order of poetry which lives, and these all unfolded from the heart of man at the touch of death.

In Memoriam differs from the others in
two things: first, in the fulness and inti-
macy with which it discloses the personal
relations and the personal loss and sorrow
out of which it grew; and, second, in the
breadth and thoroughness with which it
enters into the great questions of philoso-
phy and religion that rise out of the experi-
ence of bereavement. It has, therefore, a
twofold character; it is a glorious monu-
ment to the memory of a friend, and it is
the great English classic on the love of
immortality and the immortality of love.

It was published in 1850, and the title-
page bore no name, either of the author or
of the person to whom it was dedicated.
But every one knew that it was written by
Alfred Tennyson in memory of his friend
Arthur Henry Hallam. Their friendship
was formed at Trinity College, Cambridge,
where they had entered as students in Oc-
tober, 1828, Tennyson being then in his
twentieth year. Hallam, who was a year
and a half younger, was the son of Henry
Hallam, the historian, and had already dis-
tinguished himself among his contempora-
ries by the beauty and force of his character
and the brilliancy of his attainments, espe-

cially in the study of modern poetry and
art, in philosophy, and in argumentative
discussion. He did not incline strongly to
the study of the classics, and toward math-
ematics, the favourite discipline of Cam-
bridge, he was almost entirely indifferent.
These mental indispositions, together with
a lack of power or willingness to retain in
his memory the mass of uninteresting facts
and dates which are required for success
in examinations, and a delicacy of health
which at times made him subject to serious
depression of spirits, unfitted him to con-
tend for university honours. But he was
a natural leader among the high-spirited
youth who found in the reality of college
life and the freedom of intellectual inter-
course a deeper and broader education than
the routine of the class-room could give.
There was a debating society in Cam-
bridge at this time, familiarly called "The
Twelve Apostles," which included such men
of promise as Richard Monckton Milnes
(afterward Lord Houghton), W. H. Thomp-
son (afterward Master of Trinity), Richard
Chevenix Trench (afterward Archbishop of
Dublin), Henry Alford (afterward Dean of
Canterbury), Frederick Denison Maurice,

W. H. Brookfield, James Spedding, Ed-
mund Lushington, and G. S. Venables. In
this society of kindling genius, Hallam
shone with a singular lustre, not only by
reason of the depth and clearness of his
thought and the masterful vigour of his
expression, but also because of the sweet-
ness and purity of his character and the
sincerity of his religious spirit, strengthened
and ennobled by conflict with honest doubt.
One of his friends wrote of him: "I have
met with no man his superior in metaphysi-
cal subtlety; no man his equal as a philo-
sophical critic on works of taste; no man
whose views on all subjects connected with
the duties and dignities of humanity were
more large, more generous and enlight-
ened." Mr. Gladstone, recalling his in-
timacy with Hallam at Eton, bears witness
to "his unparalleled endowments and his
deep, enthusiastic affections, both religious
and human."

It was by such qualities that Alfred Ten-
nyson was drawn to Arthur Hallam; and
although, or perhaps because, they were
unlike in many things, their minds and
hearts were wedded in a friendship which
was closer than brotherhood, and in which

Hallam's influence was the stronger and more masculine element, so that Tennyson spoke of himself as "widowed" by his loss.

The comradeship of the two men was of the most intimate nature. They were together in study and in recreation, at home and abroad. In 1829 they were friendly rivals for the medal in English verse, which Tennyson won with his poem *Timbuctoo.* In 1830 they made an excursion together to the Pyrenees, carrying money and letters of encouragement to the Spanish revolutionists. This visit is alluded to in the poem called *In the Valley of Cauteretz.* About this time they were planning to bring out a volume of poems in company, after the example of Wordsworth and Coleridge; but by the wise advice of Hallam's father this project was abandoned, and Tennyson's slender volume of *Poems, Chiefly Lyrical* appeared alone. Hallam's review of this book in *The Englishman's Magazine* for August, 1831, was one of the very earliest recognitions that a new light had risen in English poetry. He said: —

" Mr. Tennyson belongs decidedly to the class we have already described as Poets of

Sensation. He sees all the forms of nature with the *eruditus oculus*, and his ear has a fairy fineness. There is a strange earnestness in his worship of beauty, which throws a charm over his impassioned song, more easily felt than described, and not to be escaped by those who have once felt it. . . . We have remarked five distinctive excellencies of his own manner. First, his luxuriance of imagination, and at the same time his control over it. Secondly, his power of embodying himself in ideal characters, or rather moods of character, with such extreme accuracy of adjustment that the circumstances of the narrative seem to have a natural correspondence with the predominant feeling, and, as it were, to be evolved from it by assimilative force. Thirdly, his vivid, picturesque delineation of objects, and the peculiar skill with which he holds all of them *fused*, to borrow a metaphor from science, in a medium of strong emotion. Fourthly, the variety of his lyrical measures, and exquisite modulation of harmonious sounds and cadences to the swell and fall of the feelings expressed. Fifthly, the elevated habits of thought implied in these compositions, and imparting a mellow soberness of tone, more impressive to our minds than if the author had drawn up a set of opinions in verse, and sought to instruct the understanding rather than to communicate the love of beauty to the heart."

This may still stand, among later and more searching criticisms, as an intelligent and suggestive appreciation of the sources of Tennyson's poetical charm and power.

Many allusions to incidents in Hallam's brief life may be discovered in *In Memoriam*. He was a frequent visitor in the home of the Tennysons at Somersby, in Lincolnshire, coming in winter and summer holidays. In 1832, the year of his gradution at Cambridge, he was engaged to Miss Emily Tennyson, the poet's sister. His home was with his father in Wimpole Street, called the longest street in London; and on leaving college he began the study of law, looking forward to the higher life of public service, in which so many of England's best young men find their mission. In August, 1833, he went with his father to Germany. On the way from Pesth to Vienna he was exposed to in-

clement weather and contracted an inter-
mittent fever. The symptoms were slight
and seemed to be abating, but the natural
frailty of his constitution involved unfore-
seen danger. There was a weakness of
the heart which the strength of the spirit
concealed. On the 15th of September,
while he seemed to be reposing quietly,
the silver cord was loosed and the golden
bowl was broken.

> In Vienna's fatal walls
> God's finger touch'd him, and he slept.

The sharp and overwhelming shock of
losing such a friend suddenly, irretrieva-
bly, in absence, with no opportunity of
speaking a word of love and farewell,
brought Tennyson face to face with the
intense and inexorable reality of death —
the great mystery which must either
darken all life and quench the springs of
poesy, or open a new world of victory to
the spirit, and refresh it with deeper and
never-failing fountains of inspiration.

In Memoriam begins with the confession
of this dreadful sense of loss, and the firm
resolve to hold fast the memory of his
grief, even though he doubts whether he
can

reach a hand through time to catch
The far-off interest of tears.

The arrangement of the poem does not
follow strictly the order of logic or the
order of time. It was not written con-
secutively, but at intervals, and the period
of its composition extends over at least
sixteen years. The Epithalamium with
which it closes was made in 1842, the
date of the marriage of Miss Cecilia Ten-
nyson to Edmund Law Lushington, the
friend addressed in the eighty-fifth canto.
The Proem, " Strong Son of God, immortal
Love," was added in 1849, to sum up and
express the final significance of the whole
lyrical epic of the inner life which had
grown so wonderfully through these long
years of spiritual experience. " The gen-
eral way of its being written," said Tenny-
son, " was so queer that if there were a
blank space I would put in a poem." And
yet there is a profound coherence in the
series of separate lyrics; and a clear ad-
vance toward a definite goal of thought
and feeling can be traced through the
freedom of structure which characterizes
the poem.

The first division of the poem, from the

first to the eighth canto (I follow here the grouping of the sections which was made by Tennyson himself), moves with the natural uncertainty of a lonely and sorrowful heart; questioning whether it is possible or wise to hold fast to sorrow; questioning whether it be not half a sin to try to put such a grief into words questioning whether the writing of a memorial poem can be anything more than a

> sad, mechanic exercise,
> Like dull narcotics, numbing pain.

But the conclusion is that, since the lost friend loved the poet's verse, the poem shall be written for his sake and consecrated to his memory, like a flower planted on a tomb, to live or die.

The second division, beginning with the ninth canto and closing with the nineteenth, describes in lyrics of wondrous beauty the home-bringing of Arthur's body in a ship from Italy, and the burial in Clevedon Church, which stands on a solitary hill overlooking the Bristol Channel. This took place on January 3, 1834. A calmer, stronger, steadier spirit now enters into the poem, and from this point it moves forward with ever deepening power and beauty, to pay its rich tribute to the immortal meaning of friendship, and to pour its triumphant light through the shadows of the grave.

The third division, beginning with the twentieth canto, returns again to the subject of personal bereavement and the possibility of expressing it in poetry. It speaks of the necessity in the poet's heart for finding such an expression, which is as natural as song is to the bird. He turns back to trace the pathway of friendship, and remembers how love made it fair and sweet, doubling all joy and dividing all pain. That companionship is now broken and the way is dreary. The love to which he longs to prove himself still loyal is now the minister of lonely sorrow. And yet the very capacity for such suffering is better than the selfish placidity of the loveless life:

> 'T is better to have loved and lost
> Than never to have loved at all.

The fourth division opens, in the twenty-eighth canto, with a Christmas poem. The poet wonders how it is possible to keep the joyous household festival under the shadow

of this great loss. But through the sad-
dened and half-hearted merry-making there
steals at last, in the silence, the sense that
those who have left the happy circle still
live and are unchanged in sympathy and
love. From the darkness of Christmas
eve rises the prayer for the dawning of
Christmas day and

> The light that shone when Hope was born.

Led by this thought, the poet turns to
the story of Lazarus, and to Mary's faith
in Him who was the Resurrection and the
Life. Such a faith is so pure and sacred
that it demands the reverence even of
those who do not share it. For what
would our existence be worth without
immortality? Effort and patience would
be vain. It would be better to drop at
once into darkness. Love itself would be
changed and degraded if we knew that
death was the end of everything. These
immortal instincts of our manhood came
to their perfect expression in the life
and teachings of Christ. And though the
poet's utterance of these divine things be
but earthly and imperfect, at least it is
a true tribute to the friend who spoke of

them so often. Thus he stands again be-
side the funereal yew-tree, of which he
wrote, in the second canto, that it never
blossomed, and sees that, after all, it has
a season of bloom, in which the dust of
tiny flowers rises from it in living smoke.
Even so his thoughts of death are now
blossoming in thoughts of a higher life
into which his friend has entered —
thoughts of larger powers and nobler
duties in the heavenly existence. But
may not this mysterious and sudden ad-
vancement divide their friendship? No;
for if the lost friend is moving onward so
swiftly now, he will be all the better fitted
to be a teacher and helper when their in-
tercourse is renewed; but if death should
prove to be "an intervital trance," then
when he awakens the old love will awaken
with him. From this assurance the poet
passes to wondering thoughts of the man-
ner of life of "the happy dead," and rises
to the conviction that it must include an
unchanged personal identity and a certain
personal recognition and fellowship. This
is not uttered by way of argument, but
only with the brevity and simplicity of
songs which move like swallows over the
depth of grief,

Whose muffled motions blindly drown
The bases of my life in tears.

The fifth division of the poem, in the
fiftieth canto, begins with a prayer that
his unseen friend may be near him in the
hours of gloom and pain and doubt and
death. Such a presence would bring with it
a serene sympathy and allowance for mor-
tal ignorance and weakness and imperfec-
tion. For doubtless this lower life of ours
is a process of discipline and education for
something better. Good must be the final
goal of ill. We feel this but dimly and
blindly; our expression of it is like the
cry of a child in the night; but at least
the desire that it may be true comes from
that which is most God-like in our souls.
Can it be that God and Nature are at
strife? Is it possible that all the hopes
and prayers and aspirations of humanity
are vain dreams, and that the last and
highest work of creation must crumble
utterly into dust? This would be the
very mockery of reason. And yet the
sure answer is not found; it lies behind
the veil. So the poet turns away, think-
ing to close his song with a last word of
farewell to the dead ; but the Muse calls

him to abide a little longer with his sor-
row, in order that he may " take a nobler
leave."

This is the theme with which the sixth
division opens, in the fifty-ninth canto.
The poet is to live with sorrow as a wife,
and to learn from her all that she has to
teach. He turns again to the thought of
the strange difference in wisdom and purity
between the blessed dead and the living,
and finds new comfort and security in the
thought that this difference cannot destroy
love. He thinks of the tablet to Hallam's
memory in Clevedon Church, silvered by
the moonlight or glimmering in the dawn.
He dreams of Hallam over and over again.
Night after night they seem to walk and
talk together, as they did on their tour
in the Pyrenees.

The seventy-second canto opens the
seventh division of the poem with the an-
niversary of Hallam's death — an autumnal
dirge, wild and dark, followed by sad
lyrics which ring the changes on the per-
ishableness of all earthly fame and beauty.
But now the Christmas-tide returns and
brings the tender household joys. This
is a brighter Christmas than the last. The

thought of how faithfully and nobly Arthur
would have borne the sorrow, if he had
been the one to be left while his friend
was taken, calms and strengthens the poet's
heart. He reconciles himself more deeply
with death; learns to believe that it has
ripened friendship even more than earthly
intercourse could have done; assures him-
self that the transplanted life is still bloom-
ing and bearing richer fruit; and at last
complains only because death has

> put our lives so far apart
> We cannot hear each other speak.

Now the spring comes, renewing the
face of the earth; and with it comes a
new tenderness and sweetness into the
poet's song. There is a pathetic vision
of all the domestic joys that might have
been centred about Arthur's life if it had
been spared, and of the calm harmony of
death if the two friends could have arrived
together at the blessed goal,

> And He that died in Holy Land
> Would reach us out the shining hand,
> And take us as a single soul.

This vision almost disturbs the new
peace that has begun in the poet's heart;

but he comes back again, in the eighty-
fifth canto (the longest in the poem, and
its turning-point), to the deep and unal-
terable feeling that love with loss is better
than life without love. Another friend,
the same who was afterward to be mar-
ried to Tennyson's sister, has asked him
whether his sorrow has darkened his faith
and made him incapable of friendship.
The answer comes from the inmost depths
of the soul; recalling all the noble and
spiritual influences of the interrupted com-
radeship; confessing that it still abides
and works as a potent, strengthening force
in his life; and seeking for the coming
years a new friendship, not to rival the
old, nor ever to supplant it, but to teach
his heart still

> to beat in time with one
> That warms another living breast.

Now the glory of the summer earth
kindles the poetic fancy once more to
rapture; now the old college haunts are
revisited and the joys of youth live again
in memory. The thought of Arthur's
spiritual presence lends a new and loftier
significance to these common delights,
brings more sweetness than sadness, makes

his letters, read in the calm summer mid-
night, seem like a living voice. The
remembrance of his brave conflict with
his doubts gives encouragement to faith.
Now he is delivered from the struggle;
he has attained unto knowledge and wis-
dom: but the poet, still lingering among
the shadows and often confused by them,
holds fast to the spiritual companionship:

> I cannot understand: I love.

The eighth division, from the ninety-
ninth to the one hundred and third canto,
opens with another anniversary of Hallam's
death, which brings the consoling thought
that, since grief is common, sympathy
must be world-wide. The old home at
Somersby is now to be forsaken, and the
poet takes farewell of the familiar scenes
in lyrics of exquisite beauty. The division
ends with a mystical dream, in which he
is summoned to a voyage upon the sea of
eternity, and the human powers and tal-
ents, in the guise of maidens who have
served him in this life, accompany him
still, and the man he loved appears on the
ship as his comrade.

The ninth and last division begins, in

the one hundred and fourth canto, with
the return of another Christmas eve. The
Tennyson family had removed in 1837 to
Beech Hill House, and now, as the time
draws near the birth of Christ, they hear,
not the fourfold peal of bells from the four
hamlets lying around the rectory at Som-
ersby, but a single peal from the tower of
Waltham Abbey, dimly seen through the
mist below the distant hill. It is a strange,
solemn, silent holiday season; but with
the ringing of the bells on the last night
of the old year there comes into it a new,
stirring melody of faith, of hope, of high
desire and victorious trust. This is a
stronger, loftier song than the poet could
ever have reached before grief ennobled
him; and from this he rises into that
splendid series of lyrics with which the
poem closes. The harmony of knowledge
with reverence; the power of the heart
of man to assert its rights against the
colder conclusions of mere intellectual
logic; the certainty that man was born
to enjoy a higher life than the physical,
and that though his body may have been
developed from the lower animals, his soul
may work itself out from the dominion of

the passions to an imperishable liberty;
the supremacy of love; the sure progress
of all things toward a hidden goal of glory;
the indomitable courage of the human will,
which is able to purify our deeds, and to
trust,

> With faith that comes of self-control,
>   The truths that never can be proved
> Until we close with all we loved,
>   And all we flow from, soul in soul, —

these are the mighty and exultant chords
with which the poet ends his music.

In Memoriam is a dead-march, but it is
a march into immortality.

The promise of Arthur Hallam's life
was not broken. Threescore years and
ten of earthly labour could hardly have
accomplished anything greater than the
work which was inspired by his early
death and consecrated to his sacred mem-
ory. The heart of man, which can win
such victory out of its darkest defeat and
reap such harvest from the furrows of the
grave, is neither sprung from dust nor
destined to return to it. A poem like *In
Memoriam*, more than all flowers of the
returning spring, more than all shining
wings that flutter above the ruins of the

chrysalis, more than all sculptured tombs and monuments of the beloved dead, is the living evidence and intimation of an endless life.

IDYLLS OF THE KING

IDYLLS OF THE KING.

I.

THE history of Tennyson's *Idylls of the King* is one of the most curious and unlikely things in all the annals of literature. Famous novels have so often been written piecemeal and produced in parts, that readers of fiction have made a necessity of virtue, and learned to add to their faith, patience. But that a great poet should be engaged with his largest theme for more than half a century; that he should touch it first with a lyric; then with an epical fragment and two more lyrics; then with a poem which was suppressed as soon as it was written; then with four romantic idylls, followed, ten years later, by four others, and two years later by two others, and thirteen years later by yet another idyll, which is to be placed, not before or after the rest, but in the very centre of the cycle; that he should begin with the end,

and continue with the beginning, and end
with the middle of the story, and produce
at last a poem which certainly has more
epical grandeur than anything that has been
made in English since Milton died, is a
thing, so marvellous that no man would
credit it save at the sword's point of fact.
And yet this is the exact record of Tenny-
son's dealing with the Arthurian legend.

The Lady of Shalott, that dreamlike
foreshadowing of the story of *Elaine*, was
published in 1832; *Sir Galahad* and *Sir
Lancelot and Queen Guinevere* in 1842.
Underneath their smooth music and dainty
form they hide the deeper conceptions of
character and life which the poet after-
wards worked out more clearly and fully.
They compare with the *Idylls* as a cameo
with a statue. But the germ of the whole
story of the fall of the Round Table lies in
this description of Guinevere : —

> She looked so lovely, as she swayed
>   The rein with dainty finger-tips,
> *A man had given all other bliss,*
> *And all his worldly worth for this,*
> *To waste his whole heart in one kiss*
>   *Upon her perfect lips.*

Morte d'Arthur was printed in the same
volume and marks the beginning of a new

manner of treatment, not lyrical, but epical. It is worth while to notice the peculiar way in which it is introduced. A brief prelude, in Tennyson's conversational style, states the poem is a fragment of an *Epic of King Arthur*, which had contained twelve cantos, but which the poet, being discontented with their antiquated style, and regarding them as

Faint Homeric echoes, nothing worth,

had determined to burn. This one book had been picked from the hearth by a friend, and was the sole relic of the conflagration.

I do not imagine that we are to interpret this preface so literally as to conclude that Tennyson had actually written and destroyed eleven other books upon this subject; for though he has exercised a larger wisdom of suppression in regard to his immature work than almost any other poet, such a wholesale consumption of his offspring would have an almost Saturnine touch about it. But we may certainly infer that he had contemplated the idea of an Arthurian epic, and had abandoned it after severe labour as impracticable, and that he had intended not to conclude the poem with

the death of Arthur, but to follow it with
a sequel; for we must observe the fact,
which has hitherto escaped the notice of
the critics, that this rescued fragment was
not the twelfth but the eleventh canto in
the original design. We cannot help won-
dering what the conclusion would have been
if this first plan had been carried out. Per-
haps some vision of the island valley of
Avilion; perhaps some description of the
return of the King in modern guise as the
founder of a new order of chivalry; but
whatever it might have been we can hardly
regret its loss, for it is evident now that
the *Morte d'Arthur* forms the true and in-
evitable close of the story.

How long the poet held to his decision
of abandoning the subject, we cannot tell.
The first sign that he had begun to work
at it again was in 1857, when he printed
a poem called *Enid and Nimue; or, The
True and the False.* • This does not seem
to have satisfied his fastidious taste, for it
was never published, though a few copies
are said to be extant in private hands.

In June, 1858, Clough " heard Tenny-
son read a third Arthur poem, — the de-
tection of Guinevere and the last interview

with Arthur." In 1859 appeared the first volume, entitled *Idylls of the King*, with a motto from the old chronicle of Joseph of Exeter,— "*Flos regum Arthurus.*" The book contained four idylls: *Enid, Vivien, Elaine,* and *Guinevere.* *Enid* has since been divided into *The Marriage of Geraint,* and *Geraint and Enid.* This first volume, therefore, contained the third, fourth, sixth, seventh, and eleventh idylls.

In 1862 there was a new edition, dedicated to the Prince Consort. In 1870, four more idylls were published: *The Coming of Arthur, The Holy Grail, Pelleas and Ettarre,* and *The Passing of Arthur,* — respectively the first, the eighth, the ninth, and the twelfth, in the order as it stands now. Of this volume, forty thousand copies were ordered in advance. In 1872, *Gareth and Lynette* and *The Last Tournament* were produced, — the second and the tenth parts of the cycle. In 1885, the volume entitled *Tiresias and Other Poems* contained an idyll with the name of *Balin and Balan,* which was designated in a note as " an introduction to *Merlin and Vivien,*" and thus takes the fifth place in the series.

I have been careful in tracing the order

of these poems because it seems to me that
the manner of their production throws
light upon several important points. Leav-
ing out of view the Arthurian lyrics, as
examples of a style of treatment which was
manifestly too light for the subject; setting
aside also the first draught of the *Morte
d'Arthur*, as a fragment whose full mean-
ing and value the poet himself did not rec-
ognize until later; we observe that the
significance of the story of Arthur and the
legends that clustered about it was clearly
seen by Tennyson somewhere about the
year 1857, and that he then began to work
upon it with a large and positive purpose.
For at least thirty years he was steadily
labouring to give it form and substance;
but the results of his work were presented
to the world in a sequence of which he
alone held the clue: the third and fourth,
the sixth, seventh, and eleventh, the first,
the eighth, the ninth, the twelfth, the sec-
ond, the tenth, the fifth, — such was the
extraordinary order of parts in which this
work was published.

    This fact will account, first of all, for the
failure of the public to estimate the poems
in their right relation and at their true

worth. Their beauty of imagery and ver-
sification was at once acknowledged; but
so long as they were regarded as separate
pictures, so long as their succession and
the connection between them were con-
cealed, it was impossible to form any com-
plete judgment of their meaning or value.
As Wagner said of his *Siegfried :* " It can-
not make its right and unquestionable im-
pression as a *single* whole, until it is allotted
its necessary place in the *complete* whole.
Nothing must be left to be supplemented
by thought or reflection : every reader of
unprejudiced human feeling must be able
to comprehend *the whole* through his artis-
tic perceptions, because then only will he
be able rightly to understand the single
incidents." [1]

In the second place, this fact makes clear
to us the reason and justification of the gen-
eral title which Tennyson has given to these
poems. He has been criticised very fre-
quently for calling them Idylls. And if we
hold the word to its narrower meaning, —
" a short, highly wrought poem of a de-
scriptive and pastoral character," — it cer-
tainly seems inappropriate. But if we go

[1] Wagner's letter to Liszt, November 20, 1851.

back to the derivation of the word, and re-
member that it comes from εἶδος, which
means not merely the form, the figure, the
appearance of anything, but more particu-
larly that form which is characteristic and
distinctive, the ideal element, correspond-
ing to the Latin *species*, we can see that
Tennyson was justified in adapting and
using it for his purpose. He intended to
make pictures, highly wrought, carefully
finished, full of elaborate and significant de-
tails. But each one of these pictures was
to be animated with an idea, clear, definite,
unmistakable. It was to make a form ex-
press a soul. It was to present a type, not
separately, but in relation to other types.
This was the method which he had chosen.
His design was not purely classical, nor
purely romantic, but something between
the two, like the Italian Gothic in archi-
tecture. He did not propose to tell a sin-
gle straightforward story for the sake of
the story; nor to bring together in one
book a mass of disconnected tales and le-
gends, each of which might just as well have
stood alone. He proposed to group about
a central figure a number of other figures,
each one of which should be as finished, as

complete, as expressive, as he could make
it, and yet none of which could be clearly
understood except as it stood in its own
place in the circle. For this kind of work
he needed to find or invent a name. It
may be that the word "Idylls" does not
perfectly express the meaning. But at
least there is no other word in the language
which comes so near to it.

In the third place, now that we see the
Idylls all together, standing in their proper
order and relation, now that we perceive
that with all their diversity they do indeed
belong to the King, and revolve about him
as stars about a central sun, we are able to
appreciate the force and grandeur of the
poet's creative idea which could sustain and
guide him through such long and intricate
labour and produce at last, from an appar-
ent chaos of material, an harmonious work
of art of a new order. For this was the
defect, hitherto, of the romantic writers,
descending by ordinary generation from
Sir Walter Scott, — that their work had
lacked unity; it was confused, fragmentary,
inorganic. And this was the defect, hith-
erto, of the classical writers, descending by
ordinary generation from Alexander Pope,

— that their work had lacked life, interest,
colour, detail. But Tennyson has suc-
ceeded, at least better than any other Eng-
lish poet, in fulfilling the prophecy which
Victor Hugo made in his criticism of *Quen-
tin Durward :* —

"Après le roman pittoresque mais pro-
saïque de Walter Scott, il restera un autre
roman à créer, plus beau et plus complet
encore selon nous. C'est le roman à la fois
drame et épopée, pittoresque mais poétique,
réel mais idéal, vrai mais grand, qui en-
châssera Walter Scott dans Homère."

II.

The material which Tennyson has used
for his poem is the strange, complex. mys-
tical story of King Arthur and his Round
Table. To trace the origin of this story
would lead us far afield and entangle us
in the thickets of controversy which are
full of thorns. Whether Arthur was a
real king who ruled in Britain after the
departure of the Romans, and founded a
new order of chivalry, and defeated the
heathen in various more or less bloody
battles, as Nennius and other professed

historians have related; or whether he
was merely "a solar myth," as the Vi-
comte de la Villemarquè has suggested;
whether that extremely patriotic Welsh-
man, Geoffrey of Monmouth, commonly
called "the veracious Geoffrey," who
wrote in 1138 a full account of Arthur's
glorious achievements, really deserved his
name; or whether his chronicle was
merely, as an irreverent Dutch writer has
said, "a great, heavy, long, thick, pal-
pable, and most impudent lie;" whether
the source of the story was among the
misty mountains of Wales or among the
castles of Brittany, — all these are ques-
tions which lead aside from the purpose of
this essay. This much is certain: in the
twelfth century the name of King Arthur
had come to stand for an ideal of royal
wisdom, chivalric virtue, and knightly
prowess which was recognized alike in
England and France and Germany.

His story was told again and again by
Trouvère and Minnesinger and prose ro-
mancer. In camp and court and cloister,
on the banks of the Loire, the Rhine, the
Thames, men and women listened with
delight to the description of his character

and glorious exploits. A vast under-
growth of legends sprang up about him.
The older story of Merlin the Enchanter;
the tragic tale of Sir Lancelot and his
fatal love; the adventures of Sir Tristram
and Sir Gawain; the mystical romance
of the Saint Graal, with its twin heroes
of purity, Percivale and Galahad, — these
and many other tales of wonder and of
woe, of amourous devotion and fierce con-
flict and celestial vision, were woven into
the Arthurian tapestry. It extended itself
in every direction, like a vast forest; the
paths crossing and recrossing each other;
the same characters appearing and disap-
pearing in ever-changing disguises; beau-
teous ladies and valiant knights and
wicked magicians and pious monks coming
and going as if there were no end of them;
so that it is almost impossible for the
modern reader to trace his way through
the confusion, and he feels like the trav-
eller who complained that he "could not
see the wood for the trees."

It was at the close of the age of chiv-
alry, in the middle of the fifteenth cen-
tury, when the inventions of gunpowder
and printing had begun to create a new

order of things in Europe, that an English
knight, Sir Thomas Mallory by name,
conceived the idea of rewriting the Arthu-
rian story in his own language, and gather-
ing as many of these tangled legends as
he could find into one complete and con-
nected narrative. He must have been a
man of genius, for his book was more than
a mere compilation from the French. He
not only succeeded in bringing some kind
of order out of the confusion; he infused
a new and vigorous life into the ancient
tales, and clothed them in fine, simple,
sonorous prose, so that his *Morte d'Arthur*
is entitled to rank among the best things
in English literature.

William Caxton, the printer, was one
of the first to recognize the merits of the
book, and issued it from his press at West-
minster, in 1485, with a delightful pref-
ace — in which he tells what he thought
of the story. After a naïve and intrepid
defence of the historical reality of Arthur,
which he evidently thinks it would be as
sacrilegious to doubt as to question the
existence of Joshua, or King David, or
Judas Maccabeus, he goes on to say:
"Herein may be seen noble chivalry,

courtesy, humanity, friendliness, hardiness, love, friendship, cowardice, murder, hate, virtue and sin. Do after the good and leave the evil, and it shall bring you to good fame and renommee. And for to pass the time this book shall be pleasant to read in, but for to give faith and belief that all is true that is contained herein, ye be at your liberty: but all is written for our doctrine, and for to beware that we fall not to vice nor sin, but to exercise and follow virtue, by the which we may come and attain to good fame and renown in this life, and after this short and transitory life to come into everlasting bliss in heaven; the which He grant us that reigneth in heaven, the blessed Trinity. Amen."

This pleasant and profitable book was for several generations the favourite reading of the gentlemen of England. After falling into comparative obscurity for a while, it was brought back into notice and favour in the early part of the present century. In 1816 two new editions of it were published, the first since 1634; and in the following year another edition was brought out, with an introduction and

notes by Southey. It was doubtless
through the pages of Mallory that Tenny-
son made acquaintance with the story of
Arthur, and from these he has drawn most
of his materials for the Idylls.

One other source must be mentioned:
In 1838 Lady Charlotte Guest published
The Mabinogion, a translation of the an-
cient Welsh legends contained in the "red
book of Hergest," which is in the library
of Jesus College at Oxford. From this
book Tennyson has taken the story of
Geraint and Enid.

When we turn now to look at the
manner in which the poet has used his
materials, we observe two things: first,
that he has taken such liberties with the
outline of the story as were necessary to
adapt it to his own purpose; and second,
that he has thrown back into it the
thoughts and feelings of his own age.

In speaking of the changes which he
has made in the story I do not allude to
the omission of minor characters and
details, nor to the alterations in the order
of the narrative, but to changes of much
deeper significance. Take for example
the legend of Merlin: Mallory tells us

that the great Mage "fell in a dotage on
a damsel that hight Nimue and would let
her have no rest, but always he would be
with her. And so he followed her over
land and sea. But she was passing weary
of him and would fain have been delivered
of him, for she was afraid of him because
he was a devil's son. And so on a time
it happed that Merlin shewed to her in a
rock, whereas was a great wonder, and
wrought by enchantment, that went under
a great stone. So by her subtle working
she made Merlin to go under that stone,
to let her into of the marvels there, but
she wrought so there for him that he came
never out for all the craft that he could
do. And so she departed and left
Merlin."

How bald and feeble is this narrative
compared with the version which Tenny-
son has given ! He has created the char-
acter of Vivien, the woman without a
conscience, a brilliant, baleful star, a fem-
inine Iago. He has made her, not the
pursued, but the pursuer, — the huntress,
but of another train than Dian's. He
has painted those weird scenes in the
forest of Broceliande, where the earthly

wisdom of the magician proves powerless
to resist the wiles of a subtler magic than
his own. He has made Merlin yield at
last to an appeal for protection which
might have deceived a nobler nature than
his. He tells the ancient charm in a
moment of weakness; and while he sleeps,
Vivien binds him fast with his own en-
chantment. He lies there, in the hollow
oak, as dead,

> And lost to life and use and name and fame,

while she leaps down the forest crying
"Fool!" and exulting in her triumph.
It is not a pleasant story. In some re-
spects it is even repulsive: it was meant
to be so. But it has a power in it that
was utterly unknown to the old legend;
it is the familiar tale of Sophocles' Ajax,
or of Samson and Delilah, told with un-
rivalled skill and beauty of language.

There is another change, of yet greater
importance, which affects not a single
idyll, but the entire cycle. Mallory has
made the downfall of the Round Table
and the death of Arthur follow, at least
in part, a great wrong which the King
himself had committed. Modred the

traitor, is represented as the son of Belli-
cent, whom Arthur had loved and be-
trayed in his youth, not knowing that she
was his own half-sister. Thus the story
becomes a tragedy of Nemesis. The King
is pursued and destroyed, like Œdipus in
the Greek drama, by the consequences of
his own sin. Tennyson has entirely elim-
inated this element. He makes the King
say of Modred,

> I must strike against *the man they call*
> *My sister's son — no kin of mine.*

He traces the ruin of the realm to other
causes, — the transgression of Lancelot
and Guinevere, the corruption of the court
through the influence of Vivien, and the
perversion of Arthur's ideals among his
own followers.

Mr. Swinburne — the most eloquent of
dogmatists — asserts that this change is
a fatal error, that the old story was infi-
nitely nobler and more poetic, and that
Tennyson has ruined it in the telling.
Lavish in his praise of other portions of
the Laureate's work, he has been equally
lavish in his blame of the Idylls. He calls
them the "Morte d'Albert, or Idylls of

the Prince Consort;" he pours out the
vials of his contempt upon the character
of "the blameless king," and declares
that it presents the very poorest and most
pitiful standard of duty or of heroism.
And all this wrath, so far as I can under-
stand it, is caused chiefly by the fact that
Tennyson has chosen to free Arthur from
the taint of incest, and represent him, not
as the victim of an inevitable tragic des-
tiny, but rather as a pure, brave soul, who
fights in one sense vainly, but in another
and a higher sense successfully, against
the forces of evil in the world around him.

But when we come to look more closely
at Mr. Swinburne's criticism, we can see
that it is radically unjust because it is
based upon ignorance. He does not seem
to know that the element of Arthur's
spiritual glory belongs to the ancient
story just as much as the darker element
of blind sin, clinging shame, and remorse-
less fate. At one time, the King is de-
scribed as the very flower of humanity,
the most perfect man that God had made
since Adam; at another time he is exhib-
ited as a slayer of innocents planning to
destroy all the " children born of lords and

ladies, on May-day," because Merlin had
predicted that one of them would be his
own rival and destroyer. Mallory has
woven together these incongruous threads
after the strangest ·fashion. But no one
who has read his book can doubt which
of the two threads is the more important.
It is the glory of Arthur, his superiority
to his own knights, his noble purity and
strength, that really control the story;
and the other, darker thread sinks gradu-
ally out of sight, becomes more and more
obscure, until finally it is lost, and Arthur's
name is inscribed upon his tomb as *Rex
quondam, rexque futurus.*

Now it was open to Tennyson to choose
which of the threads he would follow;
but it was impossible to follow both. He
would have had no hero for his poem, he
would have been unable to present any
consistent picture of the King unless he
had exercised a liberty of selection among
these incoherent and at bottom contradic-
tory elements which Mallory had vainly
tried to blend.

If he had intended to make a tragedy
after the old Greek fashion, in which Fate
should be the only real hero, that would

have been another thing: then he must
have retained the unconscious sin of
Arthur, his weakness, his impotence to
escape from its consequences, as the cen-
tral and dominant motive of the story.
But his design was diametrically the op-
posite of this. He was writing in the
modern spirit, which lays the emphasis
not on Fate, but on Free-will. He meant
to show that the soul of man is not bound
in inextricable toils and foredoomed to
hopeless struggle, but free to choose be-
tween good and evil, and that the issues
of life, at least for the individual, depend
upon the nature of that choice. It was
for this reason that he made Arthur, as
the ideal of the highest manhood, pure
from the stains of ineradicable corruption,
and showed him rising, moving onward,
and at last passing out of sight, like a
radiant star which accomplishes its course
in light and beauty.

Mr. Swinburne has a right to find fault
with Arthur's character as an ideal; he
has a right to say that there are serious
defects in it, that it lacks virility, that it
has a touch of insincerity about it, that
it comes perilously near to self-compla-

cency and moral priggishness. There may
be a grain of truth in some of these criti-
cisms. But to condemn the Idylls because
they are not built upon the lines of a
Greek Tragedy is as superfluous and un-
just as it would be to blame a pine-tree
for not resembling an oak, or to despise
a Gothic cathedral because it differs from
a Doric temple.

It was legitimate, then, for Tennyson to
select out of the mass of materials which
Mallory had collected such portions as
were adapted to form the outline of a
consistent story, and to omit the rest as
unnecessary and incapable of being brought
into harmony with the design. But was
it also legitimate for the poet to treat his
subject in a manner and spirit so dis-
tinctly modern, — to make his characters
discuss the problems and express the senti-
ments which belong to the nineteenth
century?

It cannot be denied that he has done
this. Not only are many of the questions
of morality and philosophy which arise in
the course of the Idylls, questions which
were unknown to the Middle Ages, but
the tone of some of the most suggestive

and important speeches of Merlin, of
Arthur, of Lancelot, of Tristram, is mani-
festly the tone of these latter days. Take
for example Merlin's oracular triplets in
The Coming of Arthur : —

> Rain, rain and sun! a rainbow on the lea!
> And truth is this to me, and that to thee;
> And truth or clothed or naked let it be.

We recognize here the accents of the
modern philosopher who holds that all
knowledge is relative and deals only with
phenomena, the reality being unknowable.
Or listen to Tristram as he argues with
Isolt : —

> The vows ?
> O ay — the wholesome madness of an hour.
> . . . The wide world laughs at it.
> And worldling of the world am I, and know
> The ptarmigan that whitens ere his hour
> Woos his own end ; we are not angels here,
> Nor shall be : vows — I am woodman of the woods
> And hear the garnet-headed yaffingale
> Mock them : my soul, we love but while we may ;
> And therefore is my love so large for thee,
> Seeing it is not bounded save by love.

That is the modern doctrine of free love,
not only in its conclusion, but in its argu-
ment drawn from the example of the birds,
— the untimely ptarmigan that invites de-
struction, and the red-crested woodpecker

that pursues its amours in the liberty of nature.

Or hear the speech which Arthur makes to his knights when they return from the quest of the Holy Grail: —

> And some among you held, that if the King
> Had seen the sight he would have sworn the vow:
> Not easily, seeing that the King must guard
> That which he rules, and is but as the hind,
> To whom a space of land is given to plough,
> Who may not wander from the allotted field
> Before his work be done.

That is the modern conception of kingship, the idea of responsibility as superior to authority. Public office is a public trust. The discharge of duty to one's fellow-men, the work of resisting violence and maintaining order and righting the wrongs of the oppressed, is higher and holier than the following of visions. The service of man is the best worship of God. It was not thus that kings thought, it was not thus that warriors talked in the sixth century.

But has the poet any right to transfer the ideas and feelings of his own age to men and women who did not and could not entertain them? The answer to this question depends entirely upon the view which we take of the nature and purpose of poetry. If it is to give an exact historical account of certain events, then of course every modern touch in an ancient story, every reflection of the present into the past, is a blemish. But if the object of poetry is to bring out the meaning of human life, to quicken the dead bones of narrative with a vital spirit, to show us character and action in such a way that our hearts shall be moved and purified by pity and fear, indignation and love; then certainly it is not only lawful but inevitable that the poet should throw into his work the thoughts and emotions of his own age. For these are the only ones that he can draw from the life.

There is a certain kind of realism which absolutely destroys reality in a work of art. It is the shabby realism of the French painter who took it for granted that the only way to paint a sea-beach with accuracy was to sprinkle the canvas with actual sand; the shabby realism of M. Verestschagin, who gives us coloured photographs of Palestinian Jews as a representation of the life of Christ; the shabby realism of the writers who are satisfied with reproducing the dialect, the dress, the manners of the

time and country in which the scene of their
story is laid, without caring whether their
dramatis personæ have any human nature
and life in them or not. Great pictures or
great poems have never been produced in
this way. They have always been full of
anachronisms, — intellectual and moral an-
achronisms, I mean, — and their want of
scientific accuracy is the very condition of
their poetic truth.

Every poet of the first rank has idealized
— or let us rather say, vitalized — his char-
acters by giving to them the thoughts and
feelings which he has himself experienced,
or known by living contact with men and
women of his own day. Homer did this
with Ulysses, Virgil with Æneas, Shake-
speare with Hamlet, Milton with Satan,
Goethe with Faust. From the very begin-
ning, the Arthurian legends have been
treated in the same way. Poets and prose
romancers have made them the mirror of
their own chivalric ideals and aspirations.
Compared with the Rolands and the Alis-
cans of the *chansons de geste*, Lancelot and
Gawain and Percivale are modern gentle-
men. And why? Not because the supposed
age of Arthur was really better than the age

of Charlemagne, but simply because Chré-
tien de Troyes and Wolfram von Eschen-
bach had higher and finer conceptions of
knighthood and piety and courtesy and love,
which they embodied in their heroes of the
Round Table.

No one imagines that the *Morte d'Arthur*
in any of its forms is an exact reproduction
of life and character in Britain in the time
of the Saxon invasion. It is a reflection of
the later chivalry, — the chivalry of the
Norman and Angevin kings. If the story
could be used to convey the ideals of the
twelfth and thirteenth centuries, why not
also the ideals of the nineteenth century?
If it be said that Arthur was not really a
modern gentleman, it may be answered
that it is just as certain that he was not a
mediæval gentleman; perhaps he was not
a gentleman at all. There was no more
necessity that Tennyson should be true to
Mallory, than there was that Mallory should
be true to Walter Map or Robert de Borron.
Each of them was a poet, a maker, a creator
for his own age. The only condition upon
which it was possible for Tennyson to make
a poem about Arthur and his knights was
that he should cast his own thoughts into

the mould of the ancient legends, and make them represent living ideas and types of character. This he has done so successfully that the *Idylls* stand among the most representative poems of the present age.

III.

Two things are to be considered in a work of art : the style and the substance.

So far as the outward form of the *Idylls* is concerned, they take a very high place in English verse. In music of rhythm, in beauty of diction, in richness of illustration, they are unsurpassed. They combine in a rare way two qualities which seem irreconcilable, — delicacy and grandeur, the power of observing the most minute details and painting them with absolute truth of touch, and the power of clothing large thoughts in simple, vigorous, sweeping words.

It would be an easy matter to give examples of the first of these qualities from every page of the *Idylls*. They are full of little pictures which show that Tennyson has studied Nature at first hand, and that he understands how to catch and reproduce the most fleeting and delicate expressions of her face. Take, for instance, some of his studies of trees. He has seen the ancient yew-tree tossed by the gusts of April, —

> That puff'd the swaying branches into smoke, —

little clouds of dust rising from it, as if it were on fire. He has noted the resemblance between a crippled, shivering beggar and

> An old dwarf-elm
> That turns its back on the salt blast;

and the line describes exactly the stunted, suffering, patient aspect of a tree that grows beside the sea and is bent landward by the prevailing winds. He has felt the hush that broods upon the forest when a tempest is coming, —

> And the dark wood grew darker toward the storm
> In silence.

Not less exact is his knowledge of the birds that haunt the forests and the fields. He has seen the

> Careful robins eye the delver's toil;

and listened to

> The great plover's human whistle,

and marked at sunset, in the marshes, how

> The lone hern forgets his melancholy,
> Lets down his other leg, and, stretching, dreams
> Of goodly supper in the distant pool.

He knows, also, how the waters flow and fall; how a wild brook

> Slopes o'er a little stone,
> Running too vehemently to break upon it;

how, in a sharper rapid, there is a place

> Where the crisping white
> Plays ever back upon the sloping wave;

how one

> That listens near a torrent mountain-brook
> All thro' the crash of the near cataract, hears
> The drumming thunder of the huger fall
> At distance.

Most remarkable of all is his knowledge of the sea, and his power to describe it. He has looked at it from every standpoint and caught every phase of its changing aspect. Take these four pictures. First, you stand upon the cliffs of Cornwall and watch the huge Atlantic billows, blue as sapphire and bright with sunlight, and you understand how Isolt could say,

> O sweeter than all memories of thee,
> Deeper than any yearnings after thee,
> Seem'd *those far-rolling, westward-smiling seas.*

Then, you lie upon the smooth level of some broad beach, on a summer afternoon,

And watch *the curled white of the coming wave*
Glass'd in the slippery sand before it breaks.

Then, you go into a dark cavern like that
of Staffa, and see the dumb billows rolling
in, one after another, groping their way
into the farthest recesses as if they were
seeking to find something that they had
lost, and you know how it was with Merlin
when

So dark a forethought roll'd about his brain,
As on a dull day in an ocean cave
The blind wave feeling round his long sea-hall
In silence.

Then, you stand on the deck of a vessel
in a gale, — not on the blue Atlantic, but
on the turbid German Ocean, — and you
behold how

A wild wave in the wide North-sea,
Green-glimmering toward the summit, bears with all
Its stormy crests that smoke against the skies,
Down on a bark, and overbears the bark
And him that helms it.

I think it is safe to say that these four
wave-pictures have never been surpassed,
either in truth or in power, by any artist
in words or colours.

But if it should be asserted that lines like
these prove the fineness of Tennyson's art
rather than the greatness of his poetry, the

assertion might be granted, and still we should be able to support the larger claim by pointing to passages in the *Idylls* which are unquestionably magnificent, — great not only in expression but great also in thought. There are single lines which have the felicity and force of epigrams:

Obedience is the courtesy due to kings.

He makes no friend who never made a foe.

Man dreams of fame while woman wakes to love.

A doubtful throne is ice on summer seas.

Mockery is the fume of little hearts.

There are longer passages in which the highest truths are uttered without effort, and in language so natural and inevitable that we have to look twice before we realize its grandeur. Take for example the description of human error in *Geraint and Enid:*

O purblind race of miserable men,
How many among us even at this hour
Do forge a life-long trouble for ourselves
By taking true for false, or false for true;
Here, thro' the feeble twilight of this world,
Groping, how many, until we pass and reach
That other, where we see as we are seen!

Or take Arthur's speech to Lancelot in the *Holy Grail:* —

Never yet
Could all of true and noble in knight and man
Twine round one sin, whatever it might be,
With such a closeness, but apart there grew

. . . .

Some root of knighthood and pure nobleness :
Whereto see thou, that it may bear its flower.

Or, best of all, take that splendid description of Lancelot's disloyal loyalty to Guinevere, in *Elaine :* —

The shackles of an old love straitened him :
His honour rooted in dishonour stood,
And faith unfaithful kept him falsely true.

Shakespeare himself has nothing more perfect than this. It is an admirable example of what has been called " the grand style," — terse yet spacious, vigorous yet musical, clear yet suggestive ; not a word too little or too much, and withal a sense of something larger in the thought, which words cannot fully reveal.

It would be superfluous to quote at length such a familiar passage as the parting of Arthur and Guinevere at Almesbury. But let any reader take this up and study it carefully ; mark the fluency and strength of the verse ; the absence of all sensationalism, and yet the thrill in the far-off sound of the solitary trumpet

that blows while Guinevere lies in the
dark at Arthur's feet; the purity and
dignity of the imagery, the steady onward
and upward movement of the thought,
the absolute simplicity of the language as
it is taken word by word, and yet the
richness and splendour of the effect which
it produces, — and if he is candid, I think
he must admit that there have been few
English poets masters of as grand a style
as this.

But of course the style alone does not
make a masterpiece, nor will any number
of eloquent fragments redeem a poem from
failure if it lacks the soul of greatness.
The subject of it must belong to poetry;
that is to say, it must be adapted to move
the feelings as well as to arouse the intel-
lect, it must have the element of mystery
as well as the element of clearness.
Whether the form be lyric or epic, dra-
matic or idyllic, the poet must make us
feel that he has something to say that is
not only worth saying, but also fitted to
give us pleasure through the quickening
of the emotions. The central idea of the
poem must be vital and creative; it must
have power to sustain itself in our minds

while we read; it must be worked out
coherently, and yet it must suggest that it
belongs to a larger truth whose depths are
unexplored and inaccessible. It seems to
me that these are the conditions of a great
poem. We have now to consider whether
or not they are fulfilled in the *Idylls of
the King*.

The meaning of the *Idylls* has been
distinctly stated by the poet himself, and
we are bound to take his words as the
clue to their interpretation. In the
" Dedication to the Queen " he says : —

Accept this old imperfect tale

New-old, and *shadowing Sense at war with Soul*,
Rather than that gray king, whose name, a ghost,
Streams like a cloud, man-shaped, from mountain-peak,
And cleaves to cairn and cromlech still : or him
Of Geoffrey's book, or him of Malleor's, one
Touched by the adulterous finger of a time
That hover'd between war and wantonness,
And crownings and dethronements.

This is a clear disavowal of an historical
purpose in the *Idylls*. But does it amount
to the confession that they are an allegory
pure and simple ? It is in this sense that
the critics have commonly taken the
statement. But I venture to think that
they are mistaken, and that the mistake

has been a barrier to the thorough com-
prehension of the poem and a fertile source
of errors and absurdities in some of the
essays which have been written about it.

Let us understand precisely what an
allegory is. It is not merely a represen-
tation of one thing by another which
resembles it in its properties or circum-
stances, a picture where the outward form
conveys a hidden meaning, a story

" Where more is meant than meets the ear."

It is a work in which the figures and char-
acters are confessedly unreal, a masquer-
ade in which the actors are not men and
women, but virtues and vices dressed up
in human costume. The distinguishing
mark of allegory is personification. It
does not deal with actual persons, but with
abstract qualities which are treated as if
they were persons, and made to speak and
act as if they were alive. It moves, there-
fore, altogether in a dream-world: it is
not only improbable but impossible: at
a touch its figures dissolve into thin air.

I will illustrate my meaning by examples.
Dürer's picture of *Death and the Knight*
has allegorical features in it, but it is not

an allegory because the Knight is an actual man of flesh and blood, — or perhaps one ought to say (remembering that grim figure), of bone and nerve. *Melancolia,* on the contrary, is an allegory of the purest type. Goethe's *Faust* is not an allegory, although it is full of symbolism and contains a hidden meaning. Spenser's *Fairy Queen* is an allegory, because its characters are only attributes in disguise, and its plot is altogether arbitrary and artificial.

The defect of strict allegory is that it always disappoints us. A valiant knight comes riding in, and we prepare to follow his adventures with wonder and delight. Then the poet informs us that it is not a knight at all, but only Courage, or Temperance, or Patience, in armour; and straightway we lose our interest; we know exactly what he is going to do, and we care not what becomes of him. A fair damsel appears upon the scene, and we are ready to be moved to pity by her distress, and to love by her surpassing beauty, until presently we are reminded that it is not a damsel at all, but only Purity, or Faith, or Moral Disinterestedness, running about in woman's clothes: and forthwith we are

disenchanted.   There is no speculation in
her eyes.   Her hand is like a stuffed glove.
She has no more power to stir our feelings
than a proposition in Euclid.   We would
not shed a drop of blood to win her ghostly
favour, or to rescue her from all the giants
that ever lived.

But if the method were reversed; if in-
stead of a virtue representing a person, the
poet gave us a person embodying and rep-
resenting a virtue ; if instead of the oppo-
sitions and attractions of abstract qualities,
we had the trials and conflicts and loves of
real men and women in whom these quali-
ties were living and working, — then the
poet might remind us as often as he pleased
of the deeper significance of his story ; we
should still be able to follow it with interest.

This is the point which I desire to make
in regard to the *Idylls of the King*.   It is
a distinction which, so far as I know, has
never been clearly drawn.   The poem is
not an allegory, but a parable.

Of course there are a great many purely
allegorical figures and passages in it.   The
Lady of the Lake, for example, is a personi-
fication of Religion.   She dwells in a deep
calm, far below the surface of the waters,

and when they are tossed and troubled by storms,

> Hath power to walk the water like our Lord.

She gives to the King his sword Excalibur, to represent either the spiritual weapon with which the soul wars against its enemies, or, as seems to me more probable, the temporal power of the church. For it bears the double inscription : —

> On one side
> Graven in the oldest tongue of all this world,
> "Take me," but turn the blade and ye shall see,
> And written in the speech ye speak yourselves,
> "Cast me away." And sad was Arthur's face
> Taking it, but old Merlin counsell'd him
> "Take them and strike! " the time to cast away
> Is yet far-off. So this great brand the King
> Took, and by this will beat his foemen down.

The necessity of actual flesh-and-blood warfare against the heathen is proclaimed in the ancient language; the uselessness of such weapons under the new order, in the modern conflict, is predicted in the language of to-day.

The Lady of the Lake is described as standing on the keystone of the gate of Camelot : —

> All her dress
> Wept from her sides, as water flowing away :
> But, like the cross, her great and goodly arms

Stretch'd under all the cornice, and upheld:
And drops of water fell from either hand:
And down from one a sword was hung, from one
A censer, either worn with wind and storm;
And o'er her breast floated the sacred fish;
. . . . . . and over all,
High on the top, were those three Queens, the friends
Of Arthur, who should help him at his need.

This is an allegory of the power of religion
in sustaining the fabric of society. The
forms of the church are forever changing
and flowing like water, but her great arms
are stretched out immovable, like the cross.
The sword is the symbol of her justice, the
censer is the symbol of her adoration, and
both bear the marks of time and strife.
The drops that fall from her hands are the
water of baptism, and the fish is the ancient
sign of the name of Christ.

The three Queens who sit up aloft are
the theological virtues of Faith, Hope, and
Charity.

It is a fine piece of work from the
mystical standpoint; elaborate, spiritual,
suggestive, and full of true philosophy;
Ambrogio Lorenzetti might have painted
it. But after all, it has little or nothing
to do with the substance of the poem. The
watery Lady stands like a painted figure

on the wall, and the three Queens play
no real part in the life of Arthur. Appar-
ently they continue to sit upon the cornice
in ornamental idleness while the King loves
and toils and fights and " drees his weird ; "
and we are almost surprised at their un-
wonted activity when they appear at last
in the black barge and carry him away to
the island-valley of Avilion.

There is another passage of the same char-
acter in *The Holy Grail*, which describes
the probations of Percivale. He is allured
from his quest, first by appetite under the
figure of an orchard full of pleasant fruits,
then by domestic love under the figure of
a fair woman spinning at a cottage door,
then by wealth under the figure of a knight
clad in gold and jewels, then by fame under
the figure of a mighty city filled with shouts
of welcome and applause ; but all these are
only visions, and when they vanish at Per-
civale's approach we cannot feel that there
was any reality in his trials, or that he de-
serves any great credit for resisting them.

The most distinct example of this kind
of work is found in *Gareth and Lynette*,
in the description of the carving on the
rock. There are five figures of armed

men, Phosphorous, Meridies, Hesperus,
Nox, and Mors, all chasing the human
soul,

> A shape that fled
> With broken wings, torn raiment and loose hair,
> For help and shelter to the hermit's cave.

This is definitely called an allegory, and
its significance is explained as

> The war of Time against the soul of man.

But there is all the difference in the world
between these graven images and the brave
boy Gareth riding through the forest with
the bright, petulant, audacious maiden
Lynette. If the former are properly called
allegorical, the latter must certainly be
described by some other adjective. Ga-
reth is alive, very much alive indeed, in
his ambition to become a knight, in his
quarrel with Sir Kay the crabbed senes-
chal, in his sturdy courtship of the damsel
with " the cheek of apple-blossom," in his
conflict with the four caitiffs who kept
Lyonors shut up in her castle. We follow
his adventures with such interest that we
are fairly vexed with the poet for refusing
to tell us at the end whether this cheerful
companion and good fighter married Lyn-
ette or her elder sister.

We must distinguish, then, between the allegorical fragments which Tennyson has woven into his work, and the substance of the *Idylls;* between the scenery and mechanical appliances, and the actors who move upon the stage. The attempt to interpret the poem as a strict allegory breaks down at once and spoils the story. Suppose you say that Arthur is the Conscience, and Guinevere is the Flesh, and Merlin is the Intellect; then pray what is Lancelot, and what is Geraint, and what is Vivien? What business has the Conscience to fall in love with the Flesh? What attraction has Vivien for the Intellect without any passions? If Merlin is not a man, " *Que diable allait-il faire dans cette galère?* " The whole affair becomes absurd, unreal, incomprehensible, uninteresting.

But when we take the King and his people as actual men and women, when we put ourselves into the story and let it carry us along, then we understand that it is a parable; that is to say, it casts beside itself an image, a reflection, of something spiritual, just as a man walking in the sunlight is followed by his shadow.

It is a tale of human life, and therefore,
being told with a purpose, it

Shadows Sense at war with Soul.

Let us take up this idea of the conflict
between sense and soul and carry it out
through the *Idylls.*

Arthur is intended to be a man in whom
the spirit has already conquered and reigns
supreme. It is upon this that his kingship
rests. His task is to bring his realm into
harmony with himself, to build up a spirit-
ual and social order upon which his own
character, as the best and highest, shall
be impressed. In other words, he works
for the uplifting and purification of hu-
manity. It is the problem of civilization.
His great· enemies in this task are not
outward and visible, — the heathen, — for
these he overcomes and expels. But the
real foes that oppose him to the end are
the evil passions in the hearts of men
and women about him. So long as these
exist and dominate human lives, the dream
of a perfected society must remain unreal-
ized ; and when they get the upper hand,
even its beginnings will be destroyed. But
the conflict is not an airy, abstract strife ;

it lies in the opposition between those
in whom the sensual principle is regnant
and those in whom the spiritual principle
is regnant, and in the inward struggle of
the noble heart against the evil, and of
the sinful heart against the good.

This contest may be traced through its
different phases in the successive stories
which make up the poem.

In *The Coming of Arthur,* doubt, which
judges by the senses, is matched against
faith, which follows the spirit. The ques-
tion is whether Arthur is a pretender and
the child of shamefulness, or the true King.
Against him, stand the base-minded lords
and barons who are ready to accept any
evil story of his origin rather than accept
him as their ruler. For him, stand such
knights as Bedivere, —

> For bold in heart and act and word was he
> Whenever slander breathed against the King.

Between the two classes stands Leodogran,
the father of Guinevere, uncertain whether
to believe or doubt. The arguments of
the clever Queen Bellicent do not con-
vince him. But at last he has a dream
in which he sees the King standing out

in heaven, crowned, — and faith conquers.
Guinevere is given to Arthur as his wife.
His throne is securely established, and his
reign begins prosperously.

Then comes *Gareth and Lynette.* Here
the conflict is between a true ambition and
a false pride. Gareth is an honest, ardent
fellow who longs for "good fame and re-
nommee." He wishes to rise in the world,
but he is willing to work and fight his
way upward; even to serve as a kitchen-
knave if so he may win his spurs at last
and ride among the noble knights of the
Round Table. His conception of nobility
grasps the spirit of it without caring much
for the outward form. Lynette is a society
girl, a worshipper of rank and station;
brave, high-spirited, lovable, but narrow-
minded, and scornful of every one who
lacks the visible marks of distinction. She
judges by the senses. She cannot imagine
that a man who comes from among the
lower classes can possibly be a knight, and
despises Gareth's proferred services. But
his pride, being true, is stronger than hers,
being false. He will not be rebuffed;
follows her, fights her battles, wins first
her admiration, then her love, and brings

her at last to see that true knighthood
lies not in the name but in the deed.
The atmosphere of this Idyll is alto-
gether pure and clear. There is as yet
no shadow of the storm that is coming to
disturb Arthur's realm. The chivalry of
the spirit overcomes the chivalry of the
sense in a natural, straightforward, joyous
way, and all goes well with the world.

But in *Geraint and Enid* there is a
cloud upon the sky, a trouble in the air.
The fatal love of Lancelot and Guinevere
has already begun to poison the court
with suspicions and scandals. It is in this
brooding and electrical atmosphere that
jealousy, in the person of Geraint, comes
into conflict with loyalty, in the person of
Enid. The story is the same that Boc-
caccio has told so exquisitely in the tale
of *Griselda*, and Shakespeare so tragically
in *Othello*, — the story of a woman, sweet
and true and steadfast down to the very
bottom of her heart, joined to a man
who is exacting and suspicious. Geraint
wakens in the morning to find his wife
weeping, and leaps at once to the conclu-
sion that she is false. He judges by the
sense and not by the soul. But Enid loves

him too well even to defend herself against
him. She obeys his harsh commands and
submits to his heavy, stupid tests. Yet
even in her obedience she distinguishes
between the sense and the spirit. As long
as there is no danger she rides before him
in silence as he told her to do; but when
she sees the robbers waiting in ambush
she turns back to warn him:

> I needs must disobey him for his good;
> How should I dare obey him to his harm?
> Needs must I speak, and tho' he kill me for it,
> I save a life dearer to me than mine.

So they move onward through many
perils and adventures, she like a bright,
clear, steady star, he like a dull, smoulder-
ing, smoky fire, until at last her loyalty
conquers his jealousy, and he sees that it
is better to trust than to doubt, and that a
pure woman's love has the power to vindi-
cate its own honour against the world, and
the right to claim an absolute and un-
questioning confidence. The soul is once
more victorious over the sense.

In *Balin and Balan* the cloud has grown
larger and darker, the hostile influences
in the realm begin to make themselves
more deeply felt. The tributary court of

Pellam, in which the hypocritical old king has taken to holy things in rivalry of Arthur,

> And finds himself descended from the Saint
> Arimathean Joseph,

and collects sacred relics, and drives out all women from his palace lest he should be polluted, while his son and heir, Garlon, is a secret libertine and murderer, — is a picture of religion corrupted by asceticism. Balin and Balan are two brothers, alike in daring, in. strength, in simplicity, but differing in this: Balin is called "the savage," swift in impulse, fierce in anger, unable to restrain or guide himself; Balan is master of his passion, clear-hearted and self-controlled, his brother's better angel. Both men represent force; but one is force under dominion of soul, the other is force under dominion of sense. By the false-hood of Vivien, who now appears on the scene, they are involved in conflict and ignorantly give each other mortal wounds. It would seem as if violence had con-quered. And yet, in truth not so. Balin's last words are : —

> Goodnight! for we shall never bid again
> Goodmorrow — Dark my doom was here, and dark
> It will be there.

But Balan replies with a diviner faith, drawing his brother upward in death even as he had done in life, —

> Goodnight, true brother here! goodmorrow there!

Thus far the higher principle has been victorious, though in the last instance the victory is won only in the moment of an apparent defeat. But now, in *Merlin and Vivien*, sense becomes the victor. The old magician is a man in whom the intellect appears to be supreme. One might think him almost impregnable to temptation. But the lissome snake Vivien, also a type of keen and subtle intelligence, though without learning, finds the weak point in his armour, overcomes him and degrades him to her helpless thrall.

The conflict in *Lancelot and Elaine* is between a pure, virgin love and a guilty passion. The maid of Astolat is the lily of womanhood. The Queen is the rose, full-blown and heavy with fragrance. Never has a sharper contrast been drawn than this: Elaine in her innocent simplicity and singleness of heart; Guinevere in her opulence of charms, her intensity, her jealous devotion. Between the two

stands the great Sir Lancelot, a noble
heart though erring. If he were free he
would turn to the pure love. But he is
not free ; he is bound by ties which are
interwoven with all that seems most pre-
cious in his life. He could not break them
if he would. And so the guilty passion
conquers and he turns back to the fatal
sweetness of his old allegiance.

The Holy Grail shows us the strife be-
tween superstition, which is a sensual relig-
ion, and true faith, which is spiritual. This
is in some respects the richest of the *Idylls*,
but it is also, by reason of its theme, the
most confused. Out of the mystical twi-
light which envelops the action this truth
emerges : that those knights who thought
of the Grail only as an external wonder, a
miracle which they fain would see because
others had seen it, " followed wandering
fires ; " while those to whom it became
a symbol of inward purity and grace, like
Galahad and Percivale and even the dull,
honest, simple-minded Bors and the sin-
tormented Lancelot, finally attained unto
the vision. But the King, who remained
at home and kept the plain path of daily
duty, is the real hero of the Idyll, though
he bore no part in the quest.

In *Pelleas and Ettarre* the victory falls
back to the side of sense. Pelleas is the
counterpart of Elaine, a fair soul who has
no thought of evil. Amid the increasing
darkness of the court he sees nothing but
light. He dreams that the old ideals of
chivalry are still unbroken; to him all ladies
are perfect, and all knights loyal. He is in
love with loving, *amans amare,* as St. Augus-
tine put it, — and when Ettarre crosses his
track he worships her as a star. But she
— "of the earth, earthy " — despises him
as a child, mocks him, and casts him off.
Gawain, the flower of courtesy, betrays him
basely. Driven mad by scorn and treason,
he rushes away at last into the gloom, — a
gallant knight overthrown by the perfidy
of a wicked world.

The fool is the hero of *The Last Tourna-
ment.* He knows that Arthur's dream will
never be fulfilled, knows that the Queen is
false, and the Knights are plotting treason,
and the whole realm is on the verge of ruin ;
but still he holds fast to his master, and
believes in him, and will not break his alle-
giance to follow the downward path of the
court. Arthur has lifted him out of the
baseness of his old life and made him a

man. Maimed wits and crippled body, yet
he has a soul, — this little, loyal jester, —
and he will not lose it.

> I have had my day and my philosophies, —
> And thank the Lord I am King Arthur's fool.

In contrast to him stands Sir Tristram, the
most brilliant and powerful of the new
knights who followed the King only for
glory, and despised him in their hearts, and
broke his vows as if they had never sworn
them. Poet, musician, huntsman, warrior,
perfect in face and form, victor in love and
war, Tristram is one to whom faith is fool-
ishness and the higher life an idle delusion.
He denies his soul, mocks at it, flings it
away from him.

> New leaf, new life — the days of frost are o'er:
> New life, new love, to suit the newer day;
> New loves are sweet as those that went before:
> Free love — free field — we love but while we may.

In him the triumph of the senses is com-
plete. He wins the prize in the " Tourna-
ment of the Dead Innocence," and the
shouts of the people hail him as their fav-
ourite. He clasps the jewels around the
neck of Isolt as she sits with him in her
tower of Tintagil by the sea, lightly glory-
ing in his conquests. But out of the dark-

ness the battle-axe of the craven King
Mark strikes him dead. Meanwhile, at
Camelot, Arthur comes home ; Guinevere
has fled ; —

> And while he climb'd,
> All in a death-dumb autumn-dripping gloom,
> The stairway to the wall, and look'd and saw
> The great Queen's bower was dark, — about his feet
> A voice clung sobbing till he question'd it,
> " What art thou? " and the voice about his feet
> Sent up an answer, sobbing, " I am thy fool,
> And I shall never make thee smile again."

Yes, a fool, but also a soul, and faithful
even unto death, and therefore shining
steadfastly like a star in heaven when the
false meteor of sense has dropt into end-
less night.

The next Idyll should be called *Arthur
and Guinevere*. The conflict now draws
to its final issue. It lies between these
two : one the victim of a great sin, a crime
of sense which chose the lower rather than
the higher love ; the other the hero of a
great faith, which knows that pardon fol-
lows penitence, and seeks to find some
light of hope for the fallen. Is Guinevere
to be separated from Arthur forever ? —
that is the question whose answer hangs
upon the close of this struggle. And the

Queen herself tells us the result, when
she says, —

> Ah, great and gentle lord,
> Who wast, as is the conscience of a saint
> Among his warring senses, to thy knights —
> . . . Now I see thee what thou art,
> Thou art the highest and most human too,
> Not Lancelot, nor another. Is there none
> Will tell the King I love him tho' so late?
> Now — ere he goes to that great Battle ? none:
> Myself must tell him in that purer life,
> But now it were too daring.

In *The Passing of Arthur* we have a
picture of the brave man facing death.
All the imagery of the poem is dark and
shadowy. The great battle has been
fought; the Round Table has been shat-
tered; the bodies of the slain lie upon
the field, friends and foes mingled together,
and not a voice to stir the silence.

> Only the wan wave
> Brake in among dead faces, to and fro
> Swaying the helpless hands, and up and down
> Tumbling the hollow helmets of the fallen,
> And shiver'd brands that once had fought with Rome,
> And rolling far along the gloomy shores
> The voice of days of old and days to be.

This is the tide of Time which engulfs all
things mortal. Arthur's hour has come:
he has lived his life and must pass away.
To Sir Bedivere, valiant, simple-hearted

knight, but still unable to look beyond the outward appearance of death, this seems a fatal end of all his hopes. He cannot bear to cast away his master's sword, but would fain keep it as a relic. He cries : —

> Ah! my Lord Arthur, whither shall I go ?
> Where shall I hide my forehead and my eyes ?
> For now I see the true old times are dead;
> .   .   .   .
> But now the whole Round Table is dissolved
> Which was an image of the mighty world,
> And I, the last, go forth companionless,
> And the days darken round me, and the years,
> Among new men, strange faces, other minds.

But the soul of Arthur is stronger, clearer-sighted. In this last conflict with the senses he is victorious. He answers Bedivere, with heroic confidence, that death does not end all.

> The old order changeth, yielding place to new,
> And God fulfils himself in many ways
> Lest one good custom should corrupt the world.

He believes that by prayer

> the whole round earth is every way
> Bound by gold chains about the feet of God.

He enters fearlessly upon the mysterious voyage into the future. And as the barge floats with him out of sight, from beyond the light of the horizon there come

Sounds as if some fair city were one voice
Around a king returning from his wars.

Thus the conflict is ended, and the victo-
rious soul enters its rest.

What shall we say of this picture of
life which Tennyson has given us in his
greatest poem? Is it true? Does it grasp
the facts and draw from them their real
lesson?

First of all, I think we must admit that
there is a serious defect in the very place
where it is most to be regretted, — in the
character of Arthur. He is too perfect
for perfection. Tennyson either meant to
paint a man who never had any conflict
with himself, which is impossible; or he
intended to exhibit a man in whom the
conflict had been fought out, in which
case Arthur surely would have borne some
of the scars of contest, shown some sense
of personal imperfection, manifested a
deeper feeling of comprehension and com-
passion for others in their temptations.
But he appears to regard his own char-
acter and conduct as absolutely flawless.
Even in that glorious parting interview
with Guinevere — one of the most superb
passages in all literature — his bearing

verges perilously on sublime self-compla-
cency. He shows no consciousness of any
fault on his own part. He acts and speaks
as if he were far above reproach. But
was that possible? Could such a catas-
trophe have come without blame on both
sides? Guinevere was but a girl when
she left her father's court. It was nat-
ural — yes, and it was right — that she
should desire warmth and colour in her
life. She rode among the flowers in May
with Lancelot. Is it any wonder that she
found delight in the journey? She was
married to the solemn King before the
stateliest of Britain's altar-shrines with
pompous ceremonies. Is it any wonder
that she was oppressed and made her vows
with drooping eyes? And then, at once,
the King began his state-banquets and
negotiations with the Roman ambassadors.
He was absorbed in the affairs of his king-
dom. He left the young Queen to herself,
— and to Lancelot. He seemed to be
'dreaming of fame while woman woke to
love.' Is it strange that she thought him
cold, neglectful, irresponsive, and said to
herself, " He cares not for me "? Is it to
be marvelled at that she found an outlet

for her glowing heart in her companion-
ship with Lancelot? Perhaps Arthur's
conduct was inevitable for one immersed
as he was in the cares of state; perhaps
he was unconscious that he was exposing
his wife, defenceless and alone, to a peril
from which he only could have protected
her; but when at last the consequence
was discovered, he was bound to confess
that he had a share in the transgression
and the guilt. It is the want of this note
that mars the harmony of his parting
speech. A little more humanity would
have compensated for a little less piety.
Had Arthur been a truer husband, Guin-
evere might have been a more faithful
wife. The excess of virtue is a vice. The
person who feels no consciousness of sin
must be either more or less than man.
This is the worst defect of the *Idylls*, —
that the central character comes so near to
being

<blockquote>Faultily faultless, icily regular, splendidly null.</blockquote>

But this defect is outweighed and can-
celled by the fact that the poem, after all,
does recognize, and bring out in luminous
splendour, the great truths of human life.

The first of these truths is that sin is the cause of disorder and misery, and until it is extirpated the perfect society cannot be securely established. And by sin Tennyson does not mean the desire of existence, but the transgression of law. The right to live — the right to desire to live — is not denied for a moment. It is in fact distinctly asserted, and the idea of the immortality of the soul underlies the whole poem. But life must be according to righteousness, if it is to be harmonious and happy; and righteousness consists in conformity to law. Love is the motive force of the poem. The King himself acknowledges its dominion, and says, —

> For saving I be join'd
> To her that is the fairest under heaven,
> I seem as nothing in the mighty world,
> And cannot will my will, nor work my work
> Wholly, nor make myself, in mine own realm,
> Victor and lord.

But love also must move within the bounds of law, must be true to its vows. Not even the strongest and most beautiful soul may follow the guidance of passion without restraint; for the greater the genius, the beauty, the power, of those who transgress, the more fatal will be the influence of their sin upon other lives.

This indeed is the lesson of the fall of Lancelot and Guinevere. It was because they stood so high, because they were so glorious in their manhood and womanhood, that their example had power to infect the court.

Sin is the principle of disintegration and death. It is this that corrupts societies, and brings about the decline and fall of nations; and so long as sin dwells in the heart of man all efforts to create a perfect state, or even to establish an order like the Round Table in self-perpetuating security, must fail. The redemption and purification of the earth is a long task, beyond human strength; as Tennyson has said in *Locksley Hall, Sixty Years After,* —

Ere she reach her heavenly-best a God must mingle with the game.

But side by side with this truth, and in perfect harmony with it, Tennyson teaches that the soul of man has power to resist and conquer sin within its own domain, to triumph over sense by steadfast loyalty to the higher nature, and thus to achieve

peace and final glory. When I say he
teaches this, I do not mean that he sets it
forth in any formal way as a doctrine. I
mean that he shows it in the life of Arthur
as a fact. The King chooses his ideal,
and follows it, and it lifts him up and sets
him on his course like a star. His life is
not a failure, as it has been called, but
a glorious success, for it demonstrates the
freedom of the will and the strength of
the soul against the powers of evil and
the fate of sin. Its motto might be taken
from that same poem from which we have
just quoted, — a poem which was foolishly
interpreted at first as an avowal of pes-
simism, but which is in fact a splendid
assertion of meliorism, —

Follow you the star that lights a desert pathway yours
    or mine,
Follow till you see the highest human nature is Divine;
Follow light and do the right, — for man can half con-
    trol his doom, —
Follow till you see the deathless angel seated in the
    vacant tomb!

Finally, the *Idylls* bring out the pro-
found truth that there is a vicarious ele-
ment in human life, and that no man lives
to himself alone. The characters are dis-

tinct, but they are not isolated. They
are parts of a vast organism, all bound
together, all influencing one another. The
victory of sense over soul is not a solitary
triumph; it has far-reaching results. The
evil lives of Modred, of Vivien, of Tris-
tram, spread like a poison through the
court. But no less fruitful, no less far-
reaching, is the victory of soul over sense.
Gareth, and Enid, and Balan, and Bors,
and Bedivere, and Galahad, have power to
help and to uplift others out of the lower
life. Their lives are not wasted: nor
does Arthur himself live in vain, though
his Round Table is dissolved: for he is
"joined to her that is the fairest under
heaven," not for a time only, but forever.
His faith triumphs over her sin. Guin-
evere is not lost; she is redeemed by love.
From the darkness of the convent at
Almesbury, where she lies weeping in the
dust, we hear a voice like that which
thrills through the prison of Marguerite
in *Faust.* The fiend mutters, *Sie ist
gerichtet!* But the angel cries, *Sie ist
gerettet !*

THE HISTORIC TRILOGY

THE HISTORIC TRILOGY.

THE appearance of Tennyson, in 1875, as a dramatic poet was a surprise. It is true that he had already shown that his genius was versatile and disposed to explore new methods of expression. True, also, that from the year 1842 a strong dramatic tendency had been manifest in his works. *Ulysses*, *St. Simeon Stylites*, *Love and Duty*, *Locksley Hall*, *Lucretius*, *The Northern Farmer*, *The Grandmother*, different as they are in style, are all essentially dramatic monologues. *Maud* is rightly entitled, in the late editions, *a Monodrama*. *The Princess* has been put upon the amateur stage in very pretty fashion; and the success of Mr. George Parsons Lathrop's fine acting version of *Elaine* proved not only his own ability, but also the high dramatic quality of that splendid Idyll.

But not even these hints that Tennyson had a creative impulse not yet fully satisfied were clear enough to prepare the world for his attempt to conquer another form of art.

He was acknowledged as a consummate mas-
ter of lyric and idyllic poetry. People were
not ready to see him come out in the seventh
decade of his life in a new character, and
take the stage as a dramatist. It seemed like
a rash attempt to become the rival of his
own fame.

The first feeling of the public at the pro-
duction of *Queen Mary* was undisguised
astonishment. And with this a good deal
of displeasure was mingled. For the public,
after all, is not fond of surprises. Having
formed its opinion of a great man, and
labelled him once for all as a sweet singer,
or a sound moralist, or a brilliant word-
painter, or an interesting story-teller, it
loves not to consider him in any other
light. It is confused and puzzled. The
commonplaces of easy criticism become un-
available for further use. People shrink
from the effort which is required for a new
and candid judgment ; and so they fall back
upon stale and unreasonable comparisons.
They say, " Why does the excellent cobbler
go beyond his last? The old songs were
admirable. Why does not the poet give us
more of them, instead of trying us with a
new play ? "

Thus it came to pass that *Queen Mary* was received with general dissatisfaction; respectful, of course, because it was the work of a famous man; but upon the whole the public was largely indifferent, and said in a tone of polite authority that it was not nearly so powerful as *Hamlet* or *Macbeth*, nor so melodious even as *Œnone* and *The Lotos-Eaters*. A like fate befell *Harold* in 1877, except that a few critics began to feel the scruples of literary conscience, and made an honest effort to judge the drama on its own merits.

The Falcon, a play founded upon Boccaccio's well-known story, was produced in 1879, and the accomplished Mrs. Kendal, as the heroine, made it at least a partial success. In 1881 *The Cup*, a dramatization of an incident narrated in Plutarch's treatise *De Mulierum Virtutibus*, was brought out at the Lyceum with Mr. Henry Irving and Miss Ellen Terry in the principal rôles. It received hearty and general applause, and was by far the most popular of Tennyson's dramas. But its effect upon his fame as a playwright was more than counterbalanced by the grievous failure of *The Promise of May* in 1882. This piece was intended to

be an exposure of the pernicious influences
of modern secularism. It was upon the
whole a most dismal bit of work ; and not
even the eccentric conduct of the infidel
Marquis of Queensbury, who rose from his
seat at one of the performances and violently
protested against the play as a libel upon
the free-thinkers of England, availed to give
it more than a momentary notoriety. At
the close of the year 1884 Tennyson pub-
lished the longest and most ambitious of his
dramas, *Becket*, with a distinct avowal that
it was "not intended in its present form to
meet the exigencies of the modern stage."

The wisdom of this limitation is evident.
It contains also a shrewd hint of criticism
on the present taste of the average British
play-goer. There is a demand for pungent
realism, for startling effect, for exaggerated
action easy to be followed, and for a sharp
climax in a striking tableau, — in short, for
a play which stings the nerves without tax-
ing the mind. Even Shakspere has to be
revised to meet these exigencies. To win
success nowadays he must take the stage-
manager into partnership. I suppose, when
Becket is acted, it must submit to these con-
ditions. But meantime there is a higher

standard. We may consider *Queen Mary*, *Harold*, and *Becket*, from another point of view, as dramas not for acting, but for reading.

It seems to me that this consideration is a debt of honour which we owe to the poet. These tragedies are not to be dismissed as the mistakes and follies of an over-confident and fatally fluent genius. A poet like Tennyson does not make three such mistakes in succession. They are not the idle recreations of one who has finished his life-work and retired. They are not the feeble and mechanical productions of a man in his dotage. On the contrary, they are full of fire and force; and if they err at all it is on the side of exuberance. Their intensity of passion and overflow of feeling make them sometimes turbulent and harsh and incoherent. They would do more if they attempted less. And yet in spite of their occasional overloading and confusion they have a clear and strong purpose which makes them worthy of careful study. The judgment of a critic so intelligent as George Eliot is not to be disregarded, and she has expressed her opinion that " Tennyson's plays run Shakspere's close."

The point of view from which they must

be regarded is that of historical tragedy. By
this I mean a tragedy which involves not
only individuals, but political parties and
warring classes of society. Its object is to
trace the fate of individuals as it affects the
fate of nations; to exhibit the conflict of op-
posing characters not for themselves alone,
but as the exponents of those great popular
forces and movements which play beneath the
surface; to throw the vivid colours of life
into the black and white outlines on the
screen of history and show that the figures
are not mere shadows but human beings of
like passions with ourselves.

Tennyson's dramatic trilogy is a picture
of the Making of England. The three
periods of action are chosen with the design
of touching the most critical points of the
long struggle. The three plots are so de-
veloped as to bring into prominence the
vital issues of the strife. And the different
characters, almost without exception, are ex-
hibited as the representatives of the different
races and classes and faiths which were con-
tending for supremacy. Let us take up the
plays in their historical order.

In *Harold* we see the close of that fierce
triangular duel between the Saxons, the

Danes, and the Normans, which resulted in the Norman conquest and the binding of England, still Saxon at heart, to the civilization of the Continent. The crisis of the drama is the second scene of the second act, where Harold, a prisoner in the Palace of Bayeux, is cajoled and threatened and deceived by William to swear an oath to help him to the crown of England. The fierce subtlety of the Norman is matched against the heroic simplicity and frankness of the Saxon. Craft triumphs. Harold discovers that he has sworn, not merely by the jewel of St. Pancratius, on which his hand was laid, but by the sacred bones of all the saints concealed beneath it, — an oath which admits of no evasion, the breaking of which afterwards breaks his faith in himself and makes him fight the battle of Senlac as a man foredoomed to death. Both William and Harold are superstitious. But William's superstition is of a kind which enables him to use religion as his tool; Harold's goes only far enough to weaken his heart and make him tremble before the monk even while he defies him. Harold is the better man; William is the wiser ruler. His words over the body of his fallen rival on the battlefield

are prophetic of the result of the Norman
conquest: —

> Since I knew battle,
> And that was from my boyhood, never yet —
> No, by the splendour of God — have I fought men
> Like Harold and his brethren and his guard
> Of English. Every man about his king
> Fell where he stood. They loved him: and pray God
> My Normans may but move as true with me
> To the door of death. Of one self-stock at first,
> Make them again one people — Norman, English;
> And English, Norman; — we should have a hand
> To grasp the world with, and a foot to stamp it . . .
> Flat. Praise the Saints. It is over. No more blood!
> I am king of England, so they thwart me not,
> And I will rule according to their laws.

It is worth while to remember, in this con-
nection, that Tennyson himself is of Nor-
man descent. Yet surely there never was
a man more thoroughly English than he.

In *Becket* we are made spectators of a
conflict less familiar, but more interesting
and important, — the conflict between the
church and the crown, between the ecclesias-
tical and the royal prerogatives, which shook
England to the centre for many years, and
out of the issues of which her present consti-
tution has grown.

In this conflict the Papacy played a much
smaller part than we usually imagine; and

religion, until the closing scenes, played practically no part at all. It was in fact a struggle for supreme authority in temporal affairs. First the king was contending against the nobility, and the church took sides with the king. Then the king attempted to subjugate the people, and the church, having become profoundly English, took sides with the people. Then the nobles combined against the king, and the church took sides with the nobles. Then the king revolted from the foreign domination of the church, and the people took sides with the king. Then the king endeavoured to use the church to crush the people, and the people under Cromwell rose against church and king and broke the double yoke. Then the people brought back the king, and he tried to reinstate the church as an instrument of royal absolutism. But the day for that was past. After another struggle, prolonged and bitter, but in the main bloodless, the English church lost almost the last vestige of temporal authority, and the English kingdom became simply "a crowned republic."

Now the point at which *Becket* touches this long conflict is the second stage. King Henry II., Count of Anjou, surnamed

"Plantagenet," owed his throne to the church. It was the influence of the English bishops, especially of Theobald, Anselm's great successor in the See of Canterbury, which secured Henry's succession to the crown of his uncle and enemy, King Stephen. But the wild, wicked blood of Anjou was too strong in Henry for him to remain faithful to such an alliance. He was a thoroughly irreligious man : not only dissolute in life and cruel in temper, but also destitute of the sense of reverence, which sometimes exists even in immoral men. He spent his time at church in look-ing at picture-books and whispering with his friends. He despised and neglected the confessional. He broke out, in his pas-sionate fits, with the wildest imprecations against God. The fellowship of the church was distasteful to him ; and even the bond of gratitude to so good a man as Archbishop Theobald was too irksome to be borne.

Moreover he had gotten from the church all that he wanted. He was now the most mighty monarch in Christendom. His foot was on the neck of the nobles. The royal power had broken down the feudal, and stood face to face with the ecclesiastical, as

its only rival. The English Church, whose
prerogative made her in effect the supreme
judge and ruler over all the educated classes
(that is to say over all who could read and
write and were thus entitled to claim "the
benefit of the clergy"), was the only barrier
in Henry's path to an unlimited monarchy.
He resolved that this obstacle must be re-
moved. He would brook no rivalry in Eng-
land, not even in the name of God. And
therefore he thrust his bosom - friend, his
boon - companion, his splendid chancellor,
Thomas Becket, into the Archbishopric of
Canterbury, hoping to find in him a willing
and skilful ally in the subjugation of the
church to the throne. Becket's rebellion
and Henry's wrath form the plot of Tenny-
son's longest and greatest drama.

The character of Becket is one of the
standing riddles of history. He compels our
admiration by his strength, his audacity, his
success in everything that he undertook. He
is one of those men who are so intensely
virile that they remain alive after they are
dead : we cannot be indifferent to him : we
are for him or against him. At the same
time he perplexes us and stimulates our
wonder to the highest pitch by the consistent

inconsistencies and harmonious contradic-
tions of his character. The son of an ob-
scure London merchant; the proudest and
most accomplished of England's chivalrous
youth; a student of theology in the Univer-
sity of Paris; the favourite pupil of the good
Archbishop Theobald; the boon-companion
of the riotous King Henry; a skilful diploma-
tist; the best horseman and boldest knight
of the court; the hatred of the nobles, and
the delight of the peasantry; the most lavish
and luxurious, the most chaste and laborious,
of English grandees; the most devout and
ascetic, the most ambitious and the least self-
ish, of English bishops; as unwearied in
lashing his own back with the scourge as he
had been in smiting his country's enemies
with the sword; as much at home in sack-
cloth as in purple and fine linen; the prince
of dandies and of devotees; the king's most
faithful servant and most daring rival, most
darling friend and most relentless foe, —
what was this Becket? hero or villain?
martyr or criminal? true man or traitor?
worldling or saint?

Tennyson gives us the key to the riddle in
the opening scene of the drama. The King
and Becket are playing at chess. The King's

fancy is wandering; he is thinking and talking of a hundred different things. But Becket is intent upon the game; he cannot bear to do anything which he does not do well; he pushes steadily forward and wins.

I think this scene gives us the secret of Becket's personality. An eager desire to be perfect in whatever part he played, an impulse to lead and conquer in every sphere that he entered, — this was what Henry failed to understand. He did not see that in transforming this intense and absolute man from a chancellor into an archbishop, he was thrusting him into a new part in which his passion for thoroughness would make him live up to all its requirements and become the most inflexible defender of the church against the encroachment of the throne.

But Becket understood himself and foresaw the conflict into which the King's plan would plunge him. He knew that for him a change of relations meant a change of character. He resisted the promotion. Tennyson depicts most graphically the struggle in his mind. When Henry first broaches the subject, Becket answers:

> Mock me not.   I am not even a monk.
> Thy jest — no more !   Why, look, is this a sleeve
> For an archbishop ?

But Henry lays his hand on the richly embroidered garment, and says :

> But the arm within
> Is Becket's who hath beaten down my foes.
> I lack a spiritual soldier, Thomas,
> A man of this world and the next to boot.

Now this is just what Thomas can never be. To either world he can belong, but not to both. He can change, but he cannot compromise. While he is the defender of the throne he is serviceable and devoted to the King ; when he becomes the leader of the Church he will be equally absorbed in her service.

The drama exhibits this strange transformation and its consequences. Forced by the urgency of the headstrong King, and persuaded by a message from the death-bed of his former friend and master Theobald, Becket yields at last and accepts the mitre. From this moment he is another man. With all his doubts as to his fitness for the sacred office, he has now given himself up to it, heart and soul. The tremendous mediæval idea of the Catholic Church as the visible kingdom of God upon earth takes possession

of him. He sees also that the issue of the
political conflict in England depends upon
the church, which is the people's "tower of
strength, their bulwark against Throne and
Baronage." He feels that he is called to be
the champion of the cause of God and the
people.

I am the man.
And yet I seem appall'd, — on such a sudden
At such an eagle height I stand, and see
The rift that runs between me and the king.
I serv'd our Theobald well when I was with him;
I serv'd King Henry well when I was Chancellor;
I am his no more, and I must serve the church.
And all my doubts I fling from me like dust,
Winnow and scatter all scruples to the wind,
And all the puissance of the warrior,
And all the wisdom of the Chancellor,
And all the heap'd experiences of life,
I cast upon the side of Canterbury, —
Our holy mother Canterbury, who sits
With tatter'd robes.

Here
I gash myself asunder from the king,
Though leaving each a wound: mine own, a grief
To show the scar forever — his, a hate
Not ever to be healed.

Both of these predictions are fulfilled: and
herein lies the interest of the drama. All
through the conflict between the monarch
and the prelate, Becket's inflexible resist-

ance to the royal commands is maintained
only at the cost of a perpetual struggle
with his great personal love for Henry,
and Henry's resolve to conquer the stub-
born archbishop is inflamed and embittered
by the thought that Becket was once his
dearest comrade. It is a tragic situation.
Tennyson has never shown a deeper insight
into human nature, than by making this
single combat between divided friends the
turning-point of his drama.

The tragedy is enhanced by the introduc-
tion of Rosamund de Clifford — the King's

One sweet rose of the world.

Her beauty, her innocence, the childlike con-
fidence of her affection for the fierce mon-
arch, who is gentle only with her and whom
she loves as her true husband, her songs and
merry games with her little boy in the hid-
den bower, fall like gleams of summer sun-
light into the stormy gloom of the play.

Becket becomes her guardian and protec-
tor against the cruel, murderous jealousy of
Queen Eleanor. A most perilous position:
a priest charged by the King whom he is re-
sisting with the duty of defending and guard-
ing the loveliest of women, and keeping her
safe and secret for a master whom he cannot

but condemn. What a conflict of duty and
desire, of conscience and loyalty, of passion
and friendship! How did Becket meet it?
Did he love Rosamund? Would he have
loved her if he had not been bound by
straiter vows? Was there anything of dis-
loyalty in his persuading her to flee from
her bower and take refuge with the nuns at
Godstow? Tennyson thinks not. He paints
his hero as a man true to his duty even in
this sharpest trial; upright, steadfast, fear-
less, seeking only to save the woman whom
his former master loved, and to serve the
King even while seeming to disobey him.
But Henry cannot believe it. When he
hears of Rosamund's flight, his anger against
Becket is poisoned with the madness of jeal-
ousy. He breaks out with a cry of fierce
desire for his death. And at this hint, four
of the Barons, who have long hated Becket,
set out to assassinate him.

The final scene in the Cathedral is full of
strength and splendour. Even here a ray
of sweetness falls into the gloom, in the
presence of Rosamund, praying for Becket
in his perils : —

> Save that dear head which now is Canterbury,
> Save him, he saved my life, he saved my child,

Save him, his blood would darken Henry's name,
Save him, till all as saintly as thyself,
He miss the searching flame of Purgatory,
And pass at once to perfect Paradise.

But the end is inevitable. Becket meets it
as fearlessly as he has lived, crying as the
blows of the assassins fall upon him before
the altar, —

At the right hand of Power —
Power and great glory — for thy church, O Lord —
Into thy hands, O Lord — into thy hands —

Two years afterwards, he was canonized as
a saint. His tomb became the richest and
most popular of English shrines. King
Henry himself came to it as a pilgrim, and
submitted to public penance at the grave of
the man who was too strong for him, even in
death. The homage of the nation may not
prove that Becket was a holy martyr, but at
least it proves that he was one of the first
of those great Englishmen " who taught the
people to struggle for their liberties," and
that Tennyson was right in choosing this
man as the hero of his noblest historic
drama.

In *Queen Mary*, we are called to watch
the third great conflict of England. Church
and people have triumphed. It has already

become clear that the English throne must
be

> Broad-bas'd upon the people's will,

and that religion will be a controlling influ-
ence in the life of the nation. But what
type of religion? The Papacy and the
Reformation have crossed swords and are
struggling together for the possession of the
sea-girt island. How sharp was the contest,
how near the friends of Spain and Italy
came to winning the victory over the friends
of Germany and Holland and Switzerland,
Tennyson has shown in his vivid picture of
Mary's reign.

The characters are sharply drawn. .Philip,
with his icy sensuality and gigantic egotism ;
Gardiner with his coarse ferocity,

> His big baldness,
> That irritable forelock which he rubs,
> His buzzard beak, and deep incavern'd eyes ;

Reginald Pole, the suave, timorous, selfish
ecclesiastic ; Sir Thomas Wyatt and Sir
Ralph Bagenhall, brave, steadfast, honest
men, English to the core ; Cranmer with
his moments of weakness and faltering, well
atoned for by his deep faith and humble pen-
itence and heroic martyrdom ; all these stand
out before us like living figures against the

background of diplomatic intrigue and popu-
lar tumult. And Mary herself, — never has
that unhappy queen, the victim of her own
intense, passionate delusions, had such jus-
tice done to her. She came near to wreck-
ing England. Tennyson does not let us
forget that; but he softens our hatred and
our horror with a touch of human pity for
her own self-wreck as he shows her sitting
upon the ground, desolate and desperate,
moaning for the treacherous Philip in

> A low voice
> Lost in a wilderness where none can hear!
> A voice of shipwreck on a shoreless sea!
> A low voice from the dust and from the grave.

The drama which most naturally invites
comparison with *Queen Mary* is Shak-
spere's *Henry VIII.* And it seems to me
that if we lay the two works side by side,
Tennyson's does not suffer even by this
hazardous propinquity. Take the song of
Queen Catherine:

> Orpheus with his lute made trees
> And the mountain-tops that freeze
>   Bow themselves when he did sing:
> To his music plants and flowers
> Ever sprung; as Sun and showers
>   There had made a lasting spring.
>
> Everything that heard him play
> Even the billows of the sea
>   Hung their heads and then lay by.

> In sweet music is such art,
> Killing care and grief of heart
> Fall asleep, or, hearing, die.

And then read Queen Mary's song : —

> Hapless doom of woman happy in betrothing!
> Beauty passes like a breath and love is lost in loathing:
> Low, my lute: speak low, my lute, but say the world
> is nothing —
> Low, lute, low!

> Love will hover round the flowers when they first
> awaken;
> Love will fly the fallen leaf and not be overtaken:
> Low, my lute! oh low, my lute! we fade and are
> forsaken —
> Low, dear lute, low!

Surely it is not too much to say that this is infinitely more pathetic as well as more musical than Shakspere's stiff little lyric.

Or if this comparison seem unfair, then try the two dramas by their strength of character-painting. Is not Tennyson's Philip as vivid and as consistent as Shakspere's Henry? Does not the later Gardiner stand out more clearly than the earlier, and the younger Howard surpass the elder? Is not the legate Pole more lifelike than the legate Campeius? Is not Cecil's description of Elizabeth more true and sharp, though less high-flown, than Cranmer's? We must admit that there are "purple patches" of elo-

quence, like Wolsey's famous speech upon
ambition, in Shakspere's work, which are
unrivalled. But taken altogether, as an
historic drama, *Queen Mary* must rank not
below, perhaps even above, *Henry VIII.*

The systematic undervaluation of Tenny-
son's dramatic work is a reproach to the in-
telligence of our critics. J. R. Green, the
late historian of *The English People*, said
that " all his researches into the annals of the
twelfth century had not given him so vivid
a conception of the character of Henry II.
and his court as was embodied in Tenny-
son's *Becket.*" Backed by an authority like
this it is not too daring to predict that the
day is coming when the study of Shak-
spere's historical plays will be reckoned no
more important to an understanding of Eng-
lish history than the study of Tennyson's
Trilogy.

THE BIBLE IN TENNYSON

THE BIBLE IN TENNYSON.

IT is safe to say that there is no other
book which has had so great an influence
upon the literature of the world as the Bible.
And it is almost as safe — at least with no
greater danger than that of starting an in-
structive discussion — to say that there is
no other literature which has felt this influ-
ence so deeply or shown it so clearly as the
English.

The cause of this latter fact is not far to
seek. It may be, as a discontented French
critic suggests, that it is partly due to the
inborn and incorrigible tendency of the An-
glo-Saxon mind to drag religion and morality
into everything. But certainly this tendency
would never have taken such a distinctly
Biblical form had it not been for the beauty
and vigour of our common English version
of the Scriptures. These qualities were felt
by the people even before they were praised
by the critics. Apart from all religious
prepossessions, men and women and children

were fascinated by the native power and
grace of the book. The English Bible was
popular, in the broadest sense, long before it
was recognized as one of our noblest English
classics. It has coloured the talk of the
household and the street, as well as moulded
the language of scholars. It has been some-
thing more than a "well of English unde-
filed;" it has become a part of the spiritual
atmosphere. We hear the echoes of its
speech everywhere; and the music of its
familiar phrases haunts all the fields and
groves of our fine literature.

It is not only to the theologians and the
sermon-makers that we look for Biblical
allusions and quotations. We often find the
very best and most vivid of them in writ-
ers professedly secular. Poets like Shak-
spere, Milton, and Wordsworth; novelists
like Scott and romancers like Hawthorne;
essayists like Bacon, Steele, and Addison;
critics of life, unsystematic philosophers, like
Carlyle and Ruskin, — all draw upon the
Bible as a treasury of illustrations, and use
it as a book equally familiar to themselves
and to their readers. It is impossible to
put too high a value upon such a universal
volume, even as a mere literary possession.

It forms a bond of sympathy between the most cultivated and the simplest of the people. The same book lies upon the desk of the scholar and in the cupboard of the peasant. If you touch upon one of its narratives, every one knows what you mean. If you allude to one of its characters or scenes, your reader's memory supplies an instant picture to illuminate your point. And so long as its words are studied by little children at their mothers' knees and recognized by high critics as the model of pure English, we may be sure that neither the jargon of science nor the slang of ignorance will be able to create a Shibboleth to divide the people of our common race. There will be a medium of communication in the language and imagery of the English Bible.

This much, by way of introduction, I have felt it necessary to say, in order to mark the spirit of this essay. For the poet whose works we are to study is at once one of the most scholarly and one of the most widely popular of English writers. At least one cause of his popularity is that there is so much of the Bible in Tennyson. How much, few even of his most ardent lovers begin to understand.

I do not know that the attempt has ever been made before to collect and collate all the Scriptural allusions and quotations in his works, and to trace the golden threads which he has woven from that source into the woof of his poetry. The delight of "fresh woods and pastures new" — so rare in this over-explored age — has thus been mine. I have found more than four hundred direct references to the Bible in the poems of Tennyson; and have given a list of them in the appendix to this book. This may have some value for professed Tennysonians, and for them alone it is given. The general reader would find it rather dry pasturage. But there is an aspect of the subject which has a wider interest. And in this essay I want to show how closely Tennyson has read the Bible, how well he understands it, how much he owes to it, and how clearly he stands out as, in the best sense, a defender of the faith.

I.

On my table lies the first publication which bears the name of Alfred Tennyson; a thin pamphlet, in faded gray paper, containing the *Prolusiones Academicæ*, recited at the University of Cambridge in 1829. Among them is one with the title : *Timbuctoo ;* A Poem which obtained the Chancellor's Medal, etc., by A. Tennyson, of Trinity College.

On the eleventh page, in a passage describing the spirit of poetry which fills the branches of the " great vine of Fable," we find these lines : —

> There is no mightier Spirit than I to sway
> The heart of man: *and teach him to attain*
> *By shadowing forth the Unattainable ;*
> And step by step to scale the mighty stair
> Whose landing place is wrapped about with clouds
> Of glory of Heaven.

And at the bottom of the page stands this foot-note : *Be ye perfect even as your Father in Heaven is perfect.*

This is the earliest Biblical allusion that we can identify in the writings of Tennyson. Even the most superficial glance will detect its beauty and power. There are few who have not felt the lofty attraction of the teachings of Christ, in which the ideal of holiness shines so far above our reach, while we are continually impelled to climb towards it. Especially these very words about perfection, which He spoke in the Sermon on the Mount, have often lifted us upward just because they point our aspirations to a goal so high that it seems inaccessible. The young poet who sets a jewel like this in his earliest work shows not only that he has understood the moral sublimity of the doctrine of Christ, but also that he has rightly conceived the mission of noble poetry, — to idealize human life. Once and again in his later writings we see the same picture of the soul rising step by step

> To higher things;

and catch a glimpse of those vast altar-stairs

> That slope through darkness up to. God.

In the poem entitled *Isabel* — one of the best in the slender volume of 1830 — there is a line which reminds us that Tennyson must have known his New Testament in the original language. He says that all the fairest forms of nature are types of the noble woman whom he is describing, —

> And thou of God in thy great charity.

No one who was not familiar with the Greek of St. Paul and St. John would have been bold enough to speak of the "charity of God." It is a phrase which throws a golden light upon the thirteenth chapter of the

First Epistle to the Corinthians, and brings the human love into harmony and union with the divine.

The May Queen is a poem which has sung itself into the hearts of the people everywhere. The tenderness of its sentiment and the exquisite cadence of its music have made it beloved in spite of its many faults. Yet I suppose that the majority of readers have read it again and again, without recognizing that one of its most melodious verses is a direct quotation from the third chapter of *Job*.

And the wicked cease from troubling and the weary are at rest.

This is one of the instances — by no means rare — in which the translators of our English Bible have fallen unconsciously into the rhythm of the most perfect poetry; and it is perhaps the best illustration of Tennyson's felicitous use of the very words of Scripture.

There are others, hardly less perfect, in the wonderful sermon which the Rector in *Aylmer's Field* delivers after the death of Edith and Leolin. It is a mosaic of Bible language, most curiously wrought, and fused into one living whole by the heat of an intense sorrow. How like a heavy, dull

refrain of prophetic grief and indignation
recurs the dreadful text,

> Your house is left unto you desolate.

The solemn association of the words lends the
force of a superhuman and unimpassioned
wrath to the preacher's language, and the
passage stands as a monumental denuncia-
tion of

> The social wants that sin against the strength of youth.

Enoch Arden's parting words to his wife
contain some beautiful fragments of Scrip-
ture embedded in the verse :

> Cast all your cares on God ; that anchor holds.
> Is He not yonder in the uttermost
> Parts of the morning ? If I flee to these
> Can I go from Him ? and the sea is His,
> The sea is His : He made it.

The Idylls of the King are full of deli-
cate and suggestive allusions to the Bible.
Take for instance the lines from the *Holy
Grail* :—

> When the Lord of all things made Himself
> Naked of glory for His mortal change.

Here is a commentary most illuminative, on
the fifth and sixth verses of the second chap-
ter of *Philippians.* Or again, in the same
Idyll, where the hermit says to Sir Perci-
vale, after his unsuccessful quest, —

Thou hast not lost thyself to find thyself,

we are reminded of the words of Christ and
the secret of all victory in spiritual things:
He that loseth his life shall find it.

In *The Coming of Arthur*, while the
trumpet blows and the city seems on fire
with sunlight dazzling on cloth of gold, the
long procession of knights pass before the
King, singing their great song of allegiance.
It is full of warrior's pride and delight
of battle, clanging battle-axe and flashing
brand, — a true song for the heavy fighters
of the days of chivalry. But it has also a
higher touch, a strain of spiritual grandeur,
which although it may have no justification
in an historical picture of the Round Table,
yet serves to lift these knights of the poet's
imagination up into an ideal realm and set
them marching as ghostly heroes of faith
and loyalty through all ages.

The King will follow Christ, and we the King.

Compare this line with the words of St.
Paul: *Be ye followers of me even as I also
am of Christ.* They teach us that the last-
ing devotion of men is rendered not to the
human, but to the divine, in their heroes.
He who would lead others must first learn

to follow One who is higher than himself.
Without faith it is not only impossible to
please God, but also impossible to rule men.
King Arthur is the ideal of one who has
heard a secret word of promise and seen a
vision of more than earthly glory, by virtue
of which he becomes the leader and master
of his knights, able to inspire their hopes
and unite their aspirations and bind their
service to himself in the fellowship of the
Round Table.

And now turn to one of the latest poems
that Tennyson has given us : *Locksley Hall*,
Sixty Years After. Sad enough is its la-
ment for broken dreams, dark with the
gloom of declining years, when the grass-
hopper has become a burden and desire has
failed and the weary heart has grown afraid
of that which is high ; but at the close the
old man rises again to the sacred strain : —

Follow you the star that lights a desert pathway, yours
  or mine,
Forward, till you see the highest Human Nature is
  divine.

Follow Light and do the Right — for man can half con-
  trol his doom —
Till you see the deathless angel seated in the vacant tomb

II.

When we come to speak of the Biblical scenes and characters to which Tennyson refers, we find so many that the difficulty is to choose. He has recognized the fact that an allusion wins half its power from its connection with the reader's memory and previous thought. In order to be forcible and effective it must be at least so familiar as to awaken a train of associations. An allusion to something which is entirely strange and unknown may make an author appear more learned, but it does not make him seem more delightful. Curiosity may be a good atmosphere for the man of science to speak in, but the poet requires a sympathetic medium. He should endeavour to touch the first notes of well-known airs, and then memory will supply the accompaniment to enrich his music. This is what Tennyson has done, with the instinct of genius, in his references to the stories and personages of the Bible.

His favourite allusion is to Eden and the mystical story of Adam and Eve. This occurs again and again, in *The Day-Dream, Maud, In Memoriam, The Gardener's Daughter, The Princess, Milton, Enid,* and *Lady Clara Vere de Vere.* The last instance is perhaps the most interesting, on account of a double change which has been made in the form of the allusion. In the edition of 1842 (the first in which the poem appeared) the self-assertive peasant who refuses to become a lover says to the lady of high degree, —

> Trust me, Clara Vere de Vere,
>   From yon blue heavens above us bent,
> The gardener Adam and his wife
>   Smile at the claims of long descent.

In later editions this was altered to " the grand old gardener and his wife." But in this form the reference was open to misunderstanding. I remember a charming young woman, who once told me she had always thought the lines referred to some particularly pious old man who had formerly taken care of Lady Clara's flower-beds, and who now smiled from heaven at the foolish pride of his mistress. So perhaps it is just as well that Tennyson restored the line, in 1875, to its original form, and gave us " the gardener Adam " again, to remind us of the quaint distich —

> When Adam delved and Eve span,
> Who was then the gentleman?

The story of Jephtha's daughter is another of the Old Testament narratives for which the poet seems to have a predilection. It is told with great beauty and freedom in the *Dream of Fair Women; Aylmer's Field* touches upon it; and it recurs in *The Flight.*

In *The Princess* we find the Queen of Sheba, Vashti, Miriam, Jael, Lot's wife, Jonah's gourd, and the Tower of Babel. And if your copy of the Bible has the Apocrypha in it, you may add the story of Judith and Holofernes.

Esther appears in *Enid*, and Rahab in *Queen Mary.* In *Godiva* we read of the Earl's heart, —

> As rough as Esau's hand;

and in *Locksley Hall* we see the picture of the earth standing

> At gaze, like Joshua's moon in Ajalon.

The *Sonnet to Buonaparte* recalls to our memory

> Those whom Gideon school'd with briers.

In the *Palace of Art* we behold the handwriting on the wall at Belshazzar's Feast.

It would be impossible even to enumerate Tennyson's allusions to the life of Christ,

from the visit of the Magi, which appears in
Morte d'Arthur and *The Holy Grail*, down
to the line in *Balin and Balan* which tells
of

> That same spear
> Wherewith the Roman pierced the side of Christ.

But to my mind the most beautiful of all
the references to the New Testament is the
passage in *In Memoriam* which describes the
reunion of Mary and Lazarus after his re-
turn from the grave. With what a human
interest does the poet clothe the familiar
story! How reverently and yet with what
natural and simple pathos does he touch
upon the more intimate relations of the three
persons who are the chief actors! The ques-
tion which has come a thousand times to
every one that has lost a dear friend, — the
question whether love survives in the other
world, whether those who have gone before
miss those who are left behind and have any
knowledge of their grief, — this is the sug-
gestion which brings the story home to us
and makes it seem real and living.

> When Lazarus left his charnel-cave,
>   And home to Mary's house return'd,
>   Was this demanded, — if he yearn'd
> To hear her weeping by his grave?

"Where wert thou brother those four days?"
  There lives no record of reply,
  Which telling what it is to die,
Had surely added praise to praise.

From every house the neighbours met,
  The streets were fill'd with joyful sound,
  A solemn gladness even crown'd
The purple brows of Olivet.

Behold a man raised up by Christ!
  The rest remaineth unreveal'd;
  He told it not; or something seal'd
The lips of that Evangelist.

Then follows that marvellous description of Mary, — a passage which seems to me to prove the superiority of poetry, as an art, over painting and sculpture. For surely neither marble nor canvas ever held such a beautiful figure of devotion as that which breathes in these verses : —

Her eyes are homes of silent prayer,
  No other thought her mind admits
  But, he was dead, and there he sits,
And He that brought him back is there.

Then one deep love doth supersede
  All other, when her ardent gaze
  Roves from the living brother's face
And rests upon the Life indeed.

All subtle thought, all curious fears,
  Borne down by gladness so complete,
  She bows, she bathes the Saviour's feet
With costly spikenard and with tears.

Thrice blest whose lives are faithful prayers,
  Whose loves in higher love endure ;
What souls possess themselves so pure,
  Or is there blessedness like theirs ?

It does not seem possible that the chang-
ing fashions of poetic art should ever make
verses like these seem less exquisite, or that
Time should ever outwear the sweet and
simple power of this conception of religion.
  There is no passage in the range of litera-
ture which expresses more grandly the mys-
tery of death, or shows more attractively the
happiness of an unquestioning personal faith
in Him who, alone of men, has solved it and
knows the answer. I cannot bear to add
anything to it by way of comment, except
perhaps these words of Emerson : "Of im-
mortality, the soul, when well employed, is
incurious. It is so well that it is sure it
will be well. It asks no questions of the
Supreme Being."
  The poem of *Rizpah*, which was first pub--
lished in the volume of *Ballads* in 1880, is
an illustration of dramatic paraphrase from
the Bible. The story of the Hebrew mother
watching beside the dead bodies of her sons
whom the Gibeonites had hanged upon the
hill, and defending them night and day for

six months from the wild beasts and birds of
prey, is transformed into the story of an
English mother, whose son has been executed
for robbery and hung in chains upon the gib-
bet. She is driven wild by her grief; hears
her boy's voice wailing through the wind, " O
mother, come out to me; " creeps through the
rain and the darkness to the place where the
chains are creaking and groaning with their
burden; gropes and gathers all that is left
of what was once her child and carries him
home to bury him beside the churchyard
wall. And then, when she is accused of
theft, she breaks out in a passion of defence.
It is a mother's love justifying itself against
a cruel law. Those poor fragments which
the wind and the rain had spared were hers,
by a right divine, — bone of her bone, —
she had nursed and cradled her baby, and all
that was left belonged to her; justice had
no claim which could stand against hers.

Theirs? O no! they are mine, — not theirs, — *they had
    moved in my side!*

A famous writer has said of this passage,
" Nothing more piteous, more passionate,
more adorable for intensity of beauty was
ever before this wrought by human cunning
into the likeness of such words as words are
powerless to praise."

III.

In trying to estimate the general influ-
ence of the Bible upon the thought and feel-
ing of Tennyson we have a more delicate
and difficult task. For the teachings of
Christianity have become a part of the moral
atmosphere of the age; and it is hard for
us to tell just what any man would have been
without them, or just how far they have
made him what he is, while we are looking
at him through the very same medium in
which we ourselves are breathing. If we
could get out of ourselves, if we could divest
ourselves of all those views of God and
duty and human life which we have learned
so early that they seem to us natural and in-
evitable, we might perhaps be able to arrive
at a more exact discrimination. But this
would be to sacrifice a position of vital sym-
pathy for one of critical judgment. The
loss would be greater than the gain. It is
just as well for the critic to recognize that
he is hardly able

> To sit as God, holding no form of creed,
> But contemplating all.

Tennyson himself has described the mental
paralysis, the spiritual distress, which follow

that attempt. A critic ought to be free from prejudices, but surely not even for the sake of liberty should he make himself naked of convictions. To float on wings above the earth will give one a bird's-eye view; but for a man's-eye view we must have a standing-place on the earth. And after all the latter may be quite as true, even though it is not absolutely colourless.

The effect of Christianity upon the poetry of Tennyson may be felt, first of all, in its general moral quality. By this it is not meant that he is always or often preaching, or drawing pictures

" To point a moral or adorn a tale."

Didactic art sometimes misses its own end by being too instructive. We find in Tennyson's poems many narratives of action and descriptions of character which are simply left to speak for themselves and teach their own lessons. In this they are like the histories in the *Book of Judges* or the *Books of the Kings.* The writer takes it for granted that the reader has a heart and a conscience. Compare in this respect, the perfect simplicity of the domestic idyll of *Dora* with the *Book of Ruth.*

But at the same time the poet can hardly

help revealing, more by tone and accent than
by definite words, his moral sympathies.
Tennyson always speaks from the side of
virtue; and not of that new and strange vir-
tue which some of our later poets have ex-
alted, and which when it is stripped of its
fine garments turns out to be nothing else
than the unrestrained indulgence of every
natural impulse; but rather of that old-
fashioned virtue whose laws are "Self-rever-
ence, self-knowledge, self-control," and which
finds its highest embodiment in the morality
of the New Testament. Read, for example,
his poems which deal directly with the sub-
ject of marriage: *The Miller's Daughter,*
Isabel, Lady Clare, The Lord of Burleigh,
Locksley Hall, Love and Duty, The Wreck,
Aylmer's Field, Enoch Arden, the latter
part of *The Princess,* and many different
passages of the *Idylls.* From whatever side
he approaches the subject, whether he is
painting with delicate, felicitous touches the
happiness of truly-wedded hearts, or de-
nouncing the sins of avarice and pride which
corrupt the modern marriage-mart of society,
or tracing the secret evil which poisoned the
court of Arthur and shamed the golden head
of Guinevere, his ideal is always the perfect

and deathless union of two lives in one,
" which is commended of St. Paul to be hon-
ourable among all men." To him woman
seems loveliest when she has

> The laws of marriage character'd in gold
> Upon the blanched tablets of her heart,

and man strongest when he has learned

> To love one maiden only, cleave to her,
> And worship her by years of noble deeds.

The theology of Tennyson has been ac-
cused of a pantheistic tendency; and it can-
not be denied that there are expressions in
his poems which seem to look in that direc-
tion, or at least to look decidedly away from
the conception of the universe as a vast
machine and its Maker as a supernatural
machinist who has constructed the big watch
and left it to run on by itself until it wears
out. But surely this latter view, which
fairly puts God out of the world, is not the
view of the Bible. The New Testament
teaches us, undoubtedly, to distinguish be-
tween Him and His works; but it also
teaches that He is in His works, or rather
that all His works are in Him, — *in Him*,
says St. Paul, *we live and move and have our
being.* Light is His garment. Life is His
breath.

God is law say the wise; O Soul, and let us rejoice,
For if He thunder by law, the thunder is yet His voice.

But if I wished to prove, against those who doubted, Tennyson's belief in a living, personal, spiritual God, immanent in the universe, yet not confused with it, I should turn to his doctrine of prayer. There are many places in his poems where prayer is, not explained, but simply justified, as the highest activity of a human soul and a real bond between God and man. In these very lines on *The Higher Pantheism*, from which I have just quoted, there is a verse which can only be interpreted as the description of a personal intercourse between the divine and the human : —

Speak to Him, thou, for He hears, and Spirit with Spirit
    can meet, —
Closer is He than breathing, and nearer than hands and
    feet.

Of Enoch Arden in the dreadful loneliness of that rich island where he was cast away it is said that

                    Had not his poor heart
    Spoken with That, which being everywhere
    Lets none, who speaks with Him, seem all alone,
    Surely the man had died of solitude.

When he comes back, after the weary years of absence, to find his wife wedded to an-

other, and his home no longer his, it is by
prayer that he obtains strength to keep his
generous resolve

> Not to tell her, never to let her know,

and to bear the burden of his secret to the
lonely end. Edith, in the drama of Harold,
when her last hope breaks and the shadow
of gloom begins to darken over her, cries, —

> No help but prayer,
> A breath that fleets beyond this iron world
> And touches Him that made it.

King Arthur, bidding farewell to the last of
his faithful knights, says to him, —

> Pray for my soul. More things are wrought by prayer
> Than this world dreams of. Wherefore let thy voice
> Rise like a fountain for me night and day.
> For what are men better than sheep or goats
> That nourish a blind life within the brain,
> If, knowing God, they lift not hands of prayer
> Both for themselves and those who call them friend?
> For so the whole round earth is every way
> Bound by gold chains about the feet of God.

But lest any one should say that these pas-
sages are merely dramatic, and do not ex-
press the personal faith of the poet, turn to
the solemn invocation in which he has struck
the keynote of his deepest and most personal
poem, —

> Strong Son of God, immortal Love!

It is the poet's own prayer. No man could
have written it save one who believed that
God is Love, and that Love is incarnate in
the pérson of Jesus Christ.

Next to the question of the reality of
God, comes the problem of human life and
destiny. And this has a twofold aspect.
First, in regard to the present world, is
man moving upward or downward; is good
stronger than evil or evil stronger than good;
is life worth living, or is it a cheat and a
failure? Second, in regard to the future,
is there any hope of personal continuance
beyond death? To both of these inquiries
Tennyson gives an answer which is in har-
mony with the teachings of the Bible.

He finds the same difficulties and doubts
in the continual conflict between good and
evil which are expressed in Job and Eccle-
siastes. Indeed so high an authority as
Professor Plumptre has said that "the
most suggestive of all commentaries" on the
latter book are Tennyson's poems, *The Vis-*
ion of Sin, The Palace of Art, and *Two*
Voices. In the last of these he draws out
in the form of a dialogue the strife between
hope and despair in the breast of a man who
has grown weary of life and yet is not ready

to embrace death. For, after all, the sum of the reasons which the first voice urges in favour of suicide is that nothing is worth very much, no man is of any real value to the world, *il n'y pas d'homme necessaire*, no effort produces any lasting result, all things are moving round and round in a tedious circle, — vanity of vanities, — if you are tired why not depart from the play ? The tempted man — tempted to yield to the devil's own philosophy of pessimism — uses all argument to combat the enemy, but in vain, or at least with only half-success ; until at last the night is worn away ; he flings open his window and looks out upon the Sabbath morn.

> The sweet church bells began to peal.
>
> On to God's house the people prest ;
> Passing the place where each must rest,
> Each entered like a welcome guest.
>
> One walked between his wife and child,
> With measured footfall firm and mild,
> And now and then he gravely smiled.
>
> The prudent partner of his blood
> Leaned on him, faithful, gentle, good,
> Wearing the rose of womanhood.
>
> And in their double love secure,
> The little maiden walked demure,
> Pacing with downward eyelids pure.

These three made unity so sweet,
My frozen heart began to beat,
Remembering its ancient heat.

I blest them, and they wandered on:
I spoke, but answer came there none;
The dull and bitter voice was gone.

And then comes another voice whispering of
a secret hope, and bidding the soul " Re-
joice ! Rejoice ! " If we hear in the first
part of the poem the echo of the saddest
book of the Old Testament, we hear also in
the last part the tones of Him who said:
*Let not your heart be troubled, in my
Father's house are many mansions ; if it
were not so I would have told you.*

There are many places in the poems of
Tennyson where he speaks with bitterness of
the falsehood and evil that are in the world,
the corruptions of society, the downward
tendencies in human nature. He is in no
sense a rose-water optimist. But he is in
the truest sense a meliorist. He doubts not
that

Thro' the ages one increasing purpose runs,
And the thoughts of men are widened with the process of
the suns.

He believes that good

Shall be the final goal of ill.

He rests his faith upon the uplifting power
of Christianity ; —

For I count the gray barbarian lower than the Christian
child.

He hears the bells at midnight tolling the
death of the old year, and he calls them to

> Ring in the valiant man and free,
> The larger heart, the kindlier hand;
> Ring out the darkness of the land,
> Ring in the Christ that is to be!

In regard to the life beyond the grave,
he asserts with new force and beauty the
old faith in a personal immortality. The
dim conception of an unconscious survival
through the influence of our thoughts and
deeds, which George Eliot has expressed in
her poem of "the choir invisible," Tenny-
son finds to be

> A faith as vague as all unsweet.
> Eternal form shall still divide
> The eternal soul from all beside;
> And I shall know him when we meet.

The Christian doctrine of a personal recog-
nition of friends in the other world has
never been more distinctly uttered than in
these words. It is not, indeed, supported
by any metaphysical arguments; nor are we
concerned thus to justify it. Our only
purpose now is to show — and after these
verses who can doubt it — that the poet

has kept the faith which he learned in his father's house and at his mother's knee.

On many other points I fain would touch, but must forbear. There is one more, however, on which the orthodoxy of the poet has been questioned, and by some critics positively denied. It is said that he has accepted the teachings of Universalism. A phrase from *In Memoriam*,

The larger hope, —

has been made a watchword by those who defend the doctrine of a second probation, and a sign to be spoken against by those who reject it. Into this controversy I have no desire to enter. Nor is it necessary; for, whatever the poet's expectation may be, there is not a line in all his works that contradicts or questions the teachings of Christ, nor even a line that runs beyond the limit of human thought into the mysteries of the unknown and the unknowable. The wages of sin is death; the wages of virtue is to go on and not to die. This is the truth which he teaches on higher authority than his own. " The rest," as Hamlet says, " is silence." But what is the end of all these conflicts, these struggles, these probations? What the final result of this strife between sin and

virtue? What the consummation of oppug-
nancies and interworkings? The poet looks
onward through the mists and shadows and
sees only God;—

> That God, which ever lives and loves,
> One God, one law, one element,
> And one far-off divine event,
> To which the whole creation moves.

And if any one shall ask what this far-off
divine event is, we may answer in the words
of St. Paul:—

*For he must reign until he hath put all
enemies under his feet. The last enemy
that shall be abolished is death. For, he
put all things in subjection under his feet.
But when he saith, all things are put in
subjection, it is evident that he is excepted
who did subject all things unto him. And
when all things have been subjected unto
him, then shall the Son also himself be
subjected to him that did subject all things
unto him, that God may be all in all.*

And now, as we bring to a close this brief
study of a subject which I trust has proved
larger than it promised at first to those who
had never looked into it, what are our con-
clusions? Or if this word seem too exact

and formal, what are our impressions in re-
gard to the relations between Tennyson and
the Bible ?

It seems to me that we cannot help seeing
that the poet owes a large debt to the Chris-
tian Scriptures, not only for their formative
influence upon his mind and for the purely
literary material in the way of illustrations
and allusions which they have given him,
but also, and more particularly, for the crea-
tion of a moral atmosphere, a medium of
thought and feeling, in which he can speak
freely and with assurance of sympathy to a
very wide circle of readers. He does not
need to be always explaining and defining.
There is much that is taken for granted,
much that goes without saying. What a
world of unspoken convictions lies behind
such poems as *Dora* and *Enoch Arden.*
Their beauty is not in themselves alone, but
in the air that breathes around them, in the
light that falls upon them from the faith
of the centuries. Christianity is something
more than a system of doctrines; it is a life,
a tone, a spirit, a great current of memories,
beliefs and hopes flowing through millions
of hearts. And he who launches his words
upon this current finds that they are carried

with a strength beyond his own, and
freighted often with a meaning which he
himself has not fully understood as it flashed
through him.

But, on the other hand, we cannot help
seeing that the Bible gains a wider influence
and a new power over men as it flows
through the poet's mind upon the world. Its
narratives and its teachings clothe them-
selves in modern forms of speech, and find
entrance into many places which otherwise
were closed against them. I do not mean
by this that poetry is better than the Bible,
but only that poetry lends wings to Chris-
tian truth. People who would not read a
sermon will read a poem. And though its
moral and religious teachings may be indi-
rect, though they may proceed by silent
assumption rather than by formal assertion,
they exercise an influence which is perhaps
the more powerful because it is unconscious.
The Bible is in continual danger of being
desiccated by an exhaustive (and exhaust-
ing) scientific treatment. When it comes
to be regarded chiefly as a compendium of
exact statements of metaphysical doctrine,
the day of its life will be over, and it will
be ready for a place in the museum of anti-

quities. It must be a power in literature if it is to be a force in society. For literature, as a wise critic has defined it, is just "the best that has been thought and said in the world." And if this be true, literature is certain, not only to direct culture but also to mould conduct.

Is it possible, then, for wise and earnest men to look with indifference upon the course of what is often called, with a slighting accent, "mere *belles lettres*"? We might as well be careless about the air we breathe or the water we drink. Malaria is no less fatal than pestilence. The chief peril which threatens the permanence of Christian faith and morals is none other than the malaria of modern letters, — an atmosphere of dull, heavy, faithless materialism. Into this narcotic air the poetry of Tennyson blows like a pure wind from a loftier and serener height, bringing life and joy. His face looks out upon these darkening days, — grave, strong, purified by conflict, lighted by the inward glow of faith. He is become as one of the prophets, — a witness for God and for immortality.

FRUIT FROM AN OLD TREE.

FRUIT FROM AN OLD TREE.

IN the secluded garden of Christ's Col·
lege, at Cambridge, there is a mulberry-
tree of which tradition says that it was
planted by John Milton in his student days.
I remember sitting on the green turf below
it, a few years ago, and looking up at the
branches, heavy with age and propped on
crutches, and wondering to see that the old
tree still brought forth fruit. It was not
the size nor the quality of the fruit that
impressed me. I hardly thought of that.
The strange thing, the beautiful thing, was
that, after so many years, the tree was yet
bearing.

It is this feeling that comes to us when
we see the productive power of a poet con-
tinued beyond the common term of human
life. The thing is so rare that it appears
almost miraculous. " Whom the gods love
die young " seems to be the law for poets ;
or, at least, if they chance to live long, the
gods, and chiefly Apollo, cease to love them.
How few are the instances in which poetic

fertility has lasted beyond the threescore
years! Wordsworth, Landor, Victor Hugo,
Robert Browning, — among our American
singers, Bryant, Longfellow, Whittier, and
Lowell, — truly they are not many to whom
has been given the double portion of long
life and unfailing song. English literature
has no parallel, in this respect, to the
career of Tennyson. For sixty-six years
he was drawing refreshment from the wells
of poetry, and still the silver cord was not
loosed, nor the golden bowl broken.

I want to say a word or two in this essay
about the work of his later life. It has a
value of its own, apart from the wonder of
its production at such an advanced age. I
am quite sure that there is a great deal
which belongs to the real and enduring
poetry of Tennyson in the two volumes
which he gave to the world in 1886 and
1889, and in the posthumous volume
which appeared in the month of his death,
October, 1892.

I.

Locksley Hall Sixty Years After was not
received at first with notable applause.
The young critics reviled it as the work of

an old man, and raised a chorus of " Go up, thou baldhead," which made one regret that since the days of Elisha the bears have neglected one of their most beneficent functions.

The first *Locksley Hall* was beyond a doubt the strongest and most immediately successful thing in the volumes of 1842, which gave Tennyson his place as a popular poet. The billowy rush of the verse, the romantic interest of the story, the vigorous spirit of hope and enthusiasm which throbbed through the poem and made it seem alive with the breath of a new age, at once captivated all readers. It was this poem, more than any other, which lifted Tennyson beyond the admiration of a narrow circle and opened to him the heart of the world. And it is worthy of notice that, even in its outward form, this poem is one of the few which his habit of self-correction has left almost unchanged. There are but four slight verbal variations between the first and the last editions.

Forty-four years had passed when the poet took up the thread of his youthful dream once more and followed it to the end.

The dramatic nature of the poem must not be forgotten, for it is this which gives unity to the two parts. They are not disconnected strings of brilliant metaphors and comparisons, or trochaic remarks upon human life and progress. They are the expression of a character, the lyric history of a life ; they form a complete and rounded whole. They are two acts in the same play. The hero, the scene, remain the same. Only the time is changed by half a century.

It seems quite evident that Tennyson was not willing to leave his hero as he stood in the first act. For with all his attractive, not to say " magnetic," qualities, there was something about him that was unlovely and repellent, almost absurd. He made too much of himself, talked too loudly and recklessly, was too much inclined to rave and exaggerate. Tennyson doubtless wished to do for him what time really does for every man whose heart is of true metal — make him wiser and kinder and more worthy to be loved. The touches by which this change has been accomplished are most delicate and admirable.

Compare the rejected lover's jealousy of the baby rival whose lips should laugh him down, and whose hands should push him from the mother's heart, with the old man's prayer beside the marble image of Amy,

> Looking still as if she smiled,

sleeping quietly with her little child upon her breast. Or turn from the young man's scornful and unjust description of the richer suitor who had carried off his sweetheart, to the generous tribute which he lays at last upon the grave of him who

> Strove for sixty widow'd years to help his homelier brother man.

Or put his first wild complaint of the worthlessness and desolation of his life beside his later acknowledgment of the joy and strength which had come to him through the larger, deeper love of Edith. Surely, if words have any meaning, the poet means to teach us by these things that not only youthful jealousy, but also youthful despair, is false, and that, for every one who will receive its moral discipline and hold fast to its eternal hopes, life is worth the living.

So far, then, as the story of the two poems is concerned, so far as they present to us a picture of human character and trace its development through the experience of joy and sorrow, their lesson is sweet and sound and full of encouragement. It shows the frailty of exaggerated feelings of passion, born in an atmosphere of tropical heat, and unable to endure the cooler air of reality. But it shows also that the garden of life has better and more lasting blossoms, affections which survive all shock and change, a man's love which is stronger than a boy's fancy, a man's reverence for honest worth which can overcome a boy's resentment for imagined wrongs,

> A sober certainty of waking bliss

which makes divine amends for the vanished dreams of boyhood. It reminds us of the story of the " child-wife," Dora, and the woman-wife, Agnes, which Dickens has told in *David Copperfield*, or of Thackeray's history of *Henry Esmond*.

But when we come to consider the sequel of the poem in its other aspect, as a commentary on modern England, as an estimate of the result of those buoyant,

bounding hopes which seemed to swing
the earlier verses onward in the full tide
of exultation toward a near millennium,
we shall find room for a difference of
opinion among critics. There were some
who regarded the second *Locksley Hall* as
a veritable palinode, a complete recanta-
tion of the poet's youthful creed, a shame-
ful desertion from the army of progress to
the army of reaction, a betrayal of the
standard of hope into the hands of despair.
There were others, among them Mr. Glad-
stone, who thought that, though the poet
had not really deserted the good cause, he
had at least yielded too far to despond-
ency, and that he was in danger of mar-
ring the semi-centennial jubilee of Queen
Victoria's reign with unnecessarily "tragic
tones." It seems to me that both of these
views were unjust, because they both failed
to go far enough beneath the surface.
They left out of sight several things which
were necessary to a fair judgment of the
poem.

First of all is the fact that the poet does
not speak for himself, but through the lips
of a *persona*, a mask; and what he says
must be in character. Mr. Gladstone has.

indeed, noted this fact; but he has failed
to take fully into account the peculiar and
distinctive qualities of the character which
the poet has chosen. The hero of *Locksley
Hall* is a man in whom emotion is stronger
than thought; impulsive, high-strung, su-
persensitive; one to whom everything that
he sees must loom larger than life through
the mist of his own overwrought feelings.
This is his nature. And if in youth he
took too bright a view of the future, it is
quite as inevitable that in age he should
take too dark a view of the present. If
there be any exaggeration in his com-
plaints about the evils of our times, it is
but fair to set them down to the idiosyn-
crasy of the hero, and not to the opinions
of the poet.

But suppose we put this plea of dramatic
propriety aside, and make Tennyson an-
swerable for all that his hero says. We
shall find that there were some things in
the first rhapsody quite as hard and bitter
as any in the second. Take the vigourous
imprecations against the social wants, the
social lies, the sickly forms, by which the
young man is oppressed and infuriated.
Hear him cry : —

What is that which I should turn to, lighting upon days
   like these ?
Every door is barred with gold, and opens but to golden
   keys.

See his picture of the hungry people, creep-
ing like a lion toward the slothful watcher
beside a dying fire.   Here, at least, even
in the first outflow of hopeful music, are
the warning notes.   And though there may
be more severity in the old man's condem-
nation of the iniquities and follies of so-
ciety, in one point at least he has grown
milder: he does not indulge in any more
" cursing."

Observe also, if we must hold Tennyson
responsible for a retraction in the second
poem of anything that he taught in the first,
just what is the point to which that retrac-
tion applies.   He does not deny his early
hope for the future of England and the
world; he denies only the two insufficient
grounds on which that hope was based.

One of these grounds was the swift and
wonderful march of what is called modern
improvement, meaning thereby the steam-
ship, the railway, the telegraph, and the
advance of all the industrial arts.   Of these
he says now : —

Half the marvels of my morning, triumphs over time
    and space,
Staled by frequence, shrunk by usage into commonest
    commonplace.

And is not this true? Have we not all
felt the shrinkage of the much-vaunted
miracles of science into the veriest kitchen
utensils of a comfort-worshipping society?
Physical powers have been multiplied by
an unknown quantity, but it is a serious
question whether moral powers have not
had their square root extracted. A man
can go from New York to London now in
six days. But when he arrives he is no
better man than if it had taken him a
month. He can talk across three thousand
miles of ocean, but he has nothing more to
say than when he sent his letter by a
sailing-packet. All the inventions in the
world will not change man's heart, or

Lift him nearer God-like state.

The other ground of hope in the old
Locksley Hall was the advance of modern
politics, through the freedom of speech and
the extension of suffrage, which seemed to
promise at no distant date a sort of uni-
versal " Parliament of Man," a " Federation
of the World." In the new *Locksley Hall*

the poet confesses that this ground also has failed him. He no longer thinks so highly of Parliament that he desires to see it reproduced on a larger scale. The virtues of talk as a panacea for human ills appear to him more than dubious. He hazards the conjecture that

Old England may go down in babble at last.

And he breaks out in fierce indignation against the "rivals of realm-ruining party," who care more for votes than for truth, and for the preservation of their own power than for the preservation of the Empire.

What is all this but the acknowledgment of the truth which most sober men are beginning to feel? Fifty years ago material science and political theory promised large things. The promise has been kept to the ear and broken to the hope. The world has gone forward — a little — but it has not arrived at a complete millennium, nor even swept at once into a brighter day; far from it. There are heavy clouds upon the sky. The moral condition of humanity in general, and of England in particular, is certainly not free from elements of degradation and threats of danger. Let me quote two sentences from writers who deserve at least an attentive hearing:—

"British industrial existence seems fast becoming one huge poison-swamp of reeking pestilence, physical and moral; a *living* Golgotha of souls and bodies buried alive; such a Curtius' gulf communicating with the nether deeps as the sun never saw till now." That was what Thomas Carlyle thought. And, after the same fashion, Ruskin wrote: "Remember, for the last twenty years, England and all foreign nations, either tempting her or following her, have blasphemed the name of God deliberately and openly; and have done iniquity by proclamation, every man doing as much injustice to his brother as it is in his power to do."

These utterances, like the darker verses in Tennyson's poem, are not meant to be taken as complete pictures of the present time. They are only earnest and vigorous warnings against the easy-going, self-complacent optimism which talks as if the millennium had already dawned. To reply to them by an enumeration of the scientific discoveries which have been made, and the po-

litical measures which have been passed,
during the last half-century, is quite beside
the point.   The question remains, *Is human
life really higher, holier, happier?*

The answer, if it is thoughtful as well as
hopeful, must be, *A little.*   But still the
strife, the shame, the suffering, endure.

City children soak and blacken soul and sense in city
  slime;
There among the glooming alleys Progress halts on
  palsied feet,
Crime and hunger cast our maidens by the thousand on
  the street.

If we ask when and how these things
shall cease, the reply comes, not from the
fairy-tales of science nor from the blue-
books of politics, but from the heart of
Christian charity and from the promise of
Christian faith.   And this is the reply
which Tennyson has given, in words as
pure and clear and musical as he has ever
uttered : —

Follow you the Star that lights a desert pathway, yours
  or mine,
Forward, till you learn the highest Human Nature is
  divine.

Follow Light, and do the Right — for man can half con-
  trol his doom —
Till you see the deathless Angel seated in the vacant
  Tomb.

Forward, let the stormy moment fly and mingle with the
Past.
I that loathed, have come to love him. Love will con-
quer at the last.

The last line recalls us once more to the
personal interest of the poem, which, after
all, is the strongest. The hero of *Locksley
Hall* is bidding us farewell. He has played
his part through. The drama of life is
ended. In the first act we saw the youth
seeking to forget his private sorrow in the
largest public hopes; turning from the lost
embraces of his " faithless Amy," to lay
his head upon the vast bosom of the age,
and listen to the deep throbbing of cosmic
hopes. In the second act we see the old
man seeking to forget his public disap-
pointments in his private affections; turn-
ing back from that hard and unrestful
world-bosom, where he has heard nothing
better than the clank of machinery and
the words of windy oratory, to find rest in
the tender memories of Amy and Edith,
and the man whom time had changed from
his enemy into his friend; and looking
forward to the future for the fulfilment of
his hopes in an age not yet revealed.

Who that understands anything of a

young man's, or an old man's, heart can
question the truth of these two pictures?
And who will venture to say that the true
philosophy of life does not lie somewhere
between optimism and pessimism, in that
steadfast and chastened meliorism to which
old-fashioned Christianity makes its appeal
and gives its promise?

II.

The volume entitled *Demeter, and Other
Poems*, which appeared at the close of the
year 1889, does not contain any one poem
of equal interest with the second *Locksley
Hall;* but it contains several of more per-
fect workmanship, and in its wide range of
subject and style it shows some of the finest
qualities of Tennyson's poetry.

Take, first, his sympathetic interpreta-
tion of Nature. Wordsworth was the leader
here; he was the first to lift Nature to the
level of man, and utter in human language
her most intimate meanings; but Tenny-
son has added something to the scope and
beauty of this kind of poetry. He has
caught more of the throbbing and passion-
ate and joyous voices of the world; he has
not entered so deeply into the silence and

solemnity of guardian mountains and sleep-
ing lakes and broad, bare skies ; but he has
felt more keenly the thrills and flushes of
Nature — the strange, sudden, perplexed,
triumphant impulses of that eager seeking
and tremulous welcoming of love which
flows like life-blood through all animate
things.   And so he is at his best with
Nature when he comes to the springtime.
The lines on *The Oak* are Wordsworthian
in their simplicity ; the last stanza is a
model of austere expression : —

> All his leaves
>   Fall'n at length,
> Look, he stands,
> Trunk and bough,
>   Naked strength.

But in *The Throstle* we have something
that none but Tennyson could have writ-
ten.   Immortal youth throbs and pulses in
this old man's song.   The simple music of
joy, so swift and free that its cadences
break through and through one another
and overflow the edges of the verse : —

> Summer is coming, summer is coming,
>   I know it, I know it, I know it.
> Light again, leaf again, life again, love again,
>   Yes, my wild little poet.

That sings itself.

The poem of *Demeter*, which gives its
name to the volume, is valuable for several
qualities. It is an example of that opulent,
stately, and musical blank verse in which
Tennyson was the greatest master after
Milton died. It shows also his power of
reanimating an old-world legend with the
vivid feeling of present life. The ancient
myth of the earth-goddess, whose daughter
has been snatched away into the shadowy
underworld, is quickened by the poet's
genius into an impassioned utterance of
the sharp contrast between the spectral
existence of Hades and the sweet, homely
familiarities of the earth, the clinging of
the heart to simple mortal life, and the
preference of its·joys and sorrows to all
the "hard eternities" of passionless gods.
But to my apprehension, the best quality
in this poem, and the most vital, is its rev-
elation of the depth and power of the poet's
human sympathy.

Somehow or other Demeter's divinity is
forgotten and lost in her motherhood.
Take that strong, sweet, simple passage
which begins : —

> Child, when thou wert gone
> I envied human wives and nested birds.

It would be impossible to express more
directly and vividly the dependence of the
mother upon the babe who is dependent
upon her, the yearning of the maternal
breast toward the child who has been taken
from it. It is the same generous love
which is set to music in the song in *Rom-
ney's Remorse ;* but there the love is not
robbed and disappointed, but satisfied in
the outpouring of its riches : —

> Beat, little heart, I give you this and this.

That is the fragrance, the melody, the
mystery of the passion of motherhood —
profound, simple, elemental. And when a
poet can feel and interpret that for us, and
at the same time express the rude and mas-
sive emotions of the stolid peasant in a
poem like *Owd Roä*, and the troubled, sen-
sitive penitence of a vain, weak artist in a
poem like *Romney's Remorse*, he proves
that nothing human is foreign to him.

Tennyson's most distinctive trait — that
by which he is best known to those who
know him best — is the power of uttering
a delicate, vague, yet potent emotion, one
of those feelings which belong to the twi-
light of the heart, where the light of love

and the shadow of regret are mingled, in an exquisite lyric which defines nothing and yet makes everything clear. To this class belong such songs as " Tears, idle tears," " Blow, bugle, blow," and " Break, break, break." And this volume gives us another lyric with the same mystical and musical charm, " Far — far — away." This is a melody that haunts youth and age; the attraction of distance, the strange magic of the dim horizon, the enchantment of evening bells ringing beyond the bounds of sight; these are things so aërial and evanescent that they seem to elude words; but Tennyson has somehow caught them in his song.

But there is something still nobler and greater in his poetry. There is a spiritual courage in his work, a force of faith which conquers doubt and darkness, a light of inward hope which burns dauntless under the shadow of death. Tennyson is the poet of faith; faith, as distinguished from cold dogmatism and the acceptance of traditional creeds; faith, which does not ignore doubt and mystery, but triumphs over them and faces the unknown with fearless heart. The poem entitled *Vast-*

ness is an expression of this faith. But there is even a finer quality, a loftier, because a serener, power in the poem with which the book closes. Nothing that Tennyson has ever written is more beautiful in body and soul than *Crossing the Bar.*

Sunset and evening star,
    And one clear call for me !
And may there be no moaning of the bar,
    When I put out to sea,

But such a tide as moving seems asleep,
    Too full for sound and foam,
When that which drew from out the boundless deep
    Turns again home.

Twilight and evening bell,
    And after that the dark !
And may there be no sadness of farewell,
    When I embark ;

For tho' from out our bourne of Time and Place
    The flood may bear me far,
I hope to see my Pilot face to face,
    When I have crost the bar.

That is perfect poetry — simple even to the verge of austerity, yet rich with all the suggestions of wide ocean and waning light and vesper bells ; easy to understand and full of music, yet opening inward to a truth which has no words, and pointing onward to a vision which transcends all forms; it is a delight and a consolation, a song for mortal ears, and a prelude to the larger music of immortality.

III.

The Death of Œnone, Akbar's Dream, and Other Poems, came out immediately after Tennyson's death. He was at work correcting the proofs, with the loving care which he gave to all the details of his art, when I was his guest at Aldworth in the last week of August, 1892.

The volume, while it is in some respects the slightest of all that Tennyson published, containing no poem that can be ranked with his best, and making no real increment to his fame, is certainly an extraordinary piece of work for a man of eighty-three years, and does not fall below the general level of his poetry.

In *The Death of Œnone* he returns to one of the classical subjects which charmed him in his youth. In *St. Telemachus* he takes a familiar story from the ecclesiastical history of Theodoret — the story of

that first deed of monkish chivalry by
which the gladiatorial shows at Rome
were broken up — and turns it into verse.
In *Akbar's Dream* he touches the char-
acter of the famous Mogul emperor whose
name was the symbol of religious tolerance
and breadth of mind, and whose endeav-
our was to rule with fairness and an even
hand over all the people of different
creeds in his vast dominion.   The subject
is one which had strong attractions for
Tennyson, and he has handled it with
warm sympathy.   The poem closes with
a brief, splendid hymn to the Sun : —

Once again thou flamest heavenward, once again we see
    thee rise.
Every morning is thy birthday, gladdening human hearts
    and eyes.
        Every morning here we greet it, bowing lowly
            down before thee,
Thee the God-like, thee the changeless in thine ever-
    changing skies.
            Warble bird, and open flower,
                the dome of azure

Kneel adoring Him the Timeless in the flame that
    measures Time !
Shadow-maker, shadow-slayer, arrowing light from clime
    to clime,
Hear thy myriad laureates hail thee monarch in their
    woodland rhyme.

But of still greater interest are a few
short poems — *The Making of Man, Doubt
and Prayer, Faith, The Silent Voices, God
and the Universe* — in which the poet has
given utterance once more to the deepest
faith that was in him : —

Spirit, nearing yon dark portal at the limit of thy
human state,
Fear not thou the hidden purpose of that Power which
alone is great,
Nor the myriad world, His shadow, nor the silent
Opener of the Gate.

Men have assured us, in these latter
days, that faith and art have parted com-
pany ; that faith is dead, and art must
live for itself alone. But while they were
saying these things in melancholy essays
and trivial verses, which denied a spiritual
immortality and had small prospect of a
literary one, the two highest artists of the
century, Tennyson and Browning, were
setting their music to the keynote of an
endless life, and prophesying with the
harp, according as it is written : *I believe,
and therefore sing.*

A POSTSCRIPT

IN THE FORM OF A LETTER ON THE STUDY OF TENNYSON.

ON THE STUDY OF TENNYSON:

To Miss Grace Newlight, in Oldport, near Boston.

MY DEAR MISS NEWLIGHT, — It is very good of you to begin your letter by saying that you have read my book on *The Poetry of Tennyson*. Almost every candid author (except, perhaps, a few who have written, but not published, in or near your native place) will acknowledge that he has what the precise French call a *faible*, for the persons who have voluntarily become his readers, and that he inclines to form a high estimate of their wisdom, taste, and personal character. In this weakness I share, and take no shame in confessing it. Whether the opening of your letter was dictated by the natural goodness of your heart, or whether you have added a gentle diplomacy to your many other accomplishments, you have certainly put your request for "advice about the best way to study Tennyson" in such a form as to make me sincerely desirous of offering you my poor best.

Candidly, then, and after serious reflec-
tion, upon my literary honour and con-
science I believe that the very best way to
study any poet is to read his poems.

There are other ways, of course, perhaps
easier, unquestionably more in vogue. You
remember those profound lectures which Pro-
fessor Boreham gave last Lent on "The Pes-
simism of Petrarch," and how many young
women were stimulated by them to wear the
Laura hat and enter a higher life. You
know also the charming Mrs. Lucy Liebig,
in whose "Class for General Information"
it is possible to get the *extractum carnis* of
several modern poets in an hour, so that one
can thereafter speak of all their principal
characters with familiarity, and even with
accuracy. You have been a member of the
"Society for the Elucidation of the Minor
Moral Problems in Sordello," and a sub-
scriber to *The Literary Peptone*, whose ac-
complished reviewers have made the task of
digesting a book for one's self seem like an
obsolete superfluity. With all of these de-
vices for poetical study, so entertaining and
in their way so useful, you are familiar.
But, after all, if you really care to know and
love a poet, I must commend you to the sim-

ple and old-fashioned plan of reading him.
Nothing can take the place of that.

And with Tennyson, believe me, you will
not find this plan difficult. It is not an
adventure for which you will need great
preparation or many confederates. You
may safely undertake it alone, and for plea-
sure. Here and there, especially in *The
Princess*, there are hard places where good
notes will help you. And perhaps with a
few poems, notably with *In Memoriam*, one
wants an analysis or commentary. But in
the main Tennyson is a clear poet, and there-
fore a delightful one. The only book which
is indispensable for understanding him is
that thick, green volume which bears on its
back the title *The Works of Tennyson*.
Get a copy of this book for your very own ;
— and if you are wise, you will get one that
is not too fine for you to mark on the mar-
gin, and if you have a tender conscience,
you will get one that has not been pirated ;
— take it with you into a quiet place, among
the mountains, or on the seashore, or by
your fireside, and read it with a free mind
and a fresh heart. Read, not as if you were
preparing for an examination or getting
ready to make an index, — but read for the

sake of seeing what the poet has seen, and
feeling what he has felt, and knowing what
he has thought, — read the book not for idle
pastime, but for noble pleasure ; not for dry
knowledge, but for living wisdom ; and if
you read thus, I am sure it will do for you
what Dr. Johnson said that every good,
great book ought to do, — it will help you
to enjoy life and teach you to endure it.

Now I am perfectly sure that you are not
a member of the tribe of the Philistines, and
therefore you will not think of reading such
a book as you would read a treatise on logic,
straight through, from the first page to the
last. You will want a plan, a principle of
order to direct your reading. The first
question you will ask is, Where to begin
among the poems, and how to continue ? Is
it possible to classify them ? Can we "get a
line through Tennyson," which may help us
to understand the meaning of his works, and
their relation to each other ?

Well, as to classification, I am not inclined
to set a very high value upon it in the study
of poetry. There are certain broad divisions
which can be made, — none better, after all,
than the old Greek trichometry of epic, lyric,
and dramatic, corresponding to the intellect,

the emotions, and the will. But unless you use this division in a strictly formal and mechanical fashion, it will not be possible to make the works of Tennyson, or of any other modern poet, fit into it exactly. You will find that some of the poems do not belong to any one of the three divisions, and others plainly belong to several. You will not know at all what to do with *Maud*, or *Locksley Hall*, or *The Palace of Art*, or *Ulysses*, unless you put them into a border land. And when it comes to more minute classification, on the lines of psychology, — Poems of Reflection, Poems of Imagination, Poems of Fancy, Poems of Sentiment, and the like, — I doubt whether even a great poet can accomplish such a thing with his own works successfully. Wordsworth tried it, you know; and Matthew Arnold, an avowed Wordsworthian, confessed that it was not worth much. The first of Browning's commentators, Mr. Nettleship, made an even more elaborate analysis of that master's poems in the first edition of *Essays and Thoughts.* Here is a specimen of it: —

" II. A. Poems not strictly dramatic in form, but which deal with the history, or some incident in the history, of the souls of two or more individuals mutually acting on each other towards (1) progress, or (2) arrest, in development."

But in his second edition Mr. Nettleship, with amiable frankness, makes fun of his own analysis. I would rather not attempt anything of the kind with Tennyson's poems, even for the pleasure of ridiculing my own failure afterwards.

But though an exact classification may be useless or impossible, a general order, a broad grouping of the poems for the purpose of comprehending them as a whole, might be helpful, and not too difficult to make it worth trying. It would serve, at least, as a guide to your reading, and bring together the poems which are most closely related in spirit and manner. I beg you, then, to accept what follows, not as a classification, but simply as

AN ARRANGEMENT OF TENNYSON'S POEMS.

I. MELODIES AND PICTURES.

Claribel.
Leonine Elegiacs.
Nothing will Die.
All Things will Die.
"The winds as at their hour of birth."

The Owl.
The Dying Swan.
The Blackbird.
The Throstle.
The Snowdrop.
Early Spring.
Far — Far — Away.
" Move eastward, happy Earth."
" A Spirit haunts the year's last hours."
The Death of the Old Year.
A Farewell.
A Dirge.
The Merman.
The Mermaid.
The Sea-Fairies.
The Lotos-Eaters.
Child-Songs.
The Song of the Wrens.

The Kraken.
The Eagle.
The Oak.
Recollections of the Arabian Nights.
Ode to Memory.
The Progress of Spring.
The Daisy.
Mariana.
Mariana in the South.
A Dream of Fair Women.
The Day-Dream.

II. STORIES AND PORTRAITS.

Ballads.

Idylls.

2. Audley Court.
   Walking to the Mail.
   Edwin Morris.
   The Golden Year.
   The Brook.
   Sea Dreams.
   The Lover's Tale.
   The Sisters.
   The Ring.
   The Miller's Daughter.
   The Talking Oak.
   The Gardener's Daughter.
   Godiva.
   Œnone.
   The Death of Œnone.
   Dora.
   Enoch Arden.
   Aylmer's Field.

Character-Pieces.

3. A Character.
   Love and Duty.
   Tithonus. ⎫
   Teiresias. ⎬ *Classical.*
   Demeter. ⎭
   Lucretius. ⎫
   Ulysses. ⎬ *Historical.*
   Columbus. ⎭

Akbar's Dream. ⎫
St. Telemachus. ⎪
St. Simeon Stylites. ⎬ *Historical.*
Sir John Oldcastle. ⎪
Romney's Remorse. ⎭

Fatima. ⎫
St. Agnes' Eve. ⎬ *Mystical.*
Sir Galahad. ⎭

Amphion. ⎫
Will Waterproof. ⎪
The Northern Farmer.   Old Style. ⎪
The Northern Farmer.   New Style. ⎪
The Churchwarden and the Curate. ⎬ *Humorous and Dialect.*
The Northern Cobbler. ⎪
The Village Wife. ⎪
The Spinster's Sweet-Arts. ⎪
Owd Roä. ⎪
To-morrow. ⎭

The Grandmother.
Rizpah.
Despair.
The Wreck.
The Flight.
Charity.
Locksley Hall.
Locksley Hall, Sixty Years After.
Lady Clara Vere de Vere.
Maud.

III.   EPICS.

The Princess.
Idylls of the King.

IV. DRAMAS.

Queen Mary. ⎫
Harold. ⎬ *The Trilogy.*
Becket. ⎭
The Cup.
The Falcon.
The Promise of May.
The Foresters.

V. PATRIOTIC AND PERSONAL.

"You ask me why, tho' ill at ease."
"Love thou thy land."
"Of old sat Freedom on the heights."
Freedom.
England and America in 1782.
The Third of February, 1852.
Ode on the Death of the Duke of Wellington.
Hands all Round.
The Charge of the Light Brigade.
Prologue to General Hamley.
The Charge of the Heavy Brigade.
Epilogue.
To the Queen. "Revered, beloved."
To the Queen. "O loyal to the royal in thy·
self."
Dedication to Prince Albert.
A Welcome to Alexandra.
A Welcome to Alexandrovna.

Dedication to the Princess Alice.
To the Marquis of Dufferin.
To the Duke of Argyll.
To the Princess Beatrice.
To the Princess Frederica of Hanover.
Politics.
Beautiful City.
To one who ran down the English.
Ode for the International Exhibition.
Opening of the Indian and Colonial Exhibi-
tion.
On the Jubilee of Queen Victoria.
The Fleet.
On the Death of the Duke of Clarence.

To —— "Clear-headed friend."
To J. S. (James Spedding.)
To E. L., on his Travels in Greece. (Ed-
mund Lear.)
To the Rev. F. D. Maurice.
A Dedication. (To his wife.)
In the Garden of Swainston. (Sir John
Simeon.)
To E. Fitzgerald.
To Alfred Tennyson, my Grandson.
Prefatory to my Brother's Sonnets.

Epitaphs on {
Sir John Franklin,
Lord Stratford de Redcliffe,
General Gordon.
Caxton.
}

To Ulysses. (**W. G. Palgrave.**)

The Roses on the Terrace.
To Mary Boyle.
To Professor Jebb.
In Memoriam — William George Ward.

VI. POEMS OF THE INNER LIFE.

Of Art.

1. The Poet.
The Poet's Mind.
The Poet's Song.
The Palace of Art.
Merlin and the Gleam.
The Flower.
The Spiteful Letter.
Literary Squabbles.
" You might have won the Poet's name."
The Dead Prophet.
Poets and their Bibliographies.
Frater Ave atque Vale.
Parnassus.
To Virgil.
To Milton.
To Dante.
To Victor Hugo.

Of Life, Love, and Death.

2. The Deserted House.
Love and Death.
Circumstance.
The Voyage.

The Islet.
The Sailor-Boy.
The Vision of Sin.
The Voice and the Peak.
Will.
Wages.
"Flower in the crannied wall."
"My life is full of weary days."
"Come not, when I am dead."
Requiescat.
On a Mourner.
"Break, break, break."
In the Valley of Cauteretz.

Of Doubt and Faith.

3. Supposed Confessions.
The Two Voices.
The Ancient Sage.
By an Evolutionist.
In Memoriam.
The Higher Pantheism.
De Profundis.
Vastness.
Crossing the Bar.
Faith.
The Silent Voices.
God and the Universe.
Doubt and Prayer.

This arrangement may be imperfect, but I

think, at least, that it omits nothing of
importance, that it is constructed on the
lines of poetic development, and that it will
be easy to discover the inward relationship
and coherence of the principal groups, so
that you can follow a clue from poem to
poem.

You will do well to begin with the Melo-
dies and Pictures, because Tennyson began
with them, and because they belong to the
lowest form of his art, although it is the form
in which he has done some of his most ex-
quisite work. There are many people — and
not altogether illiterate people — who still
think of him chiefly as a "maker of musical
phrases." Well, he is that; and he meant
to be that, in order that he might be some-
thing more. At the very outset, he sought
to win the power of expressing sensuous
beauty in melodious language. The things
seen and heard, the rhythm, the colour, the
harmony of the outward world, — these were
the things that haunted him, and these, first
of all, he desired to convey into his verse.
He threw himself with all the passion of
youth upon the task of rendering them per-
fectly.

I call it a task, because no man has ever done this kind of work by chance. Even to the painting of a simple flower, or the making of a little song, perfectly, there goes an infinite deal of preparation, of learning, of effort; sometimes it is conscious, sometimes unconscious; sometimes it is direct, sometimes it is indirect; but always it is there, behind the music, behind the picture; for no one can do anything good in any art without labour for the mastery of its little secrets which are so hard to learn.

If, then, you find some traces of effort in Tennyson's first melodies and pictures, like *Eleänore, The Mermaid, Recollections of the Arabian Nights,* you will say that this is because he has not yet learned to conceal the effort; and if you find that in the best of them, like *The Lotos-Eaters* and *The Lady of Shalott,* the chief interest still lies in the sound, the form, the colour, you will say that it is because he has set himself to conquer the technique of his art, and to render the music and the vision beautifully, for the sake of their beauty. Mr. R. H. Hutton, who does not always see the bearing of his own criticisms, has said, "Tennyson was an artist even before he was a poet." That is true, but it does

not take anything away from his greatness
to admit such an obvious fact. Giotto was
a draughtsman before he was a painter. Mo-
zart was a pianist before he was a musician.

If you are wise, then, you will look chiefly
for the charm of perfect expression in these
melodies and pictures. Take a little piece
which has stood on the first page of Ten-
nyson's poems for sixty years, *Claribel.* It
does not mean much. Indeed, its charm
might be less if its meaning were greater. It
is mere music, — every word like a soft, clear
note, — each with its own precise value, and
yet all blending in a simple effect. The
difference between the sound of the quiet
wave "outwelling" from the spring, and
the swift runlet "crisping" over the pebbles,
is distinct; the "beetle boometh" in another
tone from that in which the "wild bee
hummeth;" but all the sounds come together
in a sad, gentle cadence with the ending
eth : —

Where Claribel low-lieth.

In the picture poems you will find a great
deal of pre-Raphaelite work. It is exact and
vivid, even to the point of seeming often too
minute. It is worth while to notice the colour
words; how few they are, and yet how per-

fectly they do their work! Here are two
lines from the *Ode to Memory* : —

> What time the *amber* morn
> Forth gushes from beneath a low-hung cloud.

That "amber" sheds all the splendour of
daybreak over the landscape.

And here, again, is a stanza from *The
Lady of Shalott* : —

> Willows *whiten*, aspens quiver,
> Little breezes dusk and shiver
> Thro' the wave that runs for ever
> By the island in the river
>> Flowing down to Camelot.
> Four gray walls, and four gray towers,
> Overlook a space of flowers,
> And the silent isle imbowers
>> The Lady of Shalott.

How exquisite is the word "whiten" to
describe the turning of the long willow-leaves
in the wind, and how well it suggests the
cool colouring of the whole picture, all in low
tones, except the little spot of flowers below
the square, gray castle.

I do not think that this is the greatest
kind of poetry, but certainly it has its own
value, and we ought to be grateful for
it. The perfection to which Tennyson has
brought it has added a new sweetness and
fluency to our language. Just as a violin

gains a richer and mellower tone by the long
and loving touch of a master, so the English
language has been enriched and softened by
the use that Tennyson has made of it in his
beauty-poems.

But already we can see that something
deeper and stronger is coming into these
beauty-poems. The melodies begin to have
a meaning, the pictures begin to have a soul.
Of many of the young women in his gallery
of female figures, — *Lilian, Adeline, Made-
line,* and the rest, — it may be said in Tenny-
son's own words : —

> The form, the form alone is eloquent,

but in *Isabel* we see a character behind the
form, and the beauty of her nature makes
her sisters seem vague and unreal beside her.
The Lady of Shalott, which I have placed
last among the Melodies and Pictures, is in
effect a mystical ballad, foreshadowing the
transition from the dream-world of fancy to
the real world of human joy and sorrow.
And so we come to the second group of
poems, the Stories and Portraits.

The interest here centres in life and per-
sonality. It is some tale of human love, or
heroism, or suffering, that the poet tells ; and

then we have a Ballad. Or it is some pic-
ture that he paints, not for its own sake alone,
but to make it the vehicle of human feeling;
and then we have an Idyll, — that is, a scene
coloured and interpreted by an emotion. Or
it is some character that he depicts, some liv-
ing personality that he clothes with language,
either in a meditative soliloquy which shows
it in all its breadth of sentiment and thought,
or in a lyrical outburst from some intense
mood; and then we have what I have ven-
tured to call a Character-Piece. The lines
between these three divisions cannot be very
clearly drawn. I have been much in doubt
as to the best place for some of the poems.
But there is a real difference among them,
after all, in the predominance of the narra-
tive, the descriptive, or the dramatic spirit;
and you will feel the difference as you read
them.

In the Ballads I think you will feel that
the secret of their charm lies quite as much
in their human sympathy as in the perfection
of their art. The clearer, simpler, more
pathetic the story, the more absolutely does
it control and clarify the music. The best
of them are those in which the beauty comes
from delicate notes, so slight that one hardly

hears them, though their effect is magical. How much the pathos of *The May Queen* is enhanced by the naïve touch in these verses : —

O look ! the sun begins to rise, the heavens are in a glow ;
He shines upon a hundred fields, *and all of them I know.*
And there I move no longer now, and there his light may
    shine —
Wild flowers in the valley for other hands than mine.

Or listen to the last lines of *The Lord of Burleigh :* —

> Then her people, softly treading,
>   Bore to earth her body, *drest*
> *In the dress that she was wed in,*
>   That her spirit might have rest.

This is perfect simplicity, — words of common life, charged with the richest and tenderest poetic meaning. No less simple in its way — which is utterly different — is the glorious fighting ballad of *The Revenge.* It is the passion of daring, now, that carries the poem onward in its strong, heroic movement. There is not a redundant ornament in the whole ballad. Every simile that it contains is full of swift motion.

At Flores in the Azores, Sir Richard Grenville lay,
And a pinnace, *like a flutter'd bird*, came flying from far
    away.

So Lord Howard past away with five ships of war that
 day,
Till he melted like a cloud in the silent summer heaven.

Sir Richard spoke, and he laugh'd, and we roar'd a
 hurrah, and so
The little " Revenge" ran on sheer into the heart of the foe.

Among the Idylls you will find a great
difference. In some of them the pictorial
element seems to count for more than the
human feeling, — and these I think are the
poorest. Of such slight sketches as *Audley
Court* and *Edwin Morris*, all that can be
said is that they have pretty passages in
them. Tennyson was right in caring little
for *The Lover's Tale*. *Aylmer's Field* is
weaker than *Enoch Arden* just in so far as
it is more ornate and complicated. *Dora* is
the best of all, and I doubt whether you can
discover one metaphor, or figure of speech,
or decorative adjective in the whole poem.
It moves like the Book of Ruth, in beauty
unadorned.

In the character-pieces you will be im-
pressed, first of all, by the breadth of their
range. They touch the whole circle of
humanity, from the Roman philosopher to
the English peasant; they even go beyond
it, and breathe into the ancient myths, like

Tithonus and *Demeter*, human life and pas-
sion. Some of them are humorous, as *Will
Waterproof* and *The Northern Farmer;*
and others are mystical, as *St. Agnes' Eve*
and *Sir Galahad;* and others are passion-
ate, springing out of the depths of life's
tragedy, as *The Wreck* and *Despair*. But
almost without exception they are true and
distinct portraits of persons.

And then you will observe that (with one
early exception, *A Character*) they are all
dramatic. The characters are not described ;
they speak for themselves, either in blank-
verse monologues, or in dramatic lyrics.
The first is the form that is used chiefly when
the mental quality is to be expressed. The
second is the form chosen to reveal the emo-
tional quality. In all of them, the thing
that you will look for, and the test by which
you will value the poems, is the truth of the
thought and the utterance to the character
from which they come. And I think that
most of them will stand the test. If Mr.
Swinburne had written them he might have
made Ulysses and Columbus and Sir Gala-
had and the Northern Cobbler all speak the
Swinburnian dialect. Mr. Browning might
have set them all to analyzing their own

souls, and talking metaphysics. But with Tennyson each character speaks in a native voice, and thinks the thoughts which belong to him. Take the subject of Love, and hear what the Northern Farmer has to say of it : —

Luvv ? What 's luvv ? thou can luvv thy lass an' 'er
   munny too,
Maakin' 'em goä togithor, as they 've good right to do.
Could n' I luvv thy muther by cause o' 'er munny laaïd
   by ?
Naäy — for I luvv'd 'er a vast sight moor fur it: reäson
   why.

And then listen to the hero of *Locksley Hall :* —

Love took up the harp of Life, and smote on all the chords
   with might ;
Smote the chord of Self, that, trembling, passed in music
   out of sight.

Or take the passion of exploration, the strong desire to push out across new seas into new worlds, and mark how differently it is felt and expressed by Ulysses and Columbus. Ulysses is the " much-experienced man," with a thirst for seeing and knowing which cannot be satiated : —

I cannot rest from travel : I will drink
Life to the lees : all times I have enjoy'd
Greatly, have suffer'd greatly .   .   .

. . . I am become a name;
For always roaming with a hungry heart
Much have I seen and known; cities of men,
And manners, climates, councils, governments,
Myself not least, but honour'd of them all;
And drunk delight of battle with my peers,
Far on the ringing plains of windy Troy.
I am a part of all that I have met;
Yet all experience is as an arch wherethro'
Gleams that untravell'd world, whose margin fades
For ever and for ever when I move.

This is the deep impulse of motion without a
goal, the mere *Reise-lust* of a restless heart.
But Columbus is a man with a mission. It
is the glory of Spain and the spread of the
Catholic faith that drives him to seek an
undiscovered continent: —

I pray you tell
King Ferdinand, who plays with me, that one,
Whose life has been no play with him and his
Hidalgos — shipwrecks, famines, fevers, fights,
Mutinies, treacheries — wink'd at, and condoned —
That I am loyal to him till the death,
And ready — tho' our Holy Catholic Queen,
Who fain had pledged her jewels on my first voyage,
Whose hope was mine to spread the Catholic faith,
Who wept with me when I return'd in chains,
Who sits beside the blessed Virgin now,
To whom I send my prayer by night and day —
She is gone — but you will tell the King, that I,
Rack'd as I am with gout, and wrench'd with pains
Gain'd in the service of His Highness, yet
Am ready to sail forth on one last voyage,
And readier, if the King would hear, to lead

One last crusade against the Saracen,
And save the Holy Sepulchre from thrall.

Or take the subject of death. To the
weary philosopher Lucretius, resolved on
suicide, it means simply absorption into
Nature : —

O Thou,
Passionless bride, divine Tranquillity,
Yearn'd after by the wisest of the wise,
Who fail to find thee, being as thou art
Without one pleasure and without one pain,
Howbeit I know thou surely must be mine
Or soon or late, yet out of season, thus
I woo thee roughly, for thou carest not
How roughly men may woo thee so they win —
Thus — thus : the soul flies out and dies in the air.

But to the peasant mother in *Rizpah* it means
the fulfilment and recompense of her intense,
unquestioning passion of maternity : —

Election, Election and Reprobation — it 's all very well.
But I go to-night to my boy, and I shall not find him in
Hell.
For I cared so much for my boy that the Lord has look'd
into my care,
And He means me I 'm sure to be happy with Willy, I
know not where.

Nothing could be sharper than the con-
trasts among these six poems; nothing more
perfect than the consistency of thought and
feeling and utterance, with the character in
each.

Maud, the largest of the character-pieces, differs from the others in its method. It is lyrical in form; but instead of being a dramatic lyric, it is a lyrical drama. It has all the elements of interest which belong to the drama, — change of scene, development of plot, sudden catastrophe; and, although only one of the characters appears upon the stage, the others are felt in the story. It is a wonderfully consistent and searching study of the action of romantic love and tragic error upon a mind with a taint of hereditary insanity. There is but one speaker in the poem; but a marvellous effect of variety is given to it by the changes in rhythm and style in the different cantos. Tennyson has never written anything which is richer in music or more alive with passionate feeling. The metre sometimes seems irregular, but there is always an air, a movement, a rhythmic beat which underlies it; and when you have found that, you understand how perfectly melodious it is. The chief beauty of the poem lies in the clearness with which it shows the redeeming, healing, purifying power of love. It transforms the hero from a selfish misanthrope to a true man.

Of Tennyson's complete dramas, I have

said elsewhere that which seemed to me
needful and fitting. Let me only beg you
to study them for yourself, — at least the
historic trilogy, — and not to be satisfied
with taking the judgment of other people.

The finished epics, also, I have tried to
criticise in another place. *The Princess* is
the one of Tennyson's poems which stands
most in need of notes. It is fortunate that
they have been supplied by such an accom-
plished scholar as Dr. W. J. Rolfe, in his
annotated edition. For my own part, I am
inclined to think that this very need, which
must arise from obscurity in the allusions
and complexity in the diction, marks the
poem as belonging to a lower order than
Tennyson's best.

The epic entitled *Idylls of the King*, be-
sides its interest as the broadest and noblest
piece of imaginative work that Tennyson has
done, is the poem in which you may most
wisely make a careful study of his poetic
manner. It is common to speak of the
Idylls as a gorgeous mediæval tapestry, full
of rich colour and crowded with elaborately
wrought figures. But I should like you to
discover whether there is not something
more precious in them; whether the very

style has not rarer and finer qualities than
mere ornament. Take some of the best
passages, in which the so-called "Tenny-
sonian manner" is quite distinct, and ex-
amine them thoroughly. For example, here
is Arthur's description of his Round Table,
from the Idyll of *Guinevere:* —

> But I was first of all the kings who drew
> The knighthood-errant of this realm and all
> The realms together under me, their Head,
> In that fair Order of my Table Round,
> A glorious company, the flower of men,
> To serve as model for the mighty world,
> And be the fair beginning of a time.
> I made them lay their hands in mine and swear
> To reverence the King, as if he were
> Their conscience, and their conscience as their King,
> To break the heathen and uphold the Christ,
> To ride abroad redressing human wrongs,
> To speak no slander, no, nor listen to it,
> To honour his own word as if his God's,
> To lead sweet lives in purest chastity,
> To love one maiden only, cleave to her,
> And worship her by years of noble deeds,
> Until they won her; for indeed I knew
> Of no more subtle master under heaven
> Than is the maiden passion for a maid,
> Not only to keep down the base in man,
> But teach high thought, and amiable words,
> And courtliness, and the desire of fame,
> And love of truth, and all that makes a man.

Now there is no mistaking this for the

work of any other poet of our century. It belongs to Tennyson as obviously as if he had signed his name to every line. But what is it that gives the style its personal flavour, what constitutes the "Tennysonianism," as Mr. Howells calls it? Certainly it is not any redundancy of ornament, or opulence of epithet. This is not elaborate, decorative verse. The words are familiar and simple; most of them are monosyllables. There is but a single instance of alliteration. I think the peculiar effect, the sense of rich and perfect art, comes from the flow of the words. It is the movement that makes the style. And this movement has three qualities. First, sweetness; not a word is harsh, abrupt, strange; the melody flows without a break. Then, certainty; this comes from the sense of order and proportion; every word fits into its place. Then, strength; the strength which consists in fulness of thought and fewness of words.

Reflect on the ideal of a true aristocracy which is expressed in this brief passage. It must begin with reverence and obedience; for only they are fit to command who have learned to obey. It must be brave and helpful, daring to resist the heathen invaders and devoted to the redress of human wrongs. It must be pure in thought and word and deed; for the thinking and speaking evil of others is one of the besetting sins of an aristocracy, and the spirit of slander is twin-sister to the spirit of lust. It must not banish the passion of love, nor brutalize it, but lift it up, and idealize it as the transfiguration of life, and make it a true worship with a ritual of noble deeds. And out of all this will come the right manhood, in thought, in speech, in manners, in ambition, in sincerity, "in all that makes a man." Now the art which can put this broad and strong conception of a class worthy to rule and to lead society, into a score of lines, so clear that they can be read without effort, and so melodious that they fill the ear with pleasure, is exquisite. I think more than anything else, it is this presence of a pure ideal shining through a refined and balanced verse, this union of moral and metrical harmony, that marks the consummation of the Tennysonian manner in the *Idylls of the King*.

I have no time to speak of the "Patriotic Poems," except to say that they ought to be studied together, because there is something in almost every one of them which is essential to the full understanding of the poet's conception of loyalty and liberty and order, as the three elements of a perfect state.

The last division in the arrangement which I have made is " Poems of the Inner Life." You can probably conjecture why it is last. Partly because it is more difficult, and partly because it is higher, in the sense that it gives a more direct revelation of the personality of the poet. It is for this reason that we should not be in haste to enter it. For it is always best to look first at the fact, and then at the explanation; first at a man's objective work, and then at the account which he gives of himself and the spirit in which he has laboured.

The group of poems in which Tennyson deals with art is important, not only for the poems themselves, but also for the light which they throw upon his artistic principles and tastes. It is not altogether by chance that the poets to whom he gives greeting are Milton, Virgil, Dante, and Victor Hugo. In *The Poet* you will find his early conception of the power of poetry; in *The Poet's Mind*, his thought of its purity; in *The Poet's Song*, his avowal that its charm depends upon faith in the immortal future.

The Palace of Art is an allegory of the impotence of art when separated from human love. *The Flower* tells, in a symbolic manner, his experience with unreasoning critics. *The Spiteful Letter* and *Literary Squabbles* are reminiscences of the critical warfare which raged around him in his youth, and made him sometimes forget his own principle of doing his work "as quietly and as well as possible without much heeding the praise or the dispraise."

But to my mind the most important, and in some respects the most beautiful, of these art-poems, is *Merlin and The Gleam*. The wonder is that none of the critics seem to have recognized it for what it really is,— the poet's own description of his life-work, and his clear confession of faith as an idealist.

> The light that never was on sea or land,
> The consecration, and the Poet's dream," —

this is the "Gleam" that Tennyson has followed. It glanced first on the world of fancy with its melodies and pictures, dancing fairies, and falling torrents. Then it touched the world of humanity; and the stories of man's toil and conflict, the faces of human love and heroism, were revealed. Then it

illuminated the world of imagination; and
the great epic of Arthur was disclosed to the
poet's vision in its spiritual meaning, the
crowning of the blameless king. Then it
passed through the valley of the shadow of
death, and clothed it with light: —

> And broader and brighter
> The Gleam flying onward,
> Wed to the melody,
> Sang thro' the world;
> And slower and fainter,
> Old and weary,
> But eager to follow,
> I saw, whenever
> In passing it glanced upon
> Hamlet or city,
> That under the Crosses
> The dead man's garden,
> The mortal hillock
> Would break into blossom;
> And so to the land's
> Last limit I came —
> And can no longer,
> But die rejoicing,
> For thro' the Magic
> Of Him the Mighty,
> Who taught me in childhood,
> There on the border
> Of boundless Ocean,
> And all but in Heaven
> Hovers The Gleam.
>
> Not of the sunlight,
> Not of the moonlight,

Not of the starlight!
O young Mariner,
Down to the haven,
Call your companions,
Launch your vessel,
And crowd your canvas,
And, ere it vanishes
Over the margin,
After it, follow it,
Follow The Gleam.

That is the confession of a poet's faith in
the Ideal. It is the cry of a prophet to the
younger singers of a faithless and irresolute
generation.

Among the poems which touch more
broadly upon the common experience of
mankind in love and sorrow and death, you
will find, first, a group which are alike only
in their manner of treatment. It is allegor-
ical, mystical, emblematic, — find a name for
it if you will. I mean that these poems
convey their meaning under a mask; they
use a symbolic language, just as *Merlin* and
The Flower do in the preceding group.
You must read *The Deserted House, The
Voyage, The Sailor Boy, The Islet, The
Vision of Sin, The Voice and the Peak*, for
their secret significance. Then come three
precious fragments of philosophy more di-
rectly uttered. *Will, Wages*, and *Flower*

in the Crannied Wall go down to the very roots of human action, and aspiration, and thought. Then follows a group of poems more personal, varied in manner, and dealing in different moods with the sorrow of death. Their deepest and sweetest note is reached in the two lyrics which sprang out of the poet's grief for the death of Arthur Hallam. The world has long since accepted the first of these as the perfect song of mourning love. "*Break, break, break,*" once heard, is never to be forgotten. It is the melody of tears. But the fragment called *In the Valley of Cauteretz* seems to me no less perfect in its way. And surely a new beauty comes into both of the poems when we read them side by side. For the early cry of longing, —

> But O for the touch of a vanish'd hand
> And the sound of a voice that is still!

finds an answer in the later assurance of consolation, —

> And all along the valley, by rock and cave and tree,
> The voice of the dead was a living voice to me.

Of the final group of poems I shall say nothing, because it will not be possible to say enough. *In Memoriam* alone would require a volume, if one attempted to speak of it adequately. Indeed, no less than six

such volumes have been written, four in Eng-
land by F. W. Robertson, Alfred Gatty,
Elizabeth R. Chapman, and Joseph Jacobs,
two in America by Profs. Thomas Davidson
and John F. Genung. If you need an anal-
ysis or commentary on the poem you can
find it easily. The one thing that I hope
you will feel in reading this great poem and
the others which are grouped with it, is that
they are real records of the inward conflict
between doubt and faith, and that in this
conflict faith has the victory. And you may
well ask yourself whether this very victory
has not meant the winning, and unsealing,
and guarding, of the fountain-head of Ten-
nyson's poetic power. How many of his
noblest poems, *Locksley Hall, The May
Queen, The Leper's Bride, Rizpah, Guine-
vere, Enoch Arden*, find their uplifting in-
spiration, and reach their climax, in " the
evidence of things not seen, the substance of
things hoped for." Could he have written
anything of his best without that high faith
in an immortal life which he has expressed
in the rolling lines of *Vastness*, and in that
last supreme, faultless lyric *Crossing the
Bar?* Can any man be a poet without
faith in God and his own soul?

An answer to this question, clear and solemn as a voice from beyond the grave, comes in the posthumous volume entitled *The Death of Œnone, Akbar's Dream, and Other Poems.* Among the longer pieces there are three short poems, profoundly and unmistakably personal, which are like majestic chords preluding the large and perfect music of immortality.

The first is *Doubt and Prayer*, closing with the splendid lines : —

> Let blow the trumpet strongly when I pray,
> Till this embattled wall of unbelief,
> My prison, not my fortress, fall away !
> Then, if Thou willest, let my day be brief,
> So Thou wilt strike Thy glory through the day.

The second is *God and the Universe*, in which the courage of the soul to believe in God is asserted against the belittling and overwhelming immensity of " the myriad worlds, His shadow."

The third is that swan-song of the dying poet, *The Silent Voices*, reëchoed and prolonged by the choral music that flowed around him as he was carried to his last repose in the Abbey of Westminster, —

> Call me not so often back,
> Silent voices of the dead !

Call me rather, silent voices,
Forward to the starry track
Glimmering up the heights beyond me,
On, and always on !

And now when you turn to look back on
your study of Tennyson, what are you to
think of him? Is he a great poet? Your
reply to that will depend on whether you
think the Nineteenth Century is a great cen-
tury. For there can be no doubt that he
represents the century better than any other
man. The thoughts, the feelings, the desires,
the conflicts, the aspirations of our age are
mirrored in his verse. And if you say that
this alone prevents him from being great,
because greatness must be solitary and inde-
pendent, I answer, No; for the great poet
does not anticipate the conceptions of his
age, he only anticipates their expression.
He says what is in the heart of the people,
and says it so beautifully, so lucidly, so
strongly, that he becomes their voice. Now
if this age of ours, with its renaissance of art
and its catholic admiration of the beautiful
in all forms, classical and romantic ; with its
love of science and its joy in mastering the
secrets of Nature ; with its deep passion of
humanity protesting against social wrongs

and dreaming of social regeneration; with its introspective spirit searching the springs of character and action; with its profound interest in the problems of the unseen, and its reaction from the theology of the head to the religion of the heart, — if this age of ours is a great age, then Tennyson is a great poet, for he is the clearest, sweetest, strongest voice of the century.

A VALEDICTION

TENNYSON

IN LUCEM TRANSITUS.

OCTOBER 6, 1892.

FROM the misty shores of midnight, touched with splen-
dours of the moon,
To the singing tides of heaven, and the light more clear
than noon,
Passed a soul that grew to music till it was with God in
tune.

Brother of the greatest poets, true to nature, true to art;
Lover of Immortal Love, uplifter of the human heart,
Who shall cheer us with high music, who shall sing, if
thou depart?

Silence here, — for love is silent, gazing on the lessening
sail;
Silence here, — for grief is voiceless when the mighty
poets fail;
Silence here, — but far beyond us, many voices crying,
Hail!

APPENDIX

A CHRONOLOGY OF TENNYSON'S
LIFE AND WORKS.

This Chronology has been greatly enlarged since the first edition, and is now revised by reference to the admirable *Memoir of Tennyson*, by his son, Hallam, Lord Tennyson. It contains an outline of the principal events in the poet's life, a complete list of his publications, and a catalogue of the most important articles and books about him. It thus presents to the reader the materials for a careful study of the development of Tennyson's poetical art and the growth of his fame.

July, 1898.

CHRONOLOGY.

1809. ALFRED, the fourth son of the Rev. George Clayton, and Elizabeth Fytche, TENNYSON, was born at Somersby in Lincolnshire, August 6.

⁎ In regard to the accuracy of this date there need be no further doubt. Lord Tennyson has been kind enough to write me that 'he thinks that he was probably born in the early morning of the 6th, just after midnight. His mother used to keep his birthday on August 6th.' Since then Mr. C. J. Caswell has made a careful examination of the date in the Baptismal Register at Somersby, and writes that the figure is a 6, which has been mistaken for a 5 on account of the fading of the ink on the left side of the loop.

1816. Alfred Tennyson entered Louth Grammar School.

1820. Alfred Tennyson left Louth Grammar School at Christmas. Charles left at Midsummer, 1821.

1827. POEMS BY TWO BROTHERS. London: Printed for W. Simpkin and R. Marshall, and J. & J. Jackson, Louth. MDCCCXXVII., pp. xii, 228. Charles and Alfred Tennyson published this book anonymously.

⁎ For the copyright Jackson paid £20; but one half of this sum was to be taken out in books from Jackson's shop. The volume of poems was printed in two forms, one on large, the other on small paper.

1828. Alfred Tennyson entered Trinity College, Cambridge, in October.

Among his intimate friends were Arthur Henry Hallam, Richard Monckton Milnes, John Mitchell Kemble, William

354   *APPENDIX.*

Henry Brookfield, Henry Alford, James Spedding, and Rich-
ard Chevenix Trench.

1829. TIMBUCTOO: A Poem which obtained the Chan-
cellor's Medal at the Cambridge Commencement,
M.DCCC.XXIX. By A. Tennyson, of Trinity College.
Printed in "Prolusiones Academicæ; MDCCCXXIX.
Cantabrigiæ : typis academicis excudit Joannes
Smith." pp. 41.

₊ This was burlesqued by William Makepeace Thackeray
in *The Snob*, an undergraduate periodical ; and highly praised
in *The Athenæum* (July 22, 1829), of which Frederick Deni-
son Maurice and John Sterling were the editors.

1830. POEMS, CHIEFLY LYRICAL, by Alfred Tennyson.
London : Effingham Wilson, Royal Exchange,
Cornhill, 1830. pp. 154, and leaf of Errata.
Tennyson and Hallam visited the Pyrenees to-
gether.

Charles Tennyson published *Sonnets and Fugitive Pieces*,
by Charles Tennyson, Trin. Coll. Cambridge : published by
R. Bridges, Market Hill, and sold by John Richardson, 91,
Royal Exchange, London. pp. 83.

₊ William Wordsworth wrote from Cambridge : "We
have also a respectable show of blossom in poetry — two
brothers of the name of Tennyson ; one in particular not a
little promising."

1831. Contributed "Anacreontics," "No More," and
"A Fragment " to *The Gem : A Literary Annual.*
London: W. Marshall ; also a Sonnet, "Check
every outflash, every ruder sally," to *The English-
man's Magazine,* August.
Tennyson's father died at Somersby, March 16,
aged 52.

₊ The *Poems, chiefly Lyrical,* were reviewed with fa-
vour in *The Westminster Review,* January ; in *The Tatler,*
February 24 — March 3, by Leigh Hunt ; and in *The Eng-
lishman's Magazine,* August, by A. H. Hallam.

1832. POEMS by Alfred Tennyson. London : Edward
Moxon, 64, New Bond Street. MDCCCXXXIII. pp.
163. (This is properly called the edition of 1833.)

Contributed a Sonnet, " Me my own fate to last-
ing sorrow doometh," to *Friendship's Offering:
A Literary Album*. London: Smith, Elder & Co.;
and a Sonnet, " There are three things which fill
my heart with sighs," to *The Yorkshire Literary
Annual*. London: Longmans & Co.

✱ Professor John Wilson (" Christopher North ") at-
tacked Tennyson as " the pet of a Cockney coterie," in
Blackwood's Magazine for May.

The Athenæum, for December 1st, had a notice of the 1833
poems.

1833. Reprinted the Sonnet, " Check every outflash,
every ruder sally," in *Friendship's Offering*.

Printed THE LOVER'S TALE. By Alfred Tenny-
son. London: Edward Moxon, 64, New Bond
Street. MDCCCXXXIII. pp. 60. This was immedi-
ately suppressed and withdrawn from the press,
because the author felt "the imperfection of the
poem."

✱ A very severe criticism of the 1833 poems appeared in
The Quarterly Review for July, and was attributed to the
editor, John Gibson Lockhart.

A review of *Poems, chiefly Lyrical*, by W. J. Fox, in *The
Monthly Repository* for January.

Samuel Taylor Coleridge said in his " Table Talk : " " I
have not read through all Mr. Tennyson's poems, which have
been sent to me, but I think there are some things of a good
deal of beauty in what I have seen. The misfortune is, that
he has begun to write verses without very well understand-
ing what metre is."

On September 15, Arthur Henry Hallam died
suddenly at Vienna.

1834. *✱* *Remains in Verse and Prose of Arthur Henry Hallam*.
Printed by W. Nicol, 51 Pall Mall. MDCCCXXXIV. pp. xl, 363.

1835. *✱* John Stuart Mill reviewed Tennyson's poems with
great fairness and appreciation in *The Westminster Review*
for July.

1837. Contributed Stanzas, " O, that 't were possible "
(the germ of " Maud "), to *The Tribute:* edited by
Lord Northampton. London: John Murray. "St.
Agnes" to *The Keepsake:* edited by Lady Emme-
line Stuart Wortley. London: Longmans & Co.

The Tennyson family left Somersby, and moved
to High Beach in Epping Forest.

⁎⁎ *The Edinburgh Review* for October noticed Tennyson
for the first time, and said that his stanzas in *The Tribute*
" showed the hand of a true poet."

Walter Savage Landor wrote to a friend on December 9:
" Yesterday a Mr. Moreton, a young man of rare judgment,
read to me a manuscript by Mr. Tennyson very different in
style from his printed poems. The subject is the death of
Arthur. It is more Homeric than any poem of our time,
and rivals some of the noblest parts of the Odyssea."

1841. The Tennyson family moved to Boxley, near
Maidstone. Tennyson spent much time in Lou-
don with Fitzgerald, Sterling, Milnes, Thackeray,
Landor, Carlyle, etc.

1842. MORTE D'ARTHUR, DORA, AND OTHER IDYLS.
By Alfred Tennyson. London: Edward Moxon,
Dover Street. MDCCCXLII. pp. 67.

(A trial book, printed but never published, con-
taining eight blank verse poems, subsequently in-
cluded in the following publication.)

POEMS by Alfred Tennyson. In Two Volumes.
London: Edward   Moxon,   Dover   Street.
MDCCCXLII.   pp. vii, 233 ; vii, 231.

⁎⁎ These volumes were reviewed by Richard Monckton
Milnes (Lord Houghton) in *The Westminster Review*, Octo-
ber ; by John Sterling in *The Quarterly Review:* and
anonymously in *The Examiner*, May 28 ; *Tait's Edinburgh
Magazine*, August ; *The London University Magazine*, De-
cember ; and *The Christian Examiner*, Boston, U. S. A.,
November. All of the criticisms were respectful, and most
of them highly laudatory.

Within a year Carlyle, Dickens, Miss Mitford, Margaret Fuller, Emerson, and Poe were speaking of Tennyson with enthusiasm.

Five hundred copies had been sold by September 8th.

1843. Second edition of Poems in Two Volumes.

** Several malicious parodies of Tennyson appeared in the "Bon Gaultier Ballads," in *Tait's* and *Fraser's* magazines.

Tennyson's Poems reviewed by James Spedding in *Edinburgh Review*, April.

1844. About this time Tennyson passed through serious money troubles, losing nearly all his small property. His health failed, and he was obliged to spend some time at a water-cure establishment to obtain relief from severe hypochondria.

** Tennyson's portrait and a sketch of his character in Richard Hengist Horne's *A New Spirit of the Age*. London: Smith, Elder & Co.

** In *The Democratic Review*, New York, January, Mrs. Kemble reviewed Tennyson's poems, and Edgar Allan Poe wrote in the December number, "I am not sure that Tennyson is not the greatest of poets."

1845. Received a pension of £200, through Sir Robert Peel; and published a third edition of Poems in Two Volumes.

** Sir Edward Bulwer Lytton attacked Tennyson in *The New Timon: a Romance of London*. Henry Colburn.

Wordsworth wrote in a letter to Professor Henry Reed of Philadelphia: "Tennyson is decidedly the first of our living poets, and I hope will live to give the world still better things."

Living Poets; and their services to the causes of Political Freedom and Human Progress. By W. J. Fox. Published from the Reporter's notes. London: 1845. Notice of Tennyson in Vol. i. pp. 248-265.

1846. Fourth edition of the Poems (and last in two volumes). Contributed "The New Timon and the Poets" (a bitter reply to Bulwer) to *Punch*, February 28; and "Afterthought" (a repentance for that reply) to *Punch*, March 7.

Tennyson visited Switzerland with Edward
Moxon, his publisher.

The Tennyson family were living at Cheltenham.

₊ James Russell Lowell on Keats and Tennyson in *Con-
versations on the Poets.* Cambridge (U. S. A.), 1846.

1847. THE PRINCESS; A MEDLEY. By Alfred Tenny-
son. London: Edward Moxon, Dover Street.
MDCCCXLVII. pp. 164.

₊ A sketch of Tennyson in William Howitt's *Homes and
Haunts of the Most Eminent British Poets.*

1848. Second edition of the Princess; with a dedication
to Henry Lushington. Fifth edition of the Poems,
in one volume.

1849. Contributed lines, "To ——, You might have won
the poet's fame," to *The Examiner*, March 24.

₊ A review of the *Princess*, by Professor James Hadley
of Yale College, in *The New Englander*, May: another in *The
Edinburgh Review*, October, by Aubrey de Vere.

An extended criticism of the Fifth edition of Tennyson's
Poems in *The Westminster Review*, July.

1850. IN MEMORIAM. London: Edward Moxon, Dover
Street. MDCCCL. pp. vii, 210.

The second and third editions (with no change
but the correction of two typographical errors)
appeared in the same year.

Third edition of the Princess, very much altered,
and with the Songs added.

Sixth edition of the Poems.

Contributed lines, " Here often, when a child, I
lay reclin'd," to *The Manchester Athenæum Album*.

On June 13, Alfred Tennyson and Emily Sell-
wood were married at Shiplake Church, Oxford-
shire.

On November 19, Alfred Tennyson was ap-
pointed to succeed William Wordsworth (died
April 23) as Poet Laureate.

₊ Charles Kingsley published an essay on Tennyson in *Fraser's Magazine*, September.

In Memoriam was reviewed in *The Westminster Review*, October.

1851. Contributed Stanzas, "What time I wasted youthful hours," and "Come not when I am dead," to *The Keepsake:* edited by Miss Power. London: David Bogue.

Sonnet to W. C. Macready, read at the valedictory dinner to the actor, and printed in *The Household Narrative of Current Events*, February–March.

Seventh edition of the Poems, containing three new pieces, and the dedication "To the Queen."

Fourth edition of the Princess, with additions. Fourth edition of In Memoriam, adding section LIX, "O sorrow, wilt thou live with me?" Presented, as Poet Laureate, to the Queen, at Buckingham Palace, March 6.

Lived at Twickenham. Travelled in France and Italy.

1852. ODE ON THE DEATH OF THE DUKE OF WELLINGTON. By Alfred Tennyson, Poet Laureate. London: Edward Moxon. 1852. pp. 16. (November.)

Contributed "Britons, guard your own," to *The Examiner*, January 31; "The Third of February," and "Hands all round," to the same paper, February 7. These poems were called forth by the general excitement consequent on the *coup d'état* of Louis Napoleon.

Tennyson's oldest son, Hallam, was born at Twickenham, August 11.

1853. Eighth edition of the Poems, with additions. Fifth edition of the Princess, with additions.

Rented the estate of Farringford in the parish of Freshwater, Isle of Wight.

Second edition of the Ode on the Death of Wellington, containing additions.

1854. THE CHARGE OF THE LIGHT BRIGADE. First printed in *The Examiner*, December 9, afterwards on a quarto sheet for distribution among the soldiers before Sebastopol. (August, 1855.)

Tennyson's second son, Lionel, was born at Farringford, March 16.

₊ *Days and Hours.* By Frederick Tennyson. London: John W. Parker & Son, West Strand. 1854. pp. viii, 346.

F. D. Maurice dedicated his *Theological Essays* to Tennyson.

E. K. Kane, the Arctic explorer, named a cliff in Greenland, "Tennyson's Monument."

1855. MAUD, AND OTHER POEMS. By Alfred Tennyson, D. C. L., Poet Laureate. London: Edward Moxon. 1855. pp. 154.

The University of Oxford had conferred the degree of D. C. L. upon him in May.

₊ *Maud* was reviewed in *Blackwood's Magazine*, September; *The Edinburgh Review*, October; *The National Review*, October; and in *The North American Review*, October, by Rev. E. E. Hale.

George Brimley's essay on Tennyson was published in *Cambridge Essays*.

1856. Second edition of Maud, with many additions, pp. 164.

Purchased the estate of Farringford.

Dr. R. J. Mann published *Tennyson's 'Maud' Vindicated*, an *Explanatory Essay*. London: Jarrold & Sons.

1857. ENID AND NIMUË: THE TRUE AND THE FALSE. By Alfred Tennyson, D. C. L., Poet Laureate. London: Edward Moxon, Dover Street. 1857. pp. 139.

(A trial book, containing two Arthurian Idylls, afterwards called *Enid* and *Vivien*.)

An edition of the Poems, illustrated by Millais, Holman Hunt, Rossetti, and others, published by Moxon, and afterwards transferred to Routledge.

₊ Bayard Taylor visited Tennyson at Farringford, and walked with him along the cliffs. " I was struck with the variety of his knowledge. Not a little flower on the downs escaped his notice, and the geology of the coast, both terrestrial and submarine, was perfectly familiar to him. I thought of a remark I once heard from a distinguished English author (Thackeray), that Tennyson was the wisest man he knew."

1858. Added two stanzas to the National Anthem, on the marriage of the Princess Royal. Printed in *The Times*, January 26.

₊ Rev. F. W. Robertson gave an estimate of Tennyson in his *Lectures and Addresses*. London : Smith, Elder & Co. pp. 124–141.

1859. THE TRUE AND THE FALSE : Four Idylls of the King. By Alfred Tennyson, P. L., D. C. L. London : Edward Moxon & Co , Dover Street. 1859. pp. 261.

(A trial book, with practically the same contents as the following, except that the name Nimue stands in place of Vivien.)

IDYLLS OF THE KING. By Alfred Tennyson, D. C. L., Poet Laureate. London : Edward Moxon & Co., Dover Street. 1859. pp. 261.

Ten thousand copies were sold in the first week.

Contributed verses entitled "The Grandmother's Apology" to *Once a Week*, July 16. Visited Portugal with Francis Turner Palgrave.

The verses entitled "The War," signed "T," and printed in *The London Times*, May 9, were acknowledged by Lord Tennyson in 1891.

₊ Peter Bayne published *Tennyson and his Teachers.* James Hogg & Sons : Edinburgh and London.

The Idylls of the King were reviewed in Blackwood's

Magazine, November, and *Edinburgh Review*, July, by Coventry Patmore.

Rev. Alfred Gatty published *The Poetical Character: illustrated from the Works of Alfred Tennyson*, D. C. L., *Poet Laureate*. London: Bell & Daldy. pp. 29.

Tennyson's Poems reviewed in *The London Quarterly*, October, and in *The Westminster Review*, by John Nichol.

Henry Wadsworth Longfellow wrote in his diary: "Finished the four Idylls. The first and third could have come only from a great poet. The second and fourth do not seem to me so good." July 20, 1859. (The first and third were *Enid* and *Elaine;* the second and fourth were *Vivien* and *Guinevere*.)

1860. Contributed "Sea Dreams: An Idyll," to *Macmillan's Magazine*, January; and "Tithonus" to *The Cornhill Magazine*, February.

Tennyson made a tour to Cornwall and the Scilly Isles with Woolner, Palgrave, Holman Hunt, and Val Prinsep, — an Arthurian Pilgrimage.

⁎⁎ *Poems and Essays* by the late William Caldwell Roscoe. London: Chapman & Hall. pp. 1-37 on Tennyson.

"Poetical Works of Alfred Tennyson" reviewed by C. C. Everett in *The North American Review*, January.

1861. THE SAILOR BOY. London: Emily Faithfull & Co. Victoria Press, 1861. (25 copies for the author's use.)

This poem was contributed to THE VICTORIA REGIA: a volume of original contributions in Poetry and Prose. Edited by Adelaide A. Procter. London, 1861.

Revisited the Pyrenees, where he had travelled with Arthur Hallam.

Wrote "Helen's Tower," privately printed by Lord Dufferin.

1862. A new edition of the Idylls, with a dedication to the memory of Prince Albert.

Wrote an "Ode: May the First, 1862;" sung at

the opening of the International Exhibition; and printed in *Fraser's Magazine*, June.

A Pirated Edition of the Poems of 1830 and 1833 was printed in this year. It was suppressed by law, and has no bibliographical value whatever.

⁎ *An Index to In Memoriam.* London: Edward Moxon & Co. pp. 40.

An Analysis of In Memoriam by the late Rev. Frederick W. Robertson of Brighton. London: Smith, Elder & Co.

Remains in Verse and Prose of Arthur Henry Hallam. With a Preface and Memoir. London: John Murray, Albemarle Street. 1862. pp. lx, 305.

1863. Published on the arrival of the Princess Alexandra, March 7, A WELCOME. London: Edward Moxon & Co. pp. 4.

A WELCOME TO HER ROYAL HIGHNESS, THE PRINCESS OF WALES. From the Poet Laureate. Owen Jones, Illuminator. Day & Sons, Lithographers to the Queen. 1863.

Contributed "Attempts at Classic Metres in Quantity" to *The Cornhill Magazine*, December.

1864. ENOCH ARDEN, ETC. By Alfred Tennyson, D. C. L., Poet Laureate. London: Edward Moxon & Co., Dover Street. 1864. pp. 178.

The title of this volume in the proof sheets was IDYLLS OF THE HEARTH. A few copies were printed with this title-page.

Contributed an "Epitaph on the late Duchess of Kent" to *The Court Journal*, March 19.

⁎ "Wordsworth, Tennyson, and Browning; or, Pure, Ornate, and Grotesque Art," by Walter Bagehot in *The National Review*, November.

Enoch Arden was reviewed in *Blackwood's Magazine*, November; in the *Nouvelle Revue de Paris*, September, by A. Vermore; in *The Westminster Review*, October; in *The North British Review*, August; in *The North American Review*, October, by James Russell Lowell; in *Harper's Magazine*, October, by George William Curtis.

Hippolyte Adolphe Taine compared Tennyson unfavour-
ably with De Musset, in his *Histoire de la Littérature
Anglaise.* Paris: 1864.

Garibaldi visited Tennyson at Farringford.

Sonnets. By the Rev. Charles Turner, Vicar of Grasby,
Lincoln. London and Cambridge: Macmillan & Co. pp. viii,
102.

This was the brother of Tennyson who had joined with him
in writing the *Poems by Two Brothers.* He had dropped the
name of Tennyson in 1835 in order to assume an inheritance.

1865. A SELECTION FROM THE WORKS OF ALFRED
TENNYSON.   London: Edward Moxon & Co.,
Dover Street.   This volume contains six new
poems: "The Captain," "On a Mourner," "Home
they brought him slain with spears," and three
"Sonnets to a Coquette."   pp. 256.

Tennyson was elected a member of "The Club"
(Dr. Samuel Johnson's), and made a tour in France
and Germany.

Tennyson's mother died February 21, aged 84.

⁎⁎ J. Leicester Warren contributed "The Bibliography of
Tennyson" to *The Fortnightly Review*, October 1.

Three Great Teachers: Carlyle, Tennyson, and Ruskin.
By Alexander H. Japp, LL. D. London: Smith, Elder & Co.

1866. *⁎⁎* *Enoch Arden (continued)*, by C. H. P. Not by the
"LAUREATE," but a timid hand that grasped the Poet's
golden lyre, "and back recoil'd — e'en at the sound herself
had made." 1866. [No printer's or publisher's name. A
pamphlet of 12 pp. Blank verse. Exact transcript of title-
page from "Enoch" to "1866."]

*Tennysoniana: Notes Bibliographical and Critical on Early
Poems of Alfred & C. Tennyson,* etc., etc. Basil Montague
Pickering: 196, Piccadilly, London, W.: MDCCCLXVI. pp. 170.
(Pages 30–41 were omitted while the work was passing through
the press. In this edition, therefore, the *verso* of page 29 is
page 42.) The author's name is not on the title-page; but
the book is known to be the work of Richard Herne Shep-
herd.

Enoch Arden reviewed in *The London Quarterly Review*
for January, 1866.

Mr. George Grove printed a commentary on "Tears, idle Tears," in *Macmillan's Magazine* for November; and one "On a Song in the Princess," in *The Shilling Magazine* for February.

1867. THE WINDOW: OR THE LOVES OF THE WRENS. Printed at the private press of Sir Ivor Bertie Guest of Canford Manor, now Lord Wimborne.

These songs were set to music by Mr. Arthur Sullivan, and so published in December, 1870.

THE VICTIM. By Alfred Tennyson, D. C. L., Poet Laureate. Printed at the same place and in the same manner.

Tennyson purchased the Greenhill estate on the top of Blackdown on the northern border of Sussex, three miles from the village of Haslemere, in Surrey. In 1868 he began the erection of a house from designs by Mr. J. T. Knowles. The place was called Aldworth, and was the poet's summer home.

₊ John K. Ingram, LL. D., reviewed Tennyson's Works in *Afternoon Lectures on Literature and Art.* Fourth Series. London: Bell & Daldy. pp. 47-94.

"Studies in Tennyson," by W. S., in *Belgravia.*

1868. Contributed "The Victim" to *Good Words*, January; "On a Spiteful Letter," to *Once a Week*, January; "Wages" to *Macmillan's Magazine*, February; "1865-1866" to *Good Words*, March; and "Lucretius" to *Macmillan's Magazine*, May.

"Lucretius" was also printed in an American magazine called *Every Saturday*, with some lines not contained in the English version. It appeared also as a small book with the following title-page:

LUCRETIUS. By Alfred Tennyson, Poet Laureate. Cambridge, Mass. Printed for private circulation. 1868. pp. 27.

₊ Professor R. C. Jebb praised the historical accuracy of "Lucretius" in *Macmillan's Magazine*, June.

8. Cheetham printed a scholarly review of the Arthurian Legends in *The Contemporary*, April.

A Study of the Works of Alfred Tennyson. By Edward Campbell Tainsh. London: Chapman & Hall. Second edition, 1869. pp. 268.

Jerrold, Tennyson, and Macaulay. By James Hutchison Stirling, LL. D. Edinburgh: Edmunston & Douglas. pp. 243.

Henry Wadsworth Longfellow visited Farringford.

Small Tableaux. By the Rev. Charles Turner, Vicar of Grasby, Lincoln. London: Macmillan & Co. pp. viii, 114.

1869. The Holy Grail and Other Poems. By Alfred Tennyson, D. C. L., Poet Laureate. Strahan & Co., Publishers, 56, Ludgate Hill, London. 1870. pp. 222. Of this volume 40,000 copies were ordered in advance. It was published late in the year, and made two announcements: The collection of the eight Idylls of the King in proper order "to-day published;" and the Pocket Volume Edition of Mr. Tennyson's Works, in ten volumes, price, £2 5s., "now ready."

Tennyson was one of the founders of "The Metaphysical Society" in this year.

*** D. Barron Brightwell published his *Concordance to the Entire Works of Alfred Tennyson.* London: E. Moxon & Co.

An article on "The Poetry of the Period," in *Temple Bar*, for May, declared that "Mr. Tennyson has no sound pretensions to be called a great poet." This review was probably by Mr. Alfred Austin, his successor in the Poet Laureateship.

Mr. Tennyson and Mr. Browning. By Edward Dowden, in *Afternoon Lectures in Literature and Arts*, published in 1869, reprinted in *Studies in Literature.* London: Kegan Paul, Trench & Co. Fifth Edition. 1889.

1870. The Window: or, The Songs of the Wrens. Words written for music by Alfred Tennyson. The music by Arthur Sullivan. London: Strahan & Co. 1871. (Published in December, 1870.)

₊ Henry Alford printed a review of *The Idylls of the King* in *The Contemporary*, January.

"The Epic of Arthur " in *The Edinburgh Review*, April, 1870.

"Alfred Tennyson," critical article by E. Camerini, in the *Nuova Antologia*. Florence, February.

Mr. J. Hain Friswell had a chapter on Alfred Tennyson in *Modern Men of Letters Honestly Criticized*. London: Hodder & Stoughton. 1870. pp. 145-146.

A letter on the same subject was printed by J. T. Knowles in *The Spectator*.

1871. THE LAST TOURNAMENT. By Alfred Tennyson, D. C. L., Poet Laureate. Strahan & Co. 56, Ludgate Hill, London. 1871. [All rights reserved.] This was a trial book, not published.

Contributed "The Last Tournament" to *The Contemporary*, December.

₊ Rev. H. R. Haweis had an article on "The Songs of the Wrens" in *The Saint Paul's Magazine*, February.

1872. GARETH AND LYNETTE, ETC. By Alfred Tennyson, D. C. L., Poet Laureate. Strahan & Co. 56, Ludgate Hill, London. 1852. pp. 136.

The Library Edition of Tennyson's Works, in seven volumes, was published by Strahan & Co. 1872-1873. It contained important additions, viz., "Alexander," "The Bridesmaid," "The Third of February, 1852," "Literary Squabbles," "On a Spiteful Letter," and "Epilogue" to the Idylls of the King. The Idylls were now printed in their sequence of time, ten in number.

Contributed "England and America in 1782" to *The New York Ledger;* for this poem one thousand pounds were paid.

₊ Richard Holt Hutton contributed a review of Tennyson to *Macmillan's Magazine*, December.

Robert Buchanan printed an article entitled "Tennyson's Charm " in *St. Paul's Magazine*, March.

1873. Tennyson was offered a baronetcy, but declined.

⁎₊⁎ J. Hutchinson printed an article on "Tennyson as a Botanist" in *St. Paul's Magazine*, October.

Tennyson. By Walter Irving. Edinburgh: Maclachlan & Stewart. pp. 28.

A burlesque of the Idylls of the King was printed in *Blackwood's Magazine*, January, under the title of "Sir Tray: an Arthurian Idyll."

The Rev. Drummond Rawnsley published an article on "Lincolnshire Scenery and Character as illustrated by Mr. Tennyson" in *Macmillan's Magazine*, December, 1873.

Master-Spirits. By Robert Buchanan. London: Henry S. King & Co. 1873. pp. 349. Essay on "Tennyson, Heine, and De Musset." pp. 54–88.

1874. A WELCOME TO MARIE ALEXANDROVNA, DUCH-ESS OF EDINBURGH. This was first printed in *The Times*, and afterwards issued on a separate sheet.

The Cabinet Edition of Tennyson's Works, in 12 volumes, published by H. S. King & Co., 1874, contained important additions.

Tennyson was offered a baronetcy, but declined. The second offer came through Disraeli.

1875. QUEEN MARY. A DRAMA. By Alfred Tennyson. London: Henry S. King & Co. 1875. pp. viii, 278.

Prefixed a Sonnet to Lord Lyttelton's *Memoir of William Henry Brookfield*.

The author's Edition of Tennyson's Works was published by Henry S. King & Co., in six volumes, crown 8vo, 1875–1877. Important changes were made in this edition, and *Maud* was entitled "a monodrama."

⁎₊⁎ Edmund Clarence Stedman published a review of Tennyson in *Victorian Poets*. Boston: Houghton, Mifflin & Co. This was supplemented by an additional chapter in the edition of 1887.

The Religion of our Literature. By George McCrie. London: Hodder & Stoughton. pp. 110–180.

" Virgil and Tennyson," in *Blackwood's Magazine*, November. By " a Lincolnshire Rector " [Rev. Drummond Rawnsley].

In this year a pirated edition of *The Lover's Tale* was brought out by R. H. Shepherd, and suppressed by law, Tennyson paying the costs because he had heard that Shepherd was poor.

1876. HAROLD. A DRAMA. By Alfred Tennyson. London: Henry S. King & Co. 1877. pp. viii, 161.

⁎ *Queen Mary* was produced at the *Lyceum Theatre* by Miss Batemen and Henry Irving, in April.

Harold was reviewed in *The London Times*, October 18, by Professor Jebb.

Robert Browning dedicated the two volumes of his " Selections " " to Alfred Tennyson : in Poetry illustrious and consummate : in Friendship noble and sincere."

1877. Contributed a prefatory Sonnet to the first number of *The Nineteeenth Century*, March ; also " Montenegro," a Sonnet, to the May number ; a " Sonnet to Victor Hugo " to *The Nineteenth Century*, June ; " Achilles over the Trench " to *The Nineteenth Century*, August.

Lines on Sir John Franklin in Westminster Abbey.

⁎ Bayard Taylor printed a criticism of Tennyson in *The International Review*, New York, May.

Longfellow's Sonnet entitled *Wapentake* published in *The Atlantic Monthly*, December.

1878. Contributed " Sir Richard Grenville : A Ballad of the Fleet," to *The Nineteenth Century*, March.

Made a tour in Ireland.

⁎ *Studies in the Idylls*. By Henry Elsdale. London : H. S. King & Co. 1878. pp. vii, 197.

1879. THE LOVER'S TALE. By Alfred Tennyson. London : C. Kegan Paul & Co., 1, Paternoster Square. 1879. pp. 95. (Includes *The Golden Supper*, first published in *The Holy Grail* volume in 1869).

This was a revision of the poem suppressed in 1833, and the publication was made necessary by the fact that it had been pirated.

Tennyson's play of THE FALCON was produced at the St. James Theatre with Mrs. Kendal as the heroine, December, and ran sixty-seven nights.

Contributed "Dedicatory Poem to the Princess Alice" and "The Defence of Lucknow" to *The Nineteenth Century* for April.

****** *Tennysoniana.* Second edition, revised and enlarged. London: Pickering & Co., 196, Piccadilly. MDCCCLXXIX. pp. viii, 208. (By Richard Herne Shepherd.)
Lessons from My Masters. By Peter Bayne. London: John Clarke & Co., 13 and 14 Fleet St. 1879. pp. viii, 437.

Tennyson's brother, the Rev. Charles Tennyson Turner, died at Cheltenham, April 25.

1880. BALLADS AND OTHER POEMS. By Alfred Tennyson. London: C. Kegan Paul & Co., 1, Paternoster Square. 1880. pp. vi, 184.

The Cabinet Edition of Tennyson's Works, in twelve volumes, published by C. Kegan Paul & Co., was completed in this year.

Contributed two poems to *St. Nicholas,* an American magazine for children, and "De Profundis" to *The Nineteenth Century,* May.

Prefixed lines entitled "Midnight, June 30, 1879," to Charles Tennyson Turner's *Collected Sonnets, Old and New.* London: C. Kegan Paul & Co. 1880. pp. xxii, 390.

Tennyson declined the nomination for Lord Rectorship of Glasgow University, on the ground that he was unwilling to be "a party candidate for the conservative club."

****** "A New Study of Tennyson," by J. Churton Collins. in *The Cornhill Magazine,* January and July, and July, 1881.
Theodore Watts wrote a sonnet "to Alfred Tennyson, on

his publishing, in his seventy-first year, the most richly various volume of English verse that has appeared in his own century."

"Tennyson's Poems," in *The British Quarterly Review*, reprinted in *Littell's Living Age* for December 25.

1881. The play of THE CUP was produced at the Lyceum Theatre, with Henry Irving and Ellen Terry in the leading parts, January 3. It ran for more than one hundred nights and was a decided success.

Contributed "Despair" to *The Nineteenth Century;* and "The Charge of the Heavy Brigade" to *Macmillan's Magazine.*

Sat to Millais for his portrait.

*** Mr. Walter E. Wace published *Alfred Tennyson, His Life and Works.* Edinburgh : Macniven & Wallace. pp. vii, 203.

A Key to Tennyson's In Memoriam. By Alfred Gatty, D. D. London : D. Bogue. pp. xi, 144.

"Mr. Tennyson's New Volume," by Sidney Colvin, in *Macmillan's Magazine,* January.

Mr. A. C. Swinburne published an article on "Tennyson and Musset," in *The Fortnightly Review,* February 1, 1881. Reprinted in *Miscellanies.* London: Chatto & Windus, 1886.

"Alfred Tennyson and His New Poems," by Enrico Nencioni, in *Fanfulla della Domenica,* Rome, April 10.

"A Study of Tennyson," by R. H. Stoddard, in *The North American Review,* July.

1882. The play of THE PROMISE OF MAY was produced at the Globe Theatre, under the direction of Mrs. Bernard-Beere, in November : a failure.

Hands all Round was recast as a patriotic song and printed with music by Mrs. Tennyson.

*** *A Study of the Princess.* By S. E. Dawson. Montreal : Dawson Brothers, Publishers. pp. 120.

"Maud," a critical article by Enrico Nencioni, in *Domenica Letteraria.* Rome : March 19.

1883. Tennyson accompanied Mr. Gladstone on a sea trip to Copenhagen, where they were received by the King and Queen of Denmark, the Czar and Czarina, the King and Queen of Greece, and the Princess of Wales.

Later in the year it was announced that Queen Victoria had offered a peerage to Tennyson, and he had accepted it.

Tennyson wrote the epitaph on Caxton, for the memorial window in St. Margaret's, Westminster.

Contributed *"Frater Ave atque Vale"* to *The Nineteenth Century*, March.

₊ "Alfred Tennyson," by Mrs. Anne Thackeray Ritchie, in *Harper's Magazine* for December.

"Milton and Tennyson," in *The Presbyterian Review*. New York. By Henry van Dyke.

The Earlier and Less-Known Poems of Tennyson. By C. E. Mathews. Birmingham : 1883. pp. 34. "In Memoriam," and "The Idylls of the King," critical articles by Enrico Neniconi, in *Fanfulla della Domenica*. Rome : May 6, and September 9.

1884. THE CUP AND THE FALCON. By Alfred, Lord Tennyson, Poet Laureate. London : Macmillan & Co. 1884. pp. 146.

BECKET. By Alfred, Lord Tennyson, Poet Laureate. London : Macmillan & Co. 1884. pp. 213.

Also a New and Revised Edition of his complete Works, in seven volumes; and in one volume, pp. v, 640, revised text.

Tennyson was gazetted Baron of Aldworth and Farringford, January 18, and took his seat in the House of Lords, March 11.

Contributed "Freedom" to Macmillan's Magazine for December; introductory verses to *Ros Rosarum*, by E. V. B. ; a verse to a small pamphlet printed for the benefit of the Chelsea Hospital for Women, and "Early Spring" to *The Youth's Companion*, Boston.

Elected President of the Incorporated Society of Authors.

***Mr. Henry J. Jennings published *Lord Tennyson. A Biographical Sketch.* London: Chatto & Windus. pp. vii, 270.

Tennyson's In Memoriam. Its Purpose and Structure. By John F. Genung. Boston: Houghton, Mifflin & Co. 1884. pp. vi, 199.

"The Genesis of Tennyson's ' Maud,'" by Richard Herne Shepherd, in *The North American Review* for October.

1885. TIRESIAS AND OTHER POEMS. By Alfred, Lord Tennyson, D. C. L., P. L. London: Macmillan & Co. 1885. pp. viii, 204. Dedicated "To my good friend, Robert Browning."

LYRICAL POEMS: selected and annotated by F. T. Palgrave. London: Macmillan & Co. 1885. pp. vii, 270.

Contributed "The Fleet" to *The Times,* April 23; "To H. R. H. Princess Beatrice" to *The Times,* July 23; "Vastness" to *Macmillan's Magazine,* November.

***Hon. Roden Noel reviewed "The Poetry of Tennyson" in *The Contemporary Review,* February.

Mr. Conde B. Pallen published a criticism of the "Idylls of the King," in *The Catholic World,* April.

Augustin Filon published an extended critique of Tennyson in the *Revue des Deux Mondes,* September.

Urbana Scripta. By Arthur Galton. London: Elliot Stock, 62, Paternoster Row. 1885. pp. v, 237. Essay on "Lord Tennyson," pp. 36–68.

Review of *Tiresias,* by T. H. Caine, in *The Academy,* vol. xxviii, p. 403.

1886. LOCKSLEY HALL SIXTY YEARS AFTER, ETC. By Alfred, Lord Tennyson, P. L., D. C. L. London: Macmillan & Co., and New York. 1886. pp. 201.

The "Ode to India and the Colonies" was written for the opening of the Colonial Exhibition in London, May 4.

A new complete edition in ten volumes (revised text), and in one volume (slight alterations).

₊ "Locksley Hall, etc.," was reviewed by Richard Holt Hutton (?) in *The Spectator*, December 18 ; by the Rt. Hon. W. E. Gladstone in *The Nineteenth Century*, January, 1887 ; and by Walt Whitman in *The Critic*, New York, January 1, 1887.

Jack and the Bean-Stalk, by Hallam Tennyson, published by Macmillan & Co. The illustrations are from unfinished sketches by Randolph Caldecott.

Lionel Tennyson died on the homeward voyage from India, April 20.

1887. Contributed "Carmen Sæcula" to *Macmillan's Magazine*, April.

₊ "The Genesis of 'In Memoriam,'" published by Richard Herne Shepherd, in *Walford's Antiquarian*.

Article on "The Palace of Art" in *The New Princeton Review*, vol. iv., by Henry van Dyke.

1888. A new edition of Tennyson's complete works published by Macmillan & Co., 1888-1889, in eight volumes. In this edition the idyll of *Geraint* was divided into *The Marriage of Geraint* and *Geraint and Enid*, and *Balin and Balan* was put into its proper place, thus completing the Epic as it now stands.

Tennyson had a severe illness in the autumn and winter of this year.

₊ *Studies on the Legend of the Holy Grail.* By Alfred Nutt. London : David Nutt.

A Companion to In Memoriam. By Elizabeth Rachel Chapman. London : Macmillan & Co., and New York. 1888. pp. 72.

The Tennyson Flora. Three Lectures by Leo H. Grindon. Published as an Appendix to the Report of the Manchester Field Naturalists and Archæological Society for the year 1887.

"Tennysonian Trees," an article in *The Gardener's Magazine* for December 29.

"Dethroning Tennyson," by A. C. Swinburne, in *The Nineteenth Century*, January.

"Tennyson's Idylls," by Anna Vernon Dorsey, in *The American Magazine*, May; and by R. W. Boodle, in *The Canadian Monthly*, April.

An article in the *Pall Mall Gazette*, December 20, entitled "Is Tennyson a Spiritualist ?"

1889. DEMETER AND OTHER POEMS. By Alfred, Lord Tennyson, P. L., D. C. L. London: Macmillan & Co., and New York. 1889. pp. vi, 175.

This volume was published on December 13, 1889, and it is said that 20,000 copies were sold within a week.

Contributed "The Throstle" to *The New Review* for October.

An edition of the complete poems in one volume (without "Demeter"), pp. v. 807, was published early in the year. In this edition we have for the first time the title, "Idylls of the King, In Twelve Books," and an Index of First Lines.

。* *The Poetry of Tennyson.* By Henry van Dyke. New York: Charles Scribner's Sons. London: Elkin Mathews. Vigo St. 1889. pp. xiii, 296.

Prolegomena to In Memoriam. By Thomas Davidson. Boston and New York: Houghton, Mifflin & Co. 1889. pp. vi, 177.

The Idylls of the King. By Alfred, Lord Tennyson. Illustrated. In shorthand by Arthur G. Doughty, M. A. The Dominion Illustrated Press, Montreal. 1889.

A volume containing three of Tennyson's poems: "To E. L." (Edmund Lear), "The Daisy," and "The Palace of Art," illustrated with drawings by Edmund Lear, the artist's portrait and Watts' portrait of Tennyson, was published by Boussod, Valadon & Co., London. One hundred copies signed by Lord Tennyson.

In the Magazines, among others, the following articles appeared: In *The Nineteenth Century*, March, "Tennyson as Prophet," by Frederic W. H. Myers; in *Scribner's Magazine*, August, "The Two Locksley Halls," by T. R. Lounsbury, and "Tennyson's First Flight," by Henry van Dyke; in *The*

Century Magazine, "The Bible in Tennyson," by Henry van Dyke. In *The Baptist Review* (U. S. A.), January, an article on "Tennyson's Art and Genius," by Eugene Parsons.

In *The Methodist Recorder*, February 28 to March 21, four articles on "The Poets Laureate of England," by Rev. George Lester.

In *The Spectator*, February 2, an article on "Tennyson's Undertones" discussed the question of spiritualism in his poetry.

Mr. Napier printed in Glasgow, for private circulation, one hundred copies of a volume entitled, "Homes and Haunts of Alfred Lord Tennyson."

Tennyson's eightieth birthday, on August 6, called out a great number of articles.   Editorials in the New York *Times*, *Tribune*, and *Herald ;* in *The Mail and Express*, by Mr. Edmund Gosse ; in *The Hartford Daily Times*, by Mr. Frank L. Burr ; in *The Athenæum*, a sonnet by Mr. Theodore Watts ; in *Macmillan's Magazine*, a sonnet by Rev. H. D. Rawnsley, and lines "To Lord Tennyson," by Lewis Morris.

1890. A portrait of Lord Tennyson, in his robes as D. C. L., was completed by Mr. G. F. Watts, and given to Trinity College, Cambridge.

A new edition of the Poetical Works (without the Dramas) in one volume, 18mo, pp. viii, 535, issued by Macmillan & Co. Also a new edition with the Dramas, in one volume, 8vo. pp. v, 842. The same as the edition of 1889, with *Demeter and Other Poems* added.

⁂ In Tennyson Land. By John Cuming Walters. Illustrated. London : George Redway. 1890. pp. 108.

The Isles of Greece. Sappho and Alcæus. By Frederick Tennyson, author of "Days and Hours." London and New York: Macmillan & Co. 1890. pp. xiv, 443.

Alfred Austin reviewed "Lord Tennyson's New Volume" in *The National Review*, January.   Mr. C. J. Caswell printed an article on "Tennyson's Schooldays" in *The Pall Mall Gazette*, June 19.   Mr. Eugene Parsons had an essay on Tennyson in *The Examiner* (New York), February, and another in *The Chautauquan*, June.   An article was published on "Tennyson and Browning" in *The Edinburgh Review.* "Tennyson : and After ? " in *The Fortnightly Review* for

May. "In King Arthur's Capital," by J. Cuming Walters, in November number of *Igdrasil* (the Journal of the Ruskin Reading Guild). "Christmas with Lord Tennyson," by Rev. George Lester, in *The Fireside Magazine*, December. "An Arthurian Journey" in *The Atlantic Monthly*, June.

In *The Atlantic Monthly* for March, 1890, Thomas Bailey Aldrich published a poem on "Tennyson."

1891. Contributed "A Song" to *The New Review* for March.

Other verses by Lord Tennyson have since appeared in print, viz., a stanza written in a volume of his poems presented to Princess Louise of Schleswig-Holstein, by representatives of the nurses of England ; lines on the christening of the infant daughter of the Duchess of Fife ; a tribute to the memory of James Russell Lowell ; and a prefatory verse to *Pearl*.

A new Popular Edition of Tennyson in one volume, revised throughout by the Author. 1891 Macmillan & Co. pp. 842. With a new steel portrait.

*** *The Poetry of Tennyson.* By Henry van Dyke. Second edition. Revised and enlarged. New York and London.

The Laureate's Country. A Description of Places connected with the Life of Alfred, Lord Tennyson. By Alfred J. Church, M. A. With many illustrations from Drawings by Edward Hull. London : Seeley and Co., Limited, Essex Street, Strand. 1891. pp. 111.

Daphne and Other Poems. By Frederick Tennyson, Author of "Days and Hours." London and New York : Macmillan & Co. 1891. pp. 522.

Illustrations of Tennyson. By John Churton Collins. London : Chatto & Windus. 1891. pp. xii, 186.

In *The Art Journal* for January and February, two articles, by P. Anderson Graham, on "Lord Tennyson's Childhood," illustrated by H. E. Tidemarsh.

In *The Cornhill Magazine*, for February, "Illustrations of Animal Life in Tennyson's Poems."

Mr. C. J. Caswell printed an article on "Lord Tennyson's

Birthday " in *Notes and Queries*, March 14 ; and another on "A Comitia of Errors " in *The Birmingham Weekly Mercury*, April 11.

Prof. Albert S. Cook had an article on " St. Agnes' Eve," in " Poet-Lore," January 15.

1892. Lord Tennyson published verses on "The Death of the Duke of Clarence and Avondale" in *The Nineteenth Century*, February.

The play of THE FORESTERS, a romantic pastoral drama, was produced at Daly's Theatre in New York, on Thursday Night, March 19. Miss Ada Rehan played the leading part of Marian Lee. Mr. Drew appeared as Robin Hood. A purely formal production of the play was made in London, on the same day, at the Lyceum, for the purpose of securing the copyright.

THE FORESTERS: ROBIN HOOD AND MAID MARIAN. By Alfred, Lord Tennyson, Poet Laureate. New York : Macmillan & Co., and London. 1892. pp. 155. (Issued in New York in April.) Also a large-paper edition.

LORD TENNYSON DIED AT ALDWORTH, OCTOBER 6, BETWEEN ONE AND TWO IN THE MORNING.

SILENT VOICES (ten lines printed for copyright purposes, on a single sheet, October 12). Macmillan & Co. 1892.

THE DEATH OF ŒNONE, AKBAR'S DREAM, AND OTHER POEMS. By Alfred, Lord Tennyson, Poet Laureate. New York: Macmillan & Co., and London. 1892. pp. vi, 113. (Issued in New York, October 29.) Printed also on large paper. 200 copies.

The English large-paper edition contained five portraits, but omitted the song " The Bee and the Flower."

⁎ *The Poetry of Tennyson.* Third edition. By Henry van Dyke. New York: Charles Scribner's Sons. 1892. London: Elkin Mathews, Vigo St. pp. xxii, 376.

The Golden Guess. A Series of Essays, by John Vance Cheney. Boston: Lee & Shepard. 1892. (Essay on Tennyson and his Critics.)

Homes and Haunts of Alfred, Lord Tennyson, Poet Laureate. By George G. Napier, M. A. Glasgow: James Maclehose & Sons, Publishers to the University. 1892. pp. xvi, 204.

Records of Tennyson, Ruskin, and Browning. By Anne Thackeray Ritchie. New York: Harper & Brothers. 1892. pp. 190.

Tennyson's Life and Poetry: and Mistakes concerning Tennyson. By Eugene Parsons. Chicago: 1892. (Second edition, revised and enlarged, 1893. Printed for the author, 43 Bryant Ave.)

Alfred, Lord Tennyson. By A. Waugh, B. A. Oxon. London: 1892. (Second edition, United States Book Company, New York, 1893.)

Tennyson and "In Memoriam": An Appreciation and a Study. By Joseph Jacobs. London: David Nutt, in the Strand. 1892. 16mo, pp. x, 108.

"Tennyson's Foresters," in *The Athenæum,* vol. ii. pp. 461, 493. By Theodore Watts. "The Study of Tennyson," in *The Century Magazine,* by Henry van Dyke.

1893. LORD TENNYSON'S WORKS. Globe 8vo edition, in ten volumes. Vols. viii., ix., x. New York: Macmillan & Co., and London. 1893. (Vol. viii. contains "Becket" and "The Cup;" vol. ix., "The Foresters," "The Falcon," "The Promise of May;" vol. x., "Teiresias, and Other Poems," "Demeter, and Other Poems," "The Death of Œnone and Other Poems."

MAUD: A MONODRAMA. London: Macmillan & Co. Printed by William Morris, at the Kelmscott Press. 1893.

POEMS BY TWO BROTHERS. Second edition. Edited by Hallam, Lord Tennyson. New York:

Macmillan & Co., and London. 1893. Crown 8vo, pp. xx, 251. (The first reprint of the volume published in 1827, in which the late Poet Laureate made his earliest appearance before the public. As far as possible the poems have been attributed to their respective authors Four new poems have been added from the original MS., and the Cambridge prize poem on Timbuctoo has also been included in the volume. There is also a large-paper edition, with facsimiles of the MS., limited to 300 copies.)

BECKET: A TRAGEDY. In a Prologue and four Acts. By Alfred, Lord Tennyson. As arranged for the stage by Henry Irving, and presented at the Lyceum Theatre on February 6, 1893. New York: Macmillan & Co., and London. 1893. pp. 62.

BOOKS ON TENNYSON PUBLISHED SINCE 1892. PARTIAL LIST.

A Study of the Works of Alfred, Lord Tennyson. By Edward Campbell Tainsh. New edition. Macmillan & Co. 1893.

Lord Tennyson. A Biographical Sketch. By Henry J. Jennings. Second Edition. London: Chatto & Windus. 1893.

Essays on Lord Tennyson's Idylls of the King. By H. Littledale. Macmillan & Co. 1893.

The Poems of Arthur Henry Hallam Together with His Essay in the Lyrical Poems of Alfred Tennyson. Edited with an introduction by Richard le Gallienne. London: Elkin Mathews & John Lane. New York: Macmillan & Co. MDCCCXCIII.

Tennyson's Heroes and Heroines. Illustrated by Marcus Stone. London: Tuck & Sons. 1893.

The Scenery of Tennyson's Poems. Etchings after drawings by various authors. Letterpress by B. Francis. London: J. & E. Bumpus. 1893.

Alfred, Lord Tennyson, and His Friends. A series of 25 portraits and frontispiece in photogravure from the negatives of Mrs. Julia Margaret Cameron and H. H. H. Cameron.

Reminiscences by Anne Thackeray Ritchie, with an intro-
duction by H. H. Hay Cameron. London : T. Fisher Unwin,
1893.
  New Studies in Tennyson. By Morton Luce. Second
Edition. Clifton : J. Barker & Son. 1893.
  A Handbook to the Works of Alfred, Lord Tennyson.
By Morton Luce. London : George Bell & Sons. 1895.
  Tennyson : his Art and Relation to Modern Life. By
Stopford A. Brooke. London : Isbister & Co. 1894.
  *Tennyson's Idylls of the King, and Arthurian Story from
the XVIth Century.* By M. W. Maccallum. Glasgow :
Maclehose & Sons. 1894.
  A Primer of Tennyson with a Critical Essay. By William
Macneile Dixon. Litt. D., A. M., LL. B. (Mason College.)
London. Methuen & Co. 1896.
  The Growth of the Idylls of the King. By Richard Jones.
Philadelphia : Lippincott Co. 1895.
  Literary Anecdotes of the Nineteenth Century. Edited
by W. R. Nicoll and T. J. Wise. (Contains "The Building
of the Idylls," and "Tennysoniana.") New York : Dodd,
Mead & Co. 1896.
  The Poetry of Tennyson. By Henry Van Dyke. Eighth
Edition (in the Cameo Series, with new essay on *In Memor-
iam.*) New York : Scribners. 1897.
  Alfred Lord Tennyson. A Memoir by his Son. 2 vols.
London : Macmillan & Co. New York : The Macmillan Co.
1897.

ANNOTATED EDITIONS OF TENNYSON'S WORKS.

  By Dr. William J. Rolfe. Published by Houghton, Mifflin
& Co., Boston and New York : —
    The Princess.
    Select Poems of Tennyson.
    The Young People's Tennyson.
    Enoch Arden, and Other Poems.
    Idylls of the King. (2 vols.) *In Memoriam.*
  Published by Macmillan & Co., London and New York : —
    Lyrical Poems. Selected and Annotated by Francis
Turner Palgrave.
    Selections from Tennyson. With Introduction and
Notes by F. J. Rowe, M. A., and W. T. Webb, M. A.
    Tennyson for the Young. Selections from Lord Tenny-
son's Poems. Edited, with Notes, by the Rev. Alfred
Ainger, M. A., LL. D., Canon of Bristol.
    The Coming of Arthur, and the Passing of Arthur

Edited, with Introduction and Notes, by Prof. **F. J. Rowe** of Calcutta.

Enoch Arden. With Introduction and Notes, by **W. T. Webb, M. A.**

Aylmer's Field. By W. T. Webb, **M. A.**

The Princess. By P. M. Wallace, **M. A.**

Gareth and Lynette. By G. C. Macauley, **M. A.**

Geraint and Enid. By the same editor.

The Holy Grail. By the same editor.

Published by Effingham Maynard & Co., New York:—

Enoch Arden. With Introduction and Notes by Dr. Albert F. Blaisdell.

The Two Voices, etc. With Introduction and Notes by Prof. Hiram Corson of Cornell University.

Elaine.

In Memoriam.

The Holy Grail.

THE PUBLISHED WORKS OF ALFRED TENNYSON: WITH DATES, TITLES, AND NUMBER OF PAGES.

1827. POEMS BY TWO BROTHERS. London: Printed for W. Simpkin and R. Marshall, Stationers'-Hall-Court; and J. & J. Jackson, Louth. MDCCCXXVII. Crown 8vo, pp. xii, 228.

1829. TIMBUCTOO. A poem which obtained the chancellor's medal at the Cambridge Commencement, MDCCCXXIX. By A. Tennyson, of Trinity College. (Printed in *"Prolusiones Academicæ:* MDCCCXXIX. Cantabrigiæ: typis academicis excudit Joannes Smith." pp. 41.)

1830. POEMS, CHIEFLY LYRICAL. By Alfred Tennyson. London: Effingham Wilson, Royal Exchange, Cornhill. 1830. 12mo, pp. 154, and leaf of errata.

1832. POEMS. By Alfred Tennyson. London: Edward Moxon, 64 New Bond Street. MDCCCXXXIII. 12mo, pp. 163.

1842. POEMS. By Alfred Tennyson. In two volumes. London: Edward Moxon, Dover Street. MDCCCXLII. 2 vols. 12mo, pp. vii, 233 ; vii, 231.

1847. THE PRINCESS: A MEDLEY. By Alfred Tennyson. London: Edward Moxon, Dover Street. MDCCCXLVII. 12mo, pp. 164.

1850. IN MEMORIAM. London: Edward Moxon, Dover Street. MDCCCL. 12mo, pp. vii, 210.

1852. ODE ON THE DEATH OF THE DUKE OF WELLINGTON. By Alfred Tennyson, Poet Laureate. London: Edward Moxon, Dover Street. 1852. 8vo, pamphlet, pp. 16.

1855. MAUD, AND OTHER POEMS. By Alfred Tennyson, D. C. L., Poet Laureate. London: Edward Moxon. 1855. 12mo, pp. 154.

1859. IDYLLS OF THE KING. By Alfred Tennyson, D. C. L., Poet Laureate. London: Edward Moxon & Co., Dover Street. 1859. 12mo, pp. 261.

1864. ENOCH ARDEN, ETC. By Alfred Tennyson, D. C. L., Poet Laureate. London: Edward Moxon & Co., Dover Street. 1864. 12mo, pp. 178.

1869. THE HOLY GRAIL, AND OTHER POEMS. By Alfred Tennyson, D. C. L., Poet Laureate. Strahan & Co., Publishers, 56, Ludgate Hill, London. 1870. 12mo, pp. 222.

1872. GARETH AND LYNETTE, ETC. By Alfred Tennyson, D. C. L., Poet Laureate. Strahan & Co., 56, Ludgate Hill, London. 1872. 12mo, pp. 136.

1875. QUEEN MARY. A Drama. By Alfred Tennyson. London: Henry S. King & Co. 1875. 12mo, pp. viii, 278.

1876. HAROLD. A Drama. By Alfred Tennyson. London: Henry S. King & Co. 1877. 12mo, pp. viii, 161.

1879. THE LOVER'S TALE. By Alfred Tennyson. London: C. Kegan Paul & Co., 1 Paternoster Square. 1879. 12mo, pp. 95.

1880. BALLADS, AND OTHER POEMS. By Alfred Tennyson. London: C. Kegan Paul & Co., 1 Paternoster Square. 1880. 12mo, pp. vi, 184.

1884. THE CUP AND THE FALCON. By Alfred, Lord Tennyson, Poet Laureate. London: Macmillan & Co. 1884. 12mo, pp. 146.

BECKET. By Alfred, Lord Tennyson, Poet Laureate. London: Macmillan & Co. 1884. Crown 8vo, pp. 213.

1885. TIRESIAS, AND OTHER POEMS. By Alfred, Lord Tennyson, D. C. L., Poet Laureate. London: Macmillan & Co. 1885. 12mo, pp. viii, 204.

1886. LOCKSLEY HALL SIXTY YEARS AFTER, ETC. By Alfred, Lord Tennyson, D. C. L., Poet Laureate. London and New York: Macmillan & Co. 1886. 12mo, pp. 201.

1889. DEMETER, AND OTHER POEMS. By Alfred, Lord Tennyson, P. L., D. C. L. London and New York: Macmillan & Co. 1889. 12mo, pp. vi. 175.

1892. THE FORESTERS: ROBIN HOOD AND MAID MARIAN. By Alfred, Lord Tennyson, Poet Laureate. New York and London: Macmillan & Co. 1892. 12mo, pp. 155.

THE DEATH OF ŒNONE, AKBAR'S DREAM, AND OTHER POEMS. By Alfred, Lord Tennyson, Poet Laureate. New York and London: Macmillan & Co. 1892. 12mo, pp. vi, 113.

1893. POEMS BY TWO BROTHERS. "*Hæc nos novimus esse nihil.*" — Martial. New York and London: Macmillan & Co. 1893. pp. xx, 251. (Preface by Hallam, Lord Tennyson.)

A PARTIAL LIST

OF TRANSLATIONS OF TENNYSON'S WORKS.

LATIN AND GREEK.

In Memoriam, translated into Latin elegiac verse by Oswald A. Smith; for private circulation only. Noticed in *Edinburgh Review,* April, 1866.

Enoch Arden, translated into Latin by Gulielmus Selwyn. Lond. Edv. Moxon et Soc. A. D. MDCCCLXVII.

Horæ Tennysonianæ, sive Eclogæ e Tennysono, Latine Redditæ. Cura A. J. Church. Lond. et Cantab. Macmillan et Soc. MDCCCLXX. pp. viii, 139.

Crossing the Bar, and a Few Other Translations. By H. M. B. (Not published.) 1890. Cambridge, printed by C. J. Clay, M. A., & Sons, at the University Press. pp. 67. (By Dr. Butler, Master of Trinity College, Cambridge. Twelve Latin translations and seven Greek translations of "Crossing the Bar," in various metres.)

Verses and Translations by C. S. C. 1862. (C. S. Calverley.) Contains a Latin version of Section 106 of *In Memoriam.*

GERMAN.

Gedichte: übers. von W. Hertzberg. Dessau, 1853. pp. viii, 369.

In Memoriam: aus dem Engl. nach der 5ten Auflage. Braunschweig, 1854.

Königs-Idyllen: übers. von H. A. Feldmann. 2te Aufl. Hamburg, 1872. pp. viii, 277.

Königs-Idyllen: übers. von W. Schols. Berlin, 1867. pp. 223.

Enoch Arden: übers. von Schellwien. Quedlinburg, 1867. pp. 47.

Enoch Arden: übers. von Robert Waldmüller. (Ed. Duboc.) 2te–4te Aufl. Hamburg, 1868–1870. pp. 42. 33te Aufl. Hamburg, 1890.

Aylmers Feld: übers. von F. W. Weber. Leipzig, 1869.

Enoch Arden: übers. von F. W. Weber. Leipzig, 1869. pp. 42.

Aylmers Feld: übers. von H. A. Feldmann. Hamburg, 1870. pp. 44.

Enoch Arden: übers. von H. A. Feldmann. Hamburg, 1870. pp. 45.

Ausgewählte Dichtungen: übers. von H. A. Feldmann. Hamburg, 1870. pp. 89.

Freundes-Klage, nach "In Memoriam:" frei übertr. von Robert Waldmüller. Hamburg, 1870. pp. 160.

Ausgewählte Gedichte: übers. von M. Eugard. Elbing, 1872. pp. v. 126.

In Memoriam — "Zum Gedächtniss:" übers. von Agnes von Bohlen. Berlin, 1874. pp. 184.

Harald, ein Drama: deutsch von Alb. Graf Wickenburg. Hamburg, 1879–1880. pp. iv. 137.

Enoch Arden: deutsch von A. Strodtmann. Berlin, 1876. 2te verbess. Auflage, 1881. pp. 71.

Enoch Arden: deutsch von Carl Eichholz. 2te Auflage. Hamburg, 1881. pp. 56.

Königs-Idyllen: In Metrum des Orig. übers. von Carl Weiser. Universal Bibliothek, nrs. 1817, 1818. Leipzig, 1883-1886. pp. 175.

Enoch Arden: Students Tauchnitz Aufl. mit Wörterbuch, bearb. von Dr. A. Hamann. Leipzig, 1886. pp. 24. (Bibliothek der Gesammt-Literatur.)

Ausgewählte Dichtungen: übers. von A. Strodtmann. Hildburghausen, 1867. Leipzig, 1887-1890. Meyer's Volksbücher, nrs. 371-373. pp. 164.

Enoch Arden: frei bearb. für die Jugend. Hausbibliothek. Leipzig, 1888. pp. 29.

Locksley Hall: aus dem Engl. von Ferd. Freiligrath. *Locksley Hall sechsig Jahre später:* übers. von Jakob Fels. Hamburg, 1888. pp. 59.

Locksley Hall sechsig Jahre später: übers. von Karl B. Esmarch. Gotha, 1888. pp. 32.

Enoch Arden: aus dem Engl. von Griebenow. Halle, 1889. pp. 35.

Maud: übers. von F. W. Weber. 3te Auflage. Paderborn, 1891. pp. 109.

DUTCH.

De molenaars-dochter: Vrij bewerkt door A. J. de Bull. Utrecht, 1859.

Henoch Arden: Naar het Engl. door S. J. van den Bergh. 's Hage, 1869.

Henoch Arden: door J. L. Wertheim. Amsterdam, 1882.

Vier Idyllen van Koning Arthur: Amsterdam, 1883.

ITALIAN.

Dora: Traduzione di Giacomo Zanella: in *Versi di Giacomo Zanella*, vol. i. Firenze, 1868, G. Barbera. pp. 350-359.

(Another translation of the same poem by the same author appeared in *Varie Versione Poetiche* di Giacomo Zanella. Firenze, 1887. Successori Le Monnier. pp. 215-223.)

La Cena d' Oro di Alfredo Tennyson: Trad. di Lodovico Biagi. In Firenze. Coi Tipi di M. Cellini e C. 1871. pp. 22.

Appendice di Alcune Poesie Varie. pp. 23-30. (Il Premio della Virtù. Un Isoletta. La Ciocca dei Capelli. Il Fiore.)

Dora: Traduzione in versi di Giuseppe Chiarini. *Poesie, Storie, Canti, Traduzioni.* Livorno, 1874. F. Vigo. pp. 407-418.

"*The May Queen:*" Traduzione dei Marchesi Luigi e Raniero de Calboli. Roma, 1875.

Idilli, Liriche, Miti, e Legende, Enoc Arden, Quadri Dramatici: Traduzioni di Carlo Faccioli (Verona). [1st Ed. 1876, 2d Ed. 1879.] 3d Ed. 1887. Firenze, Successori Le Monnier. pp. xii, 441.

Enoch Arden di Alfredo Tennyson: Recato in Versi Italiani di Angelo Saggioni. Padova, 1876. Stabilimento Prosperini. pp. 51. *Nozze Scopoli-Naccari.* *

(This translation was reprinted in *Letture di Famiglia*. Firenze, 1885. pp. 109.)

Il Primo Divorbio (Nell' Isola di Wight): Trad. di Enrico Castelnuovo. Venezia, 1886. Stab. Tipografico Fratelli Visentini. pp. 19. *Nozze Bordica-Selvatico.*

La Prima Lite: Estratto dal Giornale "La Battaglia Bizantina: Traduzione di P. T. Pavolini. Bologna, 1888. Soc. Tip. Azzoguidi. pp. 12.

La Carica della Brigata Lyght. Le Due Sorelle. In *Fiori del Nord:* Versione di Moderne Poesie Tedesche e Inglese di Pietro Turati. Milano, 1881. Natale-Battezzatti. pp. 133–137.

Lyrical Poems by Alfred Lord Tennyson, Poet Laureate: with copious prefatory and explanatory notes for the use of Italians by Theophilus C. Cann. Florence, 1887. F. Paggi. pp. 31–68. (*Locksley Hall, Lady Clare, Lady Clara Vere de Vere, St. Agnes' Eve.*)

Italian translations, in verse and prose, from Tennyson's poems are to be found in the following articles: —

"Poeti Stranieri Moderni — Alfredo Tennyson:" di Eugenio Camerini. Nella *Nuova Antologia.* Firenze, Febbraio, 1870. Vol. xiii. pp. 229–249. Frammenti di traduzione in prosa.

"Alfredo Tennyson e le sue nuove poesie." (Ballads and other Poems, 1881.) Articolo critico di Enrico Nencioni, nel *Fanfulla della Domenica*, Roma, 10 Aprile, 1881. Traduzione in prosa della poesia *Rizpah.*

"*Maud.*" Articolo critico di Enrico Nencioni nella *Domenica Letteraria*, Roma, 19 Marzo, 1882. Frammenti di traduzione in prosa.

* It is an Italian custom at a wedding to have some little book printed, containing an original poem, a new translation, or something of literary novelty and appropriateness, to be presented to the bride and groom and their friends as a memorial of the marriage. The note indicates that Signore Saggioni had his translation of Enoch Arden printed as a gift for the wedding of his friends of the families of Scopoli and Naccari.

"**Gli** *Idilli del Re.*" Art. crit. di Enrico Nencioni, nel *Fanfulla della Domenica*, Roma, 9 Settembre, 1883. Traduzione in prosa di un frammento della *Ginevra.*

"**Lord** Tennyson: Alcuni suoi scritti minori." Art. crit. di F. Rodriguez, nella *Nuova Antologia*, Roma, 16 Luglio, 1890, Serie III, vol. xxviii, pp. 318–340. Traduzioni in versi dell' idillio *Il Ruscello*, della ballata *Rizpah*, e *La Diga Estrema.*

FRENCH.

Elaine, Genièvre, Viviane, Enide. Trad. par Francisque Michel. Ill. par Gustave Doré. Paris. Hachette et Cie. 1867–1869.

Enoch Arden. Trad. par M. de la Rive. 1870.

Enoch Arden. Trad. par X. Marmier. 1887.

Idylles et Poèmes: Enoch Arden: Locksley Hall. Trad. par A. Buisson du Berger. 1888.

Enoch Arden. Trad. par M. l'Abbé R. Courtois. 1890.

Enoch Arden. Trad. par E. Duglin. 1890.

SWEDISH.

Konung Arthur och hans Rid re: Upsala, 1876.

Elaine: A. Hjelmstjerna. 1877.

NORWEGIAN AND DANISH.

Enoch Arden: oversat af A. Munch. Copenhagen. 1866.

"*The May Queen:*" oversat af A. Falck. Christiania. 1875. (1855?)

Idyller om Kong Arthur: oversat af A. Munch. Copenhagen. 1876.

Anna og Locksley Slot: oversat af A. Hansen. 1872.

"*Sea Dreams:*" "*Aylmer's Field:*" oversat af F. L. Mynster. 1877.

SPANISH.

Enid and Elaine: translated by Lope Gisbert. 1875.

Poemes de Alfredo Tennyson: Enoch Arden, Gareth y Lynette, Merlin y Bibiana, etc. Tr. by D. Vicente de Arana. Barcelona. 1883.

NOTE. — The difficulty of making this list perfect in the present state of bibliography is immense. It is only in the German and the Italian that it approaches completeness and accuracy.

A LIST OF

BIBLICAL REFERENCES AND ALLUSIONS

FOUND IN THE

WORKS OF TENNYSON.

*** The author wishes to thank the many correspondents, in Canada, in England, and in the United States, who have kindly sent him additions to this list since it was first printed, in 1889. It might be enlarged almost indefinitely. On the other hand, perhaps it includes already some references in which the connection with Scripture is purely fanciful. The line is hard to draw. But at least the list may serve to show beyond a doubt how deeply the poetry of Tennyson is saturated with the influence of the Book which is at once "a well of English undefiled" and "a well of water springing up into everlasting life."

A LIST OF BIBLICAL REFERENCES AND ALLUSIONS FOUND IN THE WORKS OF TENNYSON.

———◆———

TIMBUCTOO.

" And teach him to attain
By shadowing forth the Unattainable." *

Matt. 5 : 48.

SUPPOSED CONFESSIONS.

" My sin was as a thorn
Among the thorns that girt Thy brow."

Matt. 27 : 29.

" In this extremest misery
Of ignorance I should require
A sign."

1 *Cor.* 1 : 22.

" That happy morn
When angels spake to men aloud,
And thou and peace to earth were born."

Luke 2 : 10.

" Brothers in Christ."

Matt. 12 : 50; *Col.* 1 : 2.

" To reconcile me with thy God."

2 *Cor.* 5 : 20.

"Bring back this lamb into thy fold."

Luke 15 : 4.

" Pride, the sin of Devils."

1 *Tim.* 3 : 6.

" These little motes and grains shall be
Clothed on with immortality."

1 *Cor.* 15 : 53.

* Be ye perfect, even as your Father in heaven is perfect.

"As manna on my wilderness."

Ex. 16 : 15.

"That God would move
And strike the hard, hard rock, and thence,
Sweet in their utmost bitterness,
Would issue tears of penitence."

Num. 20 : 11.

THE KRAKEN.

"Until the latter fire shall heat the deep."

Rev. 8 : 8; 2 *Pet.* 3 : 10.

ISABEL.

"The laws of marriage charactered in gold
Upon the blanched tablets of her heart."

Ps. 37 : 31; 2 *Cor.* 3 : 3.

"And thou of God in thy great *charity.*"

1 *John* 4 : 11.

To ——.

"Like that strange angel which of old
Until the breaking of the light
Wrestled with wandering Israel."

Gen. 32 : 24.

THE DESERTED HOUSE.

"A mansion incorruptible."

2 *Cor.* 5 : 1.

"The house was builded of the earth"

1 *Cor.* 15 : 47.

ADELINE.

"Sabæan spice."

Is. 45 : 11.

To J. M. KEMBLE.

"Arrows of lightnings."

Zech. 9 : 14.

BUONAPARTE.

"Late he learned humility
Perforce, like those whom Gideon schooled with briers."

Judges 8 : 16.

EARLY SONNETS — POLAND.

"Lord, how long."

Ps. 94 : 3.

SONNET X.
     "The deluge."
          Gen. 7 : 11.

TWO VOICES.
     " A still small voice."
         1 *Kings* 19 : 12.
     " Wonderfully made."
          Ps. 139 : 14.
    " When first the world began
Young Nature through five cycles ran
And in the sixth she moulded man."
          Gen. 1 : 26.
    " A little lower than angels."
          Ps. 8 : 5.
     " Like Stephen."
          Acts 7 : 55.
    " I toil beneath the curse."
          Gen. 3 : 17–19.
     " Naked I go."
          Eccl. 5 : 15.
" Though one should smite him on the cheek."
          Luke 6 : 29.
  " His sons grow up that bear his name,
Some grow to honour, some to shame."
          Job 14 : 26.
  "The place he knew forgetteth him."
          Ps. 103 : 16.
 " ' Omega ! Thou art Lord,' they said."
          Rev. 1 : 8.
 " He may not do the thing he would."
          Gal. 5 : 17.
  " Rejoice ! Rejoice ! "
          Phil. 4 : 4.

WILL WATERPROOF (1842).
   " Like Hezekiah's, backward runs
   The shadow of my days."
          Is. 38 : 8.
   " If old things, there are new."
          Matt. 13 : 52.

" Who shall say me nay ? "

1 *Kings* 2 : 20

" All in all."

1 *Cor.* 15 : 28

THE PALACE OF ART.

" I built myself a lordly pleasure-house,
  ' Wherein at ease for aye to dwell.
 I said, ' O Soul, make merry and carouse,
  Dear Soul, for all is well.' "

Luke 12 : 18, 19.

" Howling in outer darkness."

Matt. 8 : 12.

" Common clay taken from the common earth
 Moulded by God."

Gen. 2 : 7.

" Angels rising and descending."

Gen. 28 : 12.

" And oft some brainless devil enters in
 And drives them to the deep."

Luke 8 : 33.

" Like Herod when the shout was in his ears,
 Struck through with pangs of hell."

Acts 12 : 21-23.

" God, before whom ever lie bare
 The abysmal deeps of Personality."

Heb. 4 : 13.

" Wrote ' Mene, mene,' and divided quite
 The kingdom of her thought."

Dan. 5 : 25.

THE PALACE OF ART (Edition of 1833 : note, p. 73).

" One was the Tishbite whom the raven fed,
 As when he stood on Carmel-steeps,
With one arm stretched out bare, and mocked and said,
 ' Come cry aloud — he sleeps.'

" Tall, eager, lean, and strong, his cloak windborne
 Behind, his forehead heavenly-bright
From the clear marble pouring glorious scorn,
 Lit as with inner light."

1 *Kings* 18 : 27.

"Robed David touching holy strings."
                                    2 Sam. 6 : 5.

          "Isaiah with fierce Ezekiel,
          Swarth Moses by the Coptic sea."

               " As power and might
          Abode in Samson's hair."
                                    Judges 16 : 17.

"Far off she seem'd to hear the dully sound
          Of human footsteps fall,
As in strange lands a traveller walking slow,
          In doubt and great perplexity,
A little before moonrise hears the low
          Moan of an unknown sea,
And knows not if it be thunder, or a sound
Of rocks thrown down, or one deep cry
          Of great wild beasts."
               Wisdom of Solomon, 17 : 19 *et seq, Apocrypha.*

LADY CLARA VERE DE VERE.
     "The gardener Adam and his wife."
                                    Gen. 2 : 15.

THE MAY QUEEN. Conclusion.
          "His will be done."
                                    Matt. 6 : 10.

"He taught me all the mercy, for he showed me all the
     sin.
  Now, tho' my lamp was lighted late, there 's One will
     let me in."
                                    Matt. 25 : 1.

"And the wicked cease from troubling and the weary are
     at rest."
                                    Job 3 : 17.

THE TALKING OAK.
          "Thy leaf shall never fail."
                                    Ps. 1 : 3.

THE LOTUS EATERS.
          "The flower ripens in its place,
Ripens and fades and falls, and hath no toil."
                                    Matt. 6 : 28.

A DREAM OF FAIR WOMEN.
"The end of Time."
Rev. 10 : 6

" The daughter of the warrior Gileadite,
  A maiden pure ; as when she went along
From Mizpeh's towered gate with welcome light,
  With timbrel and with song."
Judges 11 : 34

  " A threefold cord."
Eccl. 4 : 12

  "The everlasting hills."
Gen. 49 : 26

  " Gross darkness."
Is. 60 : 2.

" Moreover it is written that my race
Hewed Ammon hip and thigh from Aroer
On Arnon unto Minneth."
Judges 11 : 33.

  " Love can vanquish death."
Cant. 8 : 6.

MORTE D'ARTHUR.
" Chaff . . . much better burnt." (In " The Epic.")
Luke 3 : 17.

" Such times have not been since the light that led
The holy Elders with the gift of myrrh."
Matt. 2 : 2, 3.

  " War shall be no more."
Is. 2 : 4.

THE GARDENER'S DAUGHTER.
  " Eden."
Gen. 2 : 8.

" Like the covenant of a God, to hold
From thence thro' all the worlds."
Is. 55 : 3.

EDWIN MORRIS.
  "Built . . . upon a rock."
Matt. 7 : 24.

" God made the woman for the man."
1 *Cor.* 11 : 9; *Gen.* 2 : 18.

ST. SIMEON STYLITES.
 " The meed of saints, the white robe and the palm."
Rev. 7 : 9.

" This home
Of sin, my flesh."
2 Cor. 5 : 6.

" Cover all my sin."
Ps. 32 : 1; 85 : 2.

" O mercy, mercy !   Wash away my sin."
Ps. 51 : 1, 2.

" They think that I am somewhat."
Gal. 2 : 6.

" Can I work miracles and not be saved ? "
1 *Cor.* 13 : 2

" Pontius and Iscariot."
Matt. 26 : 14.

" A sinful man, conceived and born in sin."
Ps. 51 : 5.

" Abaddon and Asmodeus."
Rev. 9 : 11; *Tobit* 3 : 8.

" Mortify your flesh."
Col. 3 : 5.

" Yield not me the praise,
God only."
Ps. 115 : 1.

" A man of God."
2 *Tim.* 3 : 17.

THE GOLDEN YEAR.
 " Cry like the daughters of the horse-leech, Give! "
Prov. 30 : 15.

LOCKSLEY HALL.
 " Joshua's moon in Ajalon."
Josh. 10 : 12.

" But I count the gray barbarian lower than the Christian child."
Matt. 11 : 11.

" Summer isles of Eden."
Gen. 2 : 8.

GODIVA.
"A heart as rough as Esau's hand."
Gen. 27 : 23

"An everlasting name."
Is. 56 : 5

THE DAY DREAM. L'ENVOI.
"For since the time when Adam first
Embraced his Eve in happy hour,
And every bird of Eden burst
In carol, every bud to flower."
Gen. 2 : 23.

ST. AGNES' EVE.
"So shows my soul before the Lamb."
Rev. 7 : 9 ; 5 : 8.

"So in my earthly house I am
To that I hope to be."
2 Cor. 5 : 1.

Draw me, thy bride, . . .
In raiment white and clean."
Rev. 3 : 5.

"The Heavenly bridegroom waits
To make me pure of sin."
Is. 62 : 5.

"The Sabbaths of Eternity,
One Sabbath deep and wide."
Heb. 4 : 9.

"The shining sea."
Rev. 15 : 2.

THE VISION OF SIN.
"Thou shalt not be saved by works."
Gal. 2 : 16.

"God's likeness."
Gen. 1 : 26.

"Far too naked to be shamed."
Gen. 2 : 25.

TO ——.
"The many-headed beast."
Rev. 13 : 1.

ENOCH ARDEN.

"Cast all your cares on God."

1 *Pet.* 5 : 7.

"That anchor holds."

Heb. 6 : 19.

"The uttermost parts of the morning."

Ps. 139 : 9.

"The sea is His: He made it."

Ps. 95 : 5.

"Under the palm-tree."

Judges 4 : 5.

"The Sun of Righteousness."

Mal. 4 : 2.

"These be palms
Whereof the happy people strowing cried,
'Hosanna in the highest.' "

John 12 : 13.

"Set in this Eden of all plenteousness."

Gen. 2 : 9.

"The blast of doom."

1 *Thess.* 4 : 16.

AYLMER'S FIELD.

"Dust are our frames."

Gen. 3 : 19.

"Sons of men, daughters of God."

Gen. 6 : 2.

"Pale as the Jephtha's daughter."

Judges 11 : 34.

"Stumbling blocks."

1 *Cor.* 1 : 23.

"Almost all that is, hurting the hurt,
Save Christ as we believe him."

Matt. 12 : 20.

"Behold
Your house is left unto you desolate."

Luke 13 : 35.

"Never since our bad earth became one sea."

Gen. 7.

"Gash thyself, priest, and honour thy brute Baal."

1 *Kings* 18 : 28

"The babe shall lead the lion."

Is. 11 : 6

"The wilderness shall blossom as the rose."

Is. 35 : 1

"Fares richly in fine linen."

Luke 16 : 19

"Leave all and follow me."

Luke 18 : 22

"His light about thy feet."

Ps. 119 : 105

"Carpenter's son."

Matt. 13 : 55.

"Wonderful, Prince of Peace, the Mighty God."

Is. 9 : 6.

"As not passing thro' the fire
Bodies, but souls — thy children's — thro' the smoke."

Lev. 18 : 21.

"The more base idolater."

Col. 3 : 5.

"Rachel by the palmy well."

Gen. 29 : 10.

"Ruth amid the fields of corn."

Ruth 2.

"Fair as the angel that said 'Hail.' "

Luke 1 : 28.

"She walked,
Wearing the light yoke of that Lord of love
Who stilled the rolling wave of Galilee."

Matt. 8 : 26; 11 : 30.

"O thou that killest, hadst thou known,
O thou that stonest, hadst thou understood
The things belonging to thy peace and ours.

Luke 13 : 34; 19 : 32.

"Is there no prophet but the voice that calls
Doom upon kings, or in the waste 'Repent'? "

Mark 1 : 3, 4.

" Is not our own child on the narrow way,
Who down to those that saunter in the broad
Cries ' Come up hither,' as a prophet to us."
Matt. 7 : 13.

" Poor in spirit."
Matt. 5 : 3.

" A rushing tempest of the wrath of God."
Ps. 11 : 6.

" Sent like the twelve-divided concubine
To inflame the tribes."
Judges 19 : 29.

"Pharaoh's darkness."
Ex. 10 : 21.

" Folds as dense as those
Which hid the Holiest from the people's eyes."
Matt. 27 : 45.

" Their own gray hairs with sorrow to the grave."
Gen. 42 : 38.

" Knew not what they did."
Luke 23 : 34.

" Will not another take their heritage."
Acts 1 : 20.

" Or one stone
Left on another."
Matt. 24 : 2; *Mark* 13 : 2.

"Is it a light thing ? "
Is. 7 : 13.

" Those that swore
Not by the Temple, but by the gold."
Matt. 23 : 16.

" And made
Their own traditions God, and slew the Lord."
Matt. 15 : 3; *Acts* 5 : 30.

SEA DREAMS.

" Simple Christ."
1 *Cor.* 2 : 2; 2 *Cor.* 11 : 3.

" The scarlet woman."
Rec. 17 : 3-5.

"The Apocalyptic millstone."

Rev. 18 : 21.

" That great Angel: 'Thus with violence
Shall Babylon be cast into the sea.
Then comes the close.' "

Rev. 18 : 21.

"Let not the sun go down upon your wrath."

Eph. 4 : 26.

" Dear Lord, who died for all."

2 *Cor.* 5 : 15.

" When the great Books (see Daniel seven and ten)
Were opened."

Dan. 7 : 10.

" We live by faith."

Gal. 2 : 20.

" All things work together for the good
Of those."

Rom. 8 : 28.

" Never took that useful name in vain."

Ex. 20 : 7.

" The Cross . . .
And Christ."

John 19 : 17.

" Boanerges."

Mark 3 : 17.

THE PRINCESS.

" Huge Ammonites."

Num. 21 : 24.

" A fountain sealed."

Cant. 4 : 12.

" A land of promise."

Heb. 11 : 9.

" A wolf within the fold."

Acts 20 : 29.

" All those hard things
That Sheba came to ask of Solomon."

1 *Kings* 10 : 1.

" He, the wisest man."

1 *Kings* 4 : 31.

" Feasted the woman wisest then, in halls
    Of Lebanonian ced ir."
                                            1 *Kings* 10 : 4, 5.

" O Vashti, noble Vashti! Summon'd out,
    She kept her state and left the drunken king
    To brawl at Shushan underneath the palms."
                                            Esther 1.

" Let there be light and there was light."
                                            Gen. 1: 3.

        " But we that are not all
            As parts, can see but parts."
                                            1 *Cor.* 13 : 12.

    " Their cancell'd Babels."
    " A new-world Babel, woman-built
        And worse-confounded."
                                            Gen. 11 : 9.

            " They mind us of the time
        When we made bricks in Egypt."
                                            Ex. 1 : 14.

            (Judith and Holofernes)
                            Apoc., Book of Judith.
            " A Jonah's gourd
    Up in one night and due to sudden sun."
                                            Jonah 4 : 6.

        " Touch not a hair of his head."
                                            Luke 21 : 18.

    " The old leaven leaven'd all."
                                            1 *Cor.* 5 : 6, 7.

            " This Egypt plague."
                                            Ex. 7-12.

            " The fires of Hell."
                                            Matt. 5 : 22.

" Between a cymball'd Miriam and a Jael."
                            Ex. 15 : 20; *Judges* 4.

" Like that great dame of Lapidoth she sang."
                                            Judges 5 : 1.

" Stiff as Lot's wife."

Gen. 19 : 26.

" Bond or free."

1 *Cor.* 12 : 13.

" Into the Heaven of Heavens."

Neh. 9 : 6.

THE GRANDMOTHER.

" The tongue is a fire."

James 3 : 6.

" God, not man, is the judge of us all."

Rom. 14 : 4.

TO THE REV. F. D. MAURICE.

" Anathema."

1 *Cor.* 16 : 22.

THE FLOWER.

" He that runs may read."

Hab. 2 : 2.

THE ISLET.

" To a sweet little Eden on earth."

Gen. 2 : 8.

THE SPITEFUL LETTER.

" This faded leaf, our names are as brief."

Is. 1 : 30.

LITERARY SQUABBLES.

" When one small touch of charity
    Could lift them nearer God-like state
Than if the crowded Orb should cry
    Like those who cried Diana great."

Acts 19 : 34.

NORTHERN FARMER.

" I weänt saäy men be loiars thaw summun said it in
    'aäste."

Ps. 116 : 11.

ODE ON THE DUKE OF WELLINGTON.

" The shining table lands
To which our God Himself is moon and sun."

Rev. 21 : 23.

" Dust to dust."

Gen. 3 : 9 : *Eccl.* 3 : 20

WAGES.

"The wages of sin is death."

Rom. 6 : 23.

THE HIGHER PANTHEISM.

"The sun, the moon, the stars, the seas, the hills and the
    plains —
  Are not these, O Soul, the Vision of Him who reigns ? "

Rom. 1 : 20.

"Is not the vision He ? tho' He be not that which He
    seems ?
  Dreams are true while they last, and do we not live in
    dreams ?

"Speak to Him for He hears, and Spirit with Spirit can
    meet —
  Closer is He than breathing, and nearer than hands and
    feet."

Ps. 65 : 2; *Rom.* 8 : 16; *Acts* 17 : 27.

"God is law, say the wise ; O Soul, and let us rejoice,
  For if He thunder by law the thunder is yet His voice."

Ps. 77 : 18.

"Law is God, say some : no God at all, says the fool ;
  For all we have power to see is a straight staff bent in
    a pool."

Ps. 14 : 1.

"And the ear of man cannot hear, and the eye of man
    cannot see ;
  But if we could see and hear, this Vision — were it not
    He ? "

Is. 64 : 4; 1 *Cor.* 2 : 9 (*Rev. Version*).

BOADICEA.

"Thou shalt wax and he shall dwindle."

John 3 : 30.

MILTON.

"Angel . . . Gabriel."

Luke 2 : 1–19.

"The brooks of Eden.

Gen. 2 : 10.

In Memoriam. Proem.

"Strong Son of God, immortal Love,
    Whom we, that have not seen thy face,
    By faith and faith alone embrace,
Believing where we cannot prove."

1 Pet. 1 : 8.

" Thou madest life in man and brute."

John 1 : 8.

" For knowledge is of things we see."

Rom. 8 : 24.

" For merit lives from man to man,
    And not from man, O Lord, to thee."

Ps. 143 : 2.

xv.
" And but for fancies which aver
    That all thy motions gently pass
    Athwart a plane of molten glass."

Job 37 : 18; *Rev.* 4 : 6.

xxii.
"The shadow fear'd of man."

Ps. 23 : 4.

xxiv.
" Since Adam left his garden."

Gen. 3 : 23.

xxviii.
" Peace and goodwill to all mankind."

Luke 2 : 14.

xxx.
" ' They rest,' we said ; ' their sleep is sweet.' "

1 Thess. 4 : 14.

xxxi.
" When Lazarus left his charnel-cave,
    And home to Mary's house returned,
    Was this demanded — if he yearned
To hear her weeping by his grave ? "

John 11.

XXXII.

" She bows, she bathes the Saviour's feet
With costly spikenard and with tears."

John 12 : 3.

" The life indeed."

John 11 : 25

XXXVI.

" And so the Word had breath."

John 1 : 14.

XXXVII.
" Sacred wine."

1 *Cor.* 10 : 16.

LVI.

" Who trusted God was love indeed."

1 *John* 4 : 8.

LXXXIV.

" What reed was that on which I leant ? "

Is. 36 : 6.

LXXXVII.

" The God within him light his face."

2 *Cor.* 6 : 16.

LXXXVIII.
" Rings Eden."

Gen. 2 : 8.

XCV.

" Word by word, and line by line."

Is. 28 : 13.

XCVI.

" But in the darkness and the cloud.
As over Sinai's peaks of old,
While Israel made their gods of gold,
Altho' the trumpet blew so loud."

Ex. 32 : 1-4.

CIII.

" The thews of Anakim."

Deut. 2 : 10.

CVI.

" The thousand years of peace."

Rev. 20 : 2-4.

CVIII.

"And vacant yearning, though with might,
To scale the heavens' highest height,
Or dive below the wells of Death."

Rom. 10 : 6-8.

CXIV.

"Who shall fix Her pillars ? " (Knowledge.)

Prov. 9 : 1.

CXX.

"Like Paul with beasts I fought with Death."

1 *Cor.* 15 : 32.

CXXXI.

"O living will that shalt endure
When all that is shall suffer shock,
Rise in the spiritual rock,
Flow through our deeds and make them pure."

1 *John* 2 : 17; 1 *Cor.* 10 : 4.

"To one that with us works."

1 *Cor.* 3 : 9; *Phil.* 2 : 13.

" The moon
Of Eden."

Gen. 2 : 8.

MAUD.

Part I.   I. 6.

"The spirit of Cain."

1 *John* 3 : 12.

8.

" We are ashes and dust."

Gen. 3 : 19.

"My heart as a millstone."

Job 41 : 24.

"Set my face as a flint."

Is. 50 : 7.

9.

"When only not all men lie."

Ps. 116 : 11.

12.

"Mammon."

Matt. 6 : 24.

II.
"Neither savour nor salt."

Matt. 5 : 13.

XIII. 3.
"That huge scape-goat of the race."

Lev. 16 : 10.

XVIII. 2.
"The gates of Heaven."

Rev. 21 : 21.

XVIII. 3.
(A cedar of Lebanon.) "Thy great
Forefathers of the thornless garden, there
Shadowing the snow-limbed Eve."

Gen. 2 : 8; 3 : 18.

Part II.
II. 6.
"An old song vexes my ear;
But that of Lamech is mine."

Gen. 4 : 23.

V. 4.
"I never whispered a private affair

.   .   .   .

No, not to myself in the closet alone,
But I heard it shouted at once from the top of the
house."

Luke 12 : 3.

IDYLLS OF THE KING.

THE COMING OF ARTHUR.
"Elfin Urim."

Ex. 28 : 30.

"Hath power to walk the waters like our Lord."

Matt. 14 : 25.

"Dark sayings from of old."

Ps. 78 : 2.

"The King will follow Christ and we the King."

1 Cor. 11 : 1.

"The old order changeth, yielding place to new."

Rev. 21 : 4, 5.

GARETH AND LYNETTE.

"A stone about his neck to drown him in it."
Matt. 18 : 6.

" When reviled, hast answered graciously."
1 *Pet.* 2 : 23.

GERAINT AND ENID.

" Tho' they sought
Through all the provinces like those of old
That lighted on Queen Esther."
Esther 2 : 3.

" Here through the feeble twilight of this world
Groping, how many, until we pass and reach
That other where we see as we are seen."
1 *Cor.* 13 : 12.

" Whose souls the old serpent long had drawn
Down."
Rev. 12 : 9.

" Since high in Paradise
O'er the four rivers."
Gen. 2 : 10.

" But o'er her meek eyes came a happy mist
Like that which kept the heart of Eden green
Before the useful trouble of the rain."
Gen. 2 : 6.

" He hears the judgment of the King of Kings."
1 *Tim.* 6 : 15.

BALIN AND BALAN.

" The Lost one Found was greeted as in Heaven."
Luke 15 : 32.

" Arimathæan Joseph."
Mark 15 : 43.

" Thorns of the crown."
Matt. 27 : 29.

" That same spear
Wherewith the Roman pierced the side of Christ."
John 19 : 34.

" Arm of flesh."
2 *Chron.* 32 : 8.

" I better prize
The living dog than the dead lion."
Eccl. 9 : 4.

MERLIN AND VIVIEN.
" As Love, if Love be perfect, casts out fear."
1 *John* 4 : 18.

" There is no being pure,
My cherub; saith not Holy Writ the same ? "
Rom. 3 : 10.

" But neither marry nor are given
In marriage, angels of our Lord's report."
Matt. 22 : 30.

" The sin that practice burns into the blood,
And not the one dark hour which brings remorse,
Will brand us, after, of whose fold we be :
Or else were he, the holy king whose hymns
Are chanted in our minster, worse than all."
2 *Sam.* 11.

" Seethed like the kid in its own mother's milk."
Ex. 23 : 19.

" An enemy that has left
Death in the living waters."
2 *Kings* 4 : 39, 40.

" And stirr'd this vice in you which ruin'd man
Through woman the first hour."
Gen. 3 : 12; 8 : 1–6.

" Let her tongue rage like a fire."
James 3 : 6.

" And judge all nature from her feet of clay."
Dan. 2 : 33.

LANCELOT AND ELAINE.
" His mood was often like a fiend, and rose
And drove him into wastes and solitudes."
Luke 8 : 29.

" Fire in dry stubble."
Is. 5 : 24.

"Since man's first fall."

           Gen. 3 : 1–6.

"But loved me with a love beyond all love in women."

           2 Sam. 1 : 26.

THE HOLY GRAIL.

   "The cup, the cup itself, from which our Lord
   Drank at the last sad supper with his own."

           Matt. 26 : 29.

     "After the day of darkness when the dead
     Went wandering o'er Moriah."

           Matt. 27 : 53.

       "An adulterous race."

           Matt. 12 : 39.

   "Galahad, when he heard of Merlin's doom,
   Cried, 'If I lose myself, I save myself!'"

           Matt. 10 : 39; 16 : 25.

   "When the Lord of all things made Himself
   Naked of glory for His mortal change."

           Phil. 2 : 5–7.

       "Like a flying star
   Led on the gray-hair'd wisdom of the east."

           Matt. 2 : 9.

       "But my time is hard at hand,
   And hence I go, and one will crown me King
   Far in the spiritual city."

           2 Tim. 4 : 6, 8.

       "Arimathæan Joseph."

           Matt. 27 : 57.

"Thou hast not lost thyself to save thyself."

           Matt. 10 : 39.

"For now there is a lion in the way."

           Prov. 22 : 13.

"What go ye into the wilderness to see ? "

           Matt. 11 : 7.

"Shoutings of all the sons of God."

           Job 38 : 7.

"Gateways in a glory like one pearl."

           Rev. 21 : 12.

"As ever shepherd knew his sheep."
John 10 : 14.

"Perhaps, like him of Cana in Holy Writ,
Our Arthur kept his best until the last."
John 2 : 1-10.

"Glory and joy and honour to our Lord."
Rev. 4 : 11.

"A seven-times heated furnace."
Dan. 3 : 19.

"Great angels, awful shapes, and wings and eyes."
Ezek. 10 : 12.

"That One
Who rose again."
1 *Cor.* 15 : 20; 2 *Cor.* 5 : 15.

PELLEAS AND ETTARRE.
"The flame about a sacrifice
Kindled by fire from heaven."
2 *Chron.* 7 : 1.

"Would they have risen against me in their blood
At the last day?   I might have answered them
Even before high God."
Rev. 6 : 10.

"That own no lust because they have no law."
Rom. 4 : 15.

"I have no sword, —
Then Lancelot, 'Yea, between thy lips—and sharp.'"
Is. 49 : 2.

THE LAST TOURNAMENT.
"For I have flung thee pearls and find thee swine."
Matt. 7 : 6.

"Fear God: honour the King."
1 *Pet.* 2 : 17.

"As the water Moab saw
Come round by the East."
2 *Kings* 3 : 20-23.

"The scorpion-worm that twists in Hell
And stings itself to everlasting death."
Is. 66: 24.

"Who marr'd Heaven's image in thee thus?"

Gen. 1 : 27.

"That oft I seem as he
Of whom was written, 'a sound is in his ears.'"

Job 15 : 21.

"The great lake of fire."

Rev. 20 : 14.

"Conceits himself as God that he can make
Figs out of thistles."

Matt. 7 : 16.

"Michael trampling Satan."

Rev. 12 : 7–9.

GUINEVERE.

"Late, late, so late! and dark the night and chill."

Matt. 25 : 1.

"So she did not see the face
Which then was as an angel's."

Acts 6 : 15.

QUEEN MARY.

ACT I., Sc. 2.

"'Thou shalt not wed thy brother's wife.' — 'T is written,
'They shall be childless.'"

Lev. 20 : 21.

Sc. 3.

"From thine own mouth I judge thee."

Luke 19 : 22.

"The old leaven."

1 *Cor.* 5 : 7.

Sc. 5.

"The great angel of the church."

Rev. 2 : 1.

"Whosoever
Looketh after a woman."

Matt. 5 : 28.

"Him who made Heaven and earth."

Ex. 20 : 11.

"The living waters of the Faith."

John 4 : 10.

"The palms of Christ."

John 12 : 13.

"Many wolves among you."

Acts 20 : 29.

ACT II., Sc. 2.

"They go like those old Pharisees in John
Convicted by their conscience, arrant cowards."

John 8 : 1–11.

"Fruit of mine own body."

Ps. 132 : 11.

Sc. 4.

"My foes are at my feet . . .
There let them lie, your footstool."

Ps. 110 : 1.

ACT III., Sc. 1.

"Not red like Iscariot's."

Matt. 10 : 4.

"A pale horse for Death."

Rev. 6 : 8.

"Thou shalt do no murder."

Matt. 19 : 18.

"I have ears to hear."

Matt. 11 : 15.

"*Verbum Dei* . . . Word of God."

Rom. 10 : 17.

"That cannot spell Esaias from St. Paul."

Rom. 9 : 27.

Sc. 2.

"Ave Maria, gratia plena,
Benedictu tu in mulieribus."

Luke 1 : 28.

"The scarlet thread of Rahab saved her life."

Joshua 2 : 18; 6 : 17.

"And marked me ev'n as Cain."

Gen. 4 : 15.

" Since your Herod's death
How oft hath Peter knocked at Mary's gate,
And Mary would have risen and let him in ;
But, Mary, there were those within the house
Who would not have it."

Acts 12 : 11–17.

" Sit benedictus fructus ventris tui."

Luke 1 : 42.

" Our little sister of the Song of Songs."

Cant. 8 : 8.

" Swept and garnished."

Matt. 12 : 44.

" The devils in the swine."

Matt. 8 : 28–32.

" Prince of Peace."

Is. 9 : 6.

" Who will avenge me of mine enemies."

Is. 1 : 24.

" Open, ye everlasting gates."

Ps. 24 : 7.

Sc. 3.

" The blessed angels who rejoice
Over one saved."

Luke 15 : 10.

" The Lord who hath redeem'd us
With his own blood and wash'd us from our sins."

Rev. 5 : 9.

" All her breath should, incenselike,
Rise to the heavens in grateful praise of Him."

Ps. 141 : 2.

" These are forgiven . . .
And range with . . . offal thrown
Into the blind sea of forgetfulness."

Micah 7 : 19.

" To purchase for Himself a stainless bride."

Rev. 19 : 7.

" He whom the Father hath appointed Head
Of all his church."

Eph. 5 : 23.

Sc. 4.

"Compel them to come in."

Luke 14 : 23.

"I would they were cut off
That trouble you."

Gal. 5 : 12.

"Little children,
Love one another."

1 *John* 3 : 18; 4 : 7.

"I come not to bring peace, but a sword."

Matt. 10 : 34.

"The Church on Peter's rock."

Matt. 16 : 18.

"When Herod-Henry first
Began to batter at your English Church."

Acts 12 : 1.

"The spotless bride of Christ."

Eph. 5 : 27.

"Like Christ himself on Tabor."

Matt. 17 : 2.

"God's righteous judgment."

Rom. 2 : 5.

"Ev'n Saint Peter in his time of fear
Denied his Master, ay, and thrice, my Lord."

Matt. 26 : 69–74.

"Burn and blast them root and branch."

Mal. 4 : 1.

"His fan may thoroughly purge his floor."

Matt. 3 : 12.

Sc. 5.

"The very Truth and very Word are one."

John 14 : 6; 1 : 1.

"Back again into the dust we sprang from."

Gen. 3 : 19.

ACT IV., Sc. 2.

"There is more joy in Heaven."

Luke 15 : 7.

"The trumpet of the dead."

1 *Cor.* 15 : 52.

" How are the mighty fallen."

2 Sam. 1 : 19.

" Power hath been given you."

John 19 : 11.

Sc. 3.

" Nunc dimittis."

Luke 2 : 29.

" It is expedient for one man to die."

John 11 : 50.

" The penitent thief's award
And be with Christ the Lord in Paradise."

Luke 23 : 43.

" Remember how God made the fierce fire seem
To those three children like a pleasant dew."

Dan. 4 : 20-28.

" Saint Andrew."

Luke 6 : 14.

" Whither should I flee for any help ? "

Is. 10 : 3; 20 : 6.

" I am ashamed to lift my eyes to heaven."

Luke 18 : 13.

" Refusing none
That come to Thee for succour."

John 6 : 37.

" O God the Son . . . when thou becamest
Man in the flesh."

John 1 : 14.

" O God the Father, not for little sins
Didst thou yield up thy Son to human death."

John 3 : 16.

" Unpardonable. Sin against the light."

Matt. 12 : 32.

" Forgive me, Father, for no merit of mine,
But that Thy name by man be glorified,
And Thy most blessed Son's who died for man."

John 17 : 1, 2.

" Love of this world is hatred against God."

James 4 : 4.

" Obey your King and Queen, and not for dread
Of these alone, but from the fear of Him
Whose ministers they be to govern you."

         1 Pet. 2 : 13, 14.

" But do you good to all
As much as in you lieth."

         Gal. 6 : 10.

" How hard it is
For the rich man to enter Heaven."

         Matt. 19 : 23.

" Give to the poor,
Ye give to God.   He is with us in the poor."

         Prov. 19 : 17.

" God's image."

         Gen. 1 : 26.

" Ignorance crying in the streets."

         Prov. 1 : 20, 21.

" Your original Adam-clay."

         Gen. 2 : 7.

" This hath offended, — this unworthy hand."

         Matt. 5 : 30.

ACT V., Sc. 1.

" She is none of those who loathe the honeycomb."

         Prov. 27 : 7.

Sc. 2.

" It was thought we two
Might make one flesh, and cleave unto each other
As man and wife."

         Matt. 19 : 5.

" Labour in vain."

         Ps. 127 : 1.

" A low voice from the dust."

         Is. 29 : 4.

" They say the gloom of Saul
Was lightened by young David's harp."

         1 Sam. 16 : 23.

" Bring forth death."

         James 1 : 15.

Sc. 4.

" Soft raiment."

Luke 7 : 25.

" All things in common as in the days of the first church
when Jesus Christ was King.

Acts 4 : 32.

Sc. 5.

" Garner the wheat
And burn the tares with unquenchable fire."

Matt. 3 : 12; 13 : 40.

" The shadow of death."

Ps. 23 : 4.

" And she loved much; pray God she be forgiven."

Luke 7 : 47.

HAROLD.

" All things make for good."

Rom. 8 : 28.

ACT I., Sc. 1.

" And hold their babies up to it.
I think that they would *Molochize* them too,
To have the heavens clear."

Lev. 18 : 21.

" In Heaven signs,
Signs upon earth."

Dan. 6 : 27.

" War in heaven.

Rev. 12 : 7.

" I have fought the fight and go."

2 Tim. 4 : 7.

" Gates of Pearl."

Rev. 21 : 21.

" To the deaf adder thee, that will not dance
However wisely charm'd."

Ps. 58 : 4.

" Let brethren dwell together in unity."

Ps. 133 : 1.

Sc. 2.

" Did not heaven speak to men in dreams of old."

Matt. 2 : 12.

" Scape-goat."

Lev. 16 : 8.

Act. II., Sc. 1.
" Fishers of men."

Matt. 4 : 19.

" Jonah."

Jonah.

Sc. 2.
" For having lost myself to save myself."

Matt. 10 : 39.

" Familiar spirit."

1 *Sam.* 28 : 7.

"The torch . . . among your standing corn."

Judges 15 : 4, 5.

Act III., Sc. 1.
" I have built the Lord a house."

1 *Kings* 8 : 20.

" Sing, Asaph ! clash
The cymbal, Heman ; blow the trumpet, priest."

1 *Chron.* 25 : 1.

" Fall, cloud, and fill the house."

2 *Chron.* 7 : 1; 1 *Kings* 8 : 10.

" Jachin and Boaz."

1 *Kings* 7 : 21.

" Treble denial of the tongue of flesh
Like Peter's when he fell."

Matt. 26 : 69–74.

" To wail like Peter."

Matt. 26 : 75.

" Talked with God."

Ex. 33 : 9.

" Signs in heaven."

Dan. 6 : 27.

Sc. 2.
" That which reigned called itself God."

2 *Thess.* 2 : 4.

" Render unto Cæsar."

Matt. 22 : 21.

" The Good Shepherd."

John 10 : 11.

Act IV., Sc. 1.
"The kingdoms of this world."

Rev. 11 : 15.

"A king of men
Not made but born, like the great King of all,
A light among the oxen."

Luke 2 : 7.

So. 3.

"A fast of forty days."

Matt. 4 : 2.

Act V., So. 1.

"Mock-king, I am the messenger of God,
His Norman Daniel! Mene, Mene, Tekel!"

Dan. 5 : 25.

"Evil for good."

Rom. 3 : 8.

"Evil for evil."

Rom. 12 : 17.

"The peace of God."

Phil. 4 : 7.

"Were the great trumpet blowing Doomsday dawn."

1 *Thess.* 4 : 16.

"Spear into pruning hook."

Joel 3 : 10.

"God of battles."

Ps. 24 : 8.

"There is one
Come as Goliath came of yore."

1 *Sam.* 17 : 40.

"Pastor fugatur . . . Grex trucidatur."

John 10 : 12, 13.

"Equus cum equite dejiciatur . . . praecipitatur."

Ex. 15 : 1.

"Glory to God in the highest."

Luke 2 : 14.

So. 2.

"My punishment is more that I can bear."

Gen. 4 : 13.

The Lover's Tale.

"When the outer lights are darkened."

Eccl. 12 : 3

"Till earth and heaven pass."
> *Matt.* 5 : 18.

"Length of days."
> *Ps.* 91 : 16.

"The bitterness of death."
> 1 *Sam.* 15 : 32.

"As that other gazed,
Shading his eyes till all the fiery cloud,
The prophet and the chariot and the steeds,
Sucked into oneness like a little star
Were drunk into the inmost blue."
> 2 *Kings* 2 : 11, 12.

"A land of promise flowing with the milk
And honey of delicious memories."
> *Ex.* 3 : 8.

"Exceeding sorrow unto Death."
> *Matt.* 26 : 38.

"She took the body of my past delight,
Narded and swathed and balmed it for herself.
And laid it in a sepulchre of rock."
> *John* 19 : 39–41.

"The evil flourish in the world."
> *Ps.* 37 and 73.

"Like a vain rich man,
That having always prospered in the world,
Folding his hands, deals comfortable words,
To hearts wounded forever."
> *Jas.* 2 : 15, 16.

The Lover's Tale. (Original edition.)
"So, bearing on thro' Being limitless
The triumph of this foretaste, I had merged
Glory in glory, without sense of change."
> 2 *Cor.* 3 : 18.

Rizpah.
"Rizpah."
> 2 *Sam.* 21 : 8-10.

"As the tree falls so it must lie."
> *Eccl.* 11 : 3.

"Flesh of my flesh -- bone of my bone."
> *Gen.* 2 : 23.

" My Willy 'ill rise up whole when the trumpet
of judgment 'ill sound."

1 Thess. 4 : 16.

" Full of compassion and mercy."

Ps. 86 : 15.

THE NORTHERN COBBLER.

" A beäst of the feäld."

Ex. 23 : 11.

" Like Saätan as fell
Down out o' heaven in Hell-fire."

Luke 10 : 18.

IN THE CHILDREN'S HOSPITAL.

" Ye do it to me when ye do it to these."

Matt. 25 : 40.

" Spirits in prison."

1 Pet. 3 : 19.

" Little children should come to me."

Matt. 19 : 14.

SIR JOHN OLDCASTLE.

" Not least art thou, little Bethlehem
In Judah, for in thee the Lord was born."

Micah 5 : 2.

" Hereafter thou, fulfilling Pentecost,
Must learn to speak the tongues of all the world."

Acts 2 : 1-4.

" Thou bringest
Not peace, a sword."

Matt. 10 : 34.

" Antichrist."

1 John 2 : 18.

" The kingdoms of this world."

Rev. 11 : 15.

" Lord, give thou power to thy two witnesses."

Rev. 11 : 3.

" Persecute the Lord,
And play the Saul that never will be Paul."

Acts 9 : 4

"Or such crimes
As holy Paul — a shame to speak of them —
Among the heathen."

Eph. 5 : 12.

"The Gospel, the Priest's pearl, flung down to swine."

Matt. 7 : 6.

"Thy Gospel meant
To course and range thro' all the world."

Matt. 24 : 14.

"Babylon."

Rev. 17 : 5.

"How long, O Lord, how long."

Rev. 6 : 10.

"Thou living water."

John 4 : 10.

"He that thirsteth, come and drink."

Rev. 22 : 17.

"Power of the keys."

Matt. 16 : 19.

"Those three! the fourth
Was like the Son of God! Not burnt were they."

Dan. 3 : 25.

"Caiaphas."

Matt. 26 : 57.

COLUMBUS.

"The crowd's roar fell as at the 'Peace, be still.'"

Mark 4 : 39.

"For him who gave a new heaven, a new earth,
As holy John had prophesied of me."

Rev. 21 : 1.

"And saw the rivers roll from Paradise."

Gen. 2 : 10.

"King David called the heavens a hide, a tent,
Spread over earth."

Ps. 104 : 2.

"Moriah with Jerusalem."

2 *Chron.* 3 : 1.

" And I saw
The glory of the Lord flash up."

Rev. 21 : 19-27

" From Solomon's now-recover'd Ophir, all
The gold that Solomon's navies carried home."

1 *Kings* 9 : 26-28

" O soul of little faith, slow to believe."

Matt. 14 : 31; *Luke* 24 : 25.

" Time shall be no more."

Rev. 10 : 6.

" Endure! thou hast done so well for man, that men
Cry out against thee; was it otherwise
With mine own son ? "

Matt. 10 : 24, 25.

" Be not cast down.   I lead thee by the hand,
Fear not."

Deut. 31 : 8; *Is.* 41 : 13.

THE VOYAGE OF MAELDUNE.

" Remember the words of the Lord when he told us
'Vengeance is mine.'"

Rom. 12 : 19.

DE PROFUNDIS.

" From that great deep, before our world begins,
Whereon the spirit of God moves as he will."

Gen. 1 : 2.

" Let us make man."

Gen. 1 : 26.

" That one light no man can look upon."

1 *Tim.* 6 : 16.

" Hallowed be Thy Name."

Matt. 6 : 9.

BECKET.

PROLOGUE.
" The spiritual body."

1 *Cor.* 15 : 44

" Let her eat dust like the serpent, and be driven out
of her Paradise."

Gen. 3 : 14.

ACT I., Sc. 1.
" King of Kings."

1 *Tim.* 6 : 15.

" The twelve Apostles."

Matt. 10 : 2.

" Let them be Anathema."

1 *Cor.* 16 : 22.

Sc. 3.
" The Lord be judged again by Pilate."

Matt. 27 : 2.

" When murder, common
As Nature's death, like Egypt's plague, had filled
All things with blood, — when every doorway blushed,
Dash'd red with that unhallow'd passover."

Ex. 7 : 19; 12 : 22.

" Peter's rock."

Matt. 16 : 18.

" Life for a life."

Ex. 21 : 23.

" Thou, the shepherd, hast betrayed the sheep."

John 10 : 12.

" Mortify thy flesh."

Gal. 5 : 24; *Col.* 3 : 5.

" Reeds that sway . . . to the wind."

Matt. 11 : 7.

" Who but the bridegroom dares to judge the bride ? "

John 3 : 29.

' As gold outvalues dross ; light, darkness ; Abel, Cain."

Heb. 11 : 4, 5, 8.

" Saint Lazarus."

John 11.

" Deal gently with the young man Absalom."

2 *Sam.* 18 : 5.

" Blessed is he that cometh in the name of the Lord."

Ps. 118 : 26.

Sc. 4.
" Ye have drunken of my cup."
Matt. 20 : 23.
" Bidden to our supper."
Luke 14 : 7-24.
" Steams . . . like the altar at Jerusalem."
2 *Sam.* 24 : 18.
" Call in the poor."
Matt. 22 : 9.
" The princess sat in judgment against me."
Ps. 119 : 23.
" The Lord hath prepared your table."
Ps. 23 : 5.
" Sheep without the shepherd."
Matt. 9 : 36.
" With Cain's answer, my Lord.   Am I his keeper ? "
" The Lord hath set his mark upon him that no man
should murder him."
Gen. 4 : 9-15.
" With Cain . . . in the land of Nod."
Gen. 4 : 16.
" Smite him with the edge of the sword."
Deut. 13 : 15.
" Smite the shepherd, and the sheep are scattered."
Zech. 13 : 7.
" His Lord and Master in Christ."
Matt. 20 : 27.
" Who fed you in the wilderness."
Deut. 8 : 16.

Act II., Sc. 1.
" The voice of the deep."
Hab. 3 : 10.
" Turn the world upside down."
Acts 17 : 6.

Sc. 2.
" Thief-like fled . . . no man pursuing."
Prov. 28 : 1.
" Take heed he do not turn and rend you."
Matt. 7 : 6

"None other God but me."

Ex. 20 : 3.

"Nay, if they were defective as Saint Peter
Denying Christ, who yet defied the tyrant,
We held by his defiance, not by his defect."

Matt. 26 : 70; *Acts* 4 : 19.

"What manner of man he was."

James 1 : 24.

"Yea, let a stranger spoil his heritage,
And let another take his bishoprick."

Acts 1 : 20.

"Withstood . . . to their faces."

Gal. 2 : 11.

"Out of the mouths of babes and sucklings praise."

Ps. 8 : 2.

"A fisher of men."

Matt. 4 : 19.

"Agree with him quickly."

Matt. 5 : 25.

"Still choose Barabbas rather than the Christ."

Matt. 27 : 21.

"Absolve the left-hand thief and damn the right."

Luke 23 : 43.

"On mine own self . . . had had no power except."

John 19 : 11.

"Thou art no prophet
Nor yet a prophet's son."

Amos 7 : 14.

ACT III., Sc. 1.
"Solomon-shaming flowers."

Matt. 6 : 29.

If I had been Eve in the garden, I should n't have
minded the apple.   For what 's an apple ? "

Gen. 3 : 6.

"The seventh Commandment."

Ex. 20 : 14.

Sc. 3.
"A house on sand."

Matt. 7 : 26, 27.

"Pulled . . . the church . . . down upon his own head."
                                        Judges 16 : 29.
  "A thief at night . . . hears a door open, . . .
' And thinks, 'The master.'"
                                        Matt. 24 : 43.
  "The thunder of the captains and the shouting."
                                        Job 39 : 25.
        "The miraculous draught."
                                        Luke 5 : 6.
              "Goliathizing."
                                        1 *Sam.* 17 : 4.
          "A whole Peter's sheet."
                                        Acts 10 : 11.
            "Magdalen."
                                        Luke 8 : 2.
        "The spouse of the great king."
                                        Rev. 21 : 9.
  "The daughter of Zion lies beside the way."
                                        Is. 1 : 8.
              "The priests of Baal."
                                        2 *Kings* 10 : 19.
            "The kiss of peace."
                                        1 *Thess.* 5 : 26.
  "Ay, if this if be like tne Devil's *if*,
  Thou wilt fall down and worship me."
                                        Matt. 4 : 9.
  "Thou hast trodden this winepress alone."
                                        Is. 63 : 3.
  "The drop may hollow out the dead stone."
                                        Job 14 : 19.
          "My visions in the Lord."
                                        2 *Cor.* 12 : 1.
  "Murder her one shepherd, that the sheep."
                                        Matt. 26 : 31.
              ACT IV., SC. 2.
  "The Judas-lover of our passion-play."
                                        Matt. 26 : 47.
            "Our great high-priest."
                                        Heb. 4 : 14.

ACT V., Sc. 1.
"The Decalogue."

Ex. 20.

Sc. 2.
"My kingdom is not of this world."

John 18 : 36.

"A policy of wise pardon,
Wins here, as there, to bless thine enemies."

Matt. 5 : 44, 45.

"This world's leaven."

1 *Cor.* 5 : 7.

"These wells of Marah."

Ex. 15 : 23.

"In this life and in the life to come."

1 *Tim.* 4 : 8.

"They spread their raiment down."

Matt. 21 : 8.

"Give to the King the things that are the King's,
And those of God to God."

Matt. 22 : 21.

"Mailed in the perfect panoply of faith."

Eph. 6 : 13.

"The great day
When God makes up his jewels."

Mal. 3 : 17.

"Would that I could bear thy cross."

Matt. 27 : 32.

"They seek occasion for your death."

Mark 14 : 55.

"Why do the heathen rage ? "

Ps. 2 : 1.

Sc. 3.
"Die with him and be glorified together."

Rom. 8 : 17.

"Though . . . the great deeps were broken up again."

Gen. 7 : 11.

"Knock and it shall be opened."

Matt. 7 : 7.

"Not tho' it be their hour, the power of darkness."
Luke 22 : 53.

" He is not yet ascended to the Father."
John 20 : 17.

"Fight out the good fight, die conqueror."
2 *Tim.* 4 : 7.

" At the right hand of Power
Power and great glory — for thy Church, O Lord —
Into thy hands, O Lord, into thy hands ! "
Luke 22 : 69; 23 : 46.

" Will the earth gape and swallow us ? "
Num. 16 : 32.

ACHILLES.

" Smoke from a city goes to heaven."
Josh. 8 : 20.

To E. FITZGERALD.

" As if they knew your diet spares
Whatever moved in that full sheet
Let down to Peter at his prayers."
Acts 10 : 11

" Grapes of Eshcol hugeness."
Num. 13 : 23.

THE WRECK.

" The wages of sin is death."
Rom. 6 : 23.

" I am the Jonah; the crew should cast me into the deep."
Jonah 1 : 15.

" Was it well with the child ? "
2 *Kings* 4 : 26.

DESPAIR.

" He is only a cloud and a smoke who was once a pillar
of fire."
Ex. 13: 21.

"Ah God . . . I was taking the name in vain."
Ex. 20 : 7.

"Till the sun and moon of our Science are both of them
turned into blood."
Joel 2 : 31.

"Does what he will with his own."

Matt. 20 : 15.

THE FLIGHT.
"The godless Jephtha vows his child . . .
To one cast of the dice."

Judges 11 : 30.

EARLY SPRING.
"Makes all things new."

Rev. 21 : 15.

"A Jacob's ladder falls."

Gen. 28 : 12.

LOCKSLEY HALL, SIXTY YEARS AFTER.
"Love your enemy, bless your haters, said the
Greatest of the great."

Matt. 5 : 44.

"Have we grown at last beyond the passions of the
primal clan,
Kill your enemy, for you hate him."

Matt. 5 : 43.

"Dust to dust."

Eccl. 3 : 20; *Job* 34 : 15.

"What are men that he should heed us? cried the king
of sacred song."

Ps. 8 : 4.

"The trampled serpent."

Gen. 3 : 15.

"Follow you the star that lights a desert pathway,
yours or mine,
Forward till you see the highest Human Nature is
divine."   *Matt.* 2 : 2.

"Follow Light and do the Right — for man can half
control his doom —
Till you find the deathless Angel seated in the vacant
tomb."

John 20 : 12.

THE CHARGE OF THE HEAVY BRIGADE.

EPILOGUE.

" Though carved in harder stone
The falling drop will make his name
As mortal as my own."

Job 14 : 19.

THE FALCON.

" Happy was the prodigal son."

Luke 15 : 20–23.

THE PROMISE OF MAY.

ACT I.

" Let us eat and drink for tomorrow we die."

Is. 22 : 13; 1 *Cor.* 15 : 32.

" Yes, tho' the fire should run along the ground,
As it once did in Egypt."

Ex. 9 : 23.

ACT II.

" As long as the man sarved for 'is sweet'art i'
Scripture."

Gen. 29 : 20.

ACT III.

" Forgive him seventy times and seven."

Matt. 18 : 22.

" This valley of tears."

Ps. 84 : 6.

VASTNESS.

" Innocence seethed in her mother's milk."

Ex. 34 : 26.

" He that has nail'd all flesh to the Cross."

Gal. 5 : 24.

" The dead are not dead, but alive."

Matt. 22 32; *Mark* 12 : 27; *Luke* 10 : 38.

OWD ROÄ.

" Faäithful an' True — them words be i' Scriptur'."

Rev. 22 : 6.

" Or like t'other Hangel i' Scriptur' at summun seed i'
     the flaäme,
When summun 'ed hax'd fur a son, an' 'e promised
     a son to she."

Judges 13 : 19–21.

" Judgment daäy."

Matt. 12 : 36.

THE RING.

" Father's fault visited on the children."

Ex. 20 : 5.

" The veil is rending."

Matt. 27 : 51.

FORLORN.

" Daughter of the seed of Cain."

Gen. 4.

HAPPY.

" My soldier of the cross."

2 *Tim.* 2 : 3.

" A crueller mark than Cain's."

Gen. 4 : 15.

" Creature which in Eden was divine."

Gen. 1 : 27.

" When we shall stand transfigured, like Christ on
     Hermon hill."

Matt. 17 : 1, 2.

" Clove the Moslem . . . moon . . . and changed it into
     blood."

Joel 2 : 31.

" ' Libera me, Domine ! ' you sang the Psalm."

Ps. 6.

" If man and wife be but one flesh."

Matt. 19 : 6.

To MARY BOYLE.

" Dives and Lazarus."

Luke 16 : 19–31.

MERLIN AND THE GLEAM.

" Drew to the valley
    Named of the shadow."

Ps. 23 : 4.

ROMNEY'S REMORSE.
> " Ay, but when the shout
> Of his descending peals from heaven."
>> *1 Thess.* 4 : 16.

> " Why left you wife and children ? for my sake?
> According to my word ? "
>> *Mark* 10 : 29.

> "The coals of fire you heap upon my head
> Have crazed me."
>> *Rom.* 12 : 20.

CROSSING THE BAR.
> "I hope to see my Pilot face to face,
> When I have crost the bar."
>> *1 John* 3 : 2; *1 Cor.* 13 : 12.

THE FORESTERS.
> ACT I., Sc. 1.
> " Sufficient for the day."
>> *Matt.* 6 : 34.

> ACT II., Sc. 1.
> " The serpent that had crept into the garden."
>> *Gen.* 3 : 1.

> " The palms of Paradise."
>> *Rev.* 7 : 9.

> ACT III., Sc. 1.
> "Sell all thou hast and give it to the poor."
>> *Matt.* 19 : 21.

> ACT IV., Sc. 1.
> " The King of Kings."
>> *Rev.* 17 : 14.

> "Will hang as high as Haman."
>> *Esth.* 7 : 9, 10.

> "Beelzebub."
>> *Matt.* 10 : 25.

> " I am like the man
> In Holy Writ, who brought his talent back."
>> *Matt.* 25 : 25.

AKBAR'S DREAM.
> " Allah, says their sacred book, is Love."
>> *1 John* 4 : 16.

"Love one another, little ones."
John 13 : 33, 34.

"Bless your persecutors."
Rom. 12 : 14.

"The Sun of Righteousness."
Mal. 4 : 2.

"Bear false witness."
Ex. 20 : 16.

THE CHURCH WARDEN.
"The narra gaäte."
Matt. 7 : 14.

"The tongue's sit afire o' Hell."
Jas. 3 : 6.

"By the Graäce o' the Lord — I have wot I have."
1 *Cor.* 15 : 10.

"The Kingdom o' Heaven."
Matt. 3 : 2.

CHARITY.
"For a woman ruined the world,
As God's own Scriptures tell."
Gen. 3 : 1–6.

"I had cursed — the day I was born."
Job 3 : 3.

"The Heaven of Heavens."
1 *Kings* 8 : 27.

"Face to face with her Lord."
1 *Cor.* 13 : 12.

THE DAWN.
"A babe in the red-hot palms
Of a Moloch of Tyre."
2 *Kings* 23 : 10.

THE DREAMER.
"The meek shall inherit the earth."
Matt. 5 : 5.

RIFLEMEN FORM.
"Are figs of thistles? Or grapes of thorns?"
Matt. 7 : 16.

CPSIA information can be obtained at www.ICGtesting.com
Printed in the USA
BVOW07s1310091113

335891BV00001B/5/A

9 781410 211897